D1621392

Also by EDWARD WHITTEMORE

Quin's Shanghai Circus
Sinai Tapestry
Jerusalem Poker
Nile Shadows

Jericho Mosaic

W · W · NORTON & COMPANY

New York · London

Jericho Mosaic

EDWARD WHITTEMORE

Published simultaneously in Canada by Penguin Books Canada Ltd., 2801 John Street, Markham, Ontario L3R 1B4.
Printed in the United States of America.

The text of this book is composed in Janson Alternate, with display type set in Peach Update. Composition and manufacturing by The Haddon Craftsmen Inc.
Book design by Antonina Krass

First Edition

Library of Congress Cataloging-in-Publication Data

Whittemore, Edward.
Jericho mosaic.

I. Title.
PS3573.H557J4 1987 813'.54 86-12806

ISBN 0-393-02395-8

W. W. Norton & Company, Inc., 500 Fifth Avenue, New York, N. Y. 10110
W. W. Norton & Company Ltd., 37 Great Russell Street, London WC1B 3NU

1 2 3 4 5 6 7 8 9 0

For Larry and Sarah Whittemore
and Tom and Lois Wallace

Part I

ONE

Jerusalem in the early twentieth century was a vibrant little city only newly awakened from medieval obscurity by the coming of the British at the end of the First World War—a dream from antiquity suddenly stirring to life after four hundred years of slumber under the stupefying decadence of the Ottoman Empire. With their penchant for order and proper hygiene, the British briskly built hydraulic works and piped fresh water up to Jerusalem, but many people in the walled Old City still drank from the cisterns of the past, those underground reservoirs from other ages which never saw the light of day. For Jerusalem was a place where many eras still crowded together, and where no event from history was too remote for a morning's gossip, since the very ruins of that event might well be providing shade for the day's transactions of commerce and hope.

Stately Nubian doormen reigned in splendid solemnity at the entrances of hotels. Wily merchants hovered in dim shops fingering the purses on their sleek bellies, waiting with patience for fate and guides to bring them their quota of fools who would be as deaf as they were to the cries of beggars and holy men.

Preceded by a shabbily uniformed kavass clearing a way with his thumping staff, Turkish grandees in red tarbooshes swayed by to assignations in flowering courtyards, already glassy-eyed from a nargileh or two of hashish at breakfast. Fierce bedouin and European travelers haggled side by side over bunches of garlic and sacks of dates, and over ancient coins bearing pale green profiles of Alexander the Great or some heavy-nosed emperor of Rome or Byzantium.

Black-robed monks of a dozen nationalities swirled down alleys in peaked headdresses and round and flat hats, disappearing along arcane routes devised in the Middle Ages, the Red and White monks of the Russian church looking particularly frenzied as they delved ever deeper into the plots and counterplots of their twentieth-century revolution at home.

The poor and the blind wandered among delirious lost pilgrims seeking the sites of old. Cripples in carts peered up from the cobblestones as men chanted allegiance to obscure causes or dropped to their knees in an ecstasy of prayer, or shouted out the virtues of the pots and beads and rags they had for sale.

In the Muristan where the Crusader Knights of St. John had been quartered and where the Roman Forum had once stood, stringed orchestras played in front of shops to attract customers. And everywhere in the dark recesses of the bazaars there were reaching and gesturing hands and wild rumors of forgotten magnificence being whispered into eager ears, as Jerusalem seethed again with merchandise and fervor after a drowsy sleep of centuries.

For Tajar as a boy it was a time to run through alleys and over rooftops, to hide in corners and listen to old men recall distant memories and young men dream of new dawns of glory. In the early mornings he wandered down the narrow street called el Wad near the Temple Mount, once a Jebusite donkey path and the oldest road in the Old City. And in the cool of the evenings he tarried beside the Gihon spring, beyond the walls of the city since King David's time but the original source of Jerusalem whose perennial waters first caused a town to take root on the spot, the area around the spring later to become renowned as King Solomon's rose gardens, the sacred place where perfume and incense plants were grown for the king's grand new Temple on the hill above, from seeds first brought to the king and the land by the dusky Queen of Sheba.

And so Tajar wandered back and forth through history. Being holy, Jerusalem was an endless source of myth. There were legends of intriguing mystery, such as the tale that described the original Bible having been miraculously discovered in the nineteenth century buried in a monastery deep in the Sinai, only to be secretly reburied later in Jerusalem out of fear and piety in the cause of faith, because this original Bible had turned out to be a stunningly dangerous document which denied every religious truth ever held by anyone.

And there were stories of fabulous adventure, such as the shadowy accounts of a long-term poker game which had begun in Jerusalem after the First World War and was still in progress in the back room of an antiquities dealer's shop somewhere in the Old City, a game destined to run a dozen years, it was said, its three permanent members a Moslem and a Christian and a Jew, the secret stakes of the game nothing less than control of Jerusalem itself.

Arabs and Jews and Greeks and Armenians and Europeans —Tajar learned all their languages and glimpsed all their visions of the Holy City where the patriarch-shepherd Abraham had come four millennia ago to seek the blessing of Melchizedek, mythical priest-king of the ancient Jebusite city of Jerusalem.

Tajar spied out the hidden byways of the bazaars and the dazzling silences of the great sun-washed courtyards with their towers and domes and minarets, endlessly exploring the multitude of worlds around every corner and the multiplicity of ways and tongues and costumes which were the very heart of his ancient walled city. Above all he loved being different people at different moments, imagining secret lives for himself, imagining himself to be all the men whose paths he crossed.

He had a game which he called listening to the stones of

Jerusalem. He would stop somewhere and turn his back on the crowds and close his eyes and rest his hands on a weathered stone, a wall or an abutment or arch, and soon he would find himself slipping back in time to some distant era, feeling its life surge around him and hearing its sounds and tasting its smells, so clearly the stones seemed to be whispering to him through his fingertips.

Anna smiled when he described that childhood game to her years later. She smiled and nodded in recognition at those sensations of his from long ago.

So that's where your sensualism began, she said to him, laughing. And it was true that Tajar always took enormous pleasure in textures and tastes and colors. He loved to touch things with his hands, to feel them with his fingers.

Once when he went to make coffee in Anna's house and she waited and waited and too much time had passed, she found him in the kitchen dreamily dipping his hand in and out of the jar of coffee beans, stroking the beans and letting them run through his fingers, oblivious to where he was and what he was supposed to be doing. So perhaps it was as Anna suspected, and his mystical love as a boy for the stones of Jerusalem gave him a vision that guided his entire life.

In any case, Tajar's sensual pleasure in textures and colors and his love of ideas, his delight in multiple ways and languages and especially his boyhood games of pretending, all were to provide him with a very special role in the building of his homeland. The grand rabbi of espionage, Yossi would one day call him, at a meeting of theirs in Geneva. And although Yossi laughed when he made the remark, it was no less true.

Tajar was the first director of the Mossad, its founder, and in fact his exceptional talent for secret worlds was wholly natural to him, a result of having grown up in Jerusalem at a time when all its races and tongues mingled freely, before the strife of later years caused the various communities to withdraw and isolate themselves one from the other.

Tajar had been born in Jerusalem, the son and grandson of rabbis who had also been born in Jerusalem. From the beginning ideas filled his days and Tajar could never escape them. A desert windstorm of ideas was forever swirling inside his brain and hurling him this way and that, obscuring the sun and revealing its brilliance and tossing up bits of stinging sand, tearing loose the tents of shelter and carrying off certainty and reshaping the hard wounded lines of the Judean hills from one day to the next, a never-ending struggle in his heart for recognition between man and nature, between man and his own nature, between the world and an immutable divine presence which never stopped changing.

A struggle called history, the human soul, God. A way of wrestling with life, deep in his heart, which was also his own way of rejoicing in the gifts of his fathers, those erudite men who had struggled for air in the real Jerusalem of oppression and squalor under the Turks, while dreaming of a heavenly city.

Not surprisingly, Tajar found his vocation early in life. His first foray into professional secrecy was as a very young man in Baghdad in the 1930s. He went there ostensibly as a teacher and journalist but actually he was working for Shai, the Zionist intelligence network run by the Haganah in Palestine. He traveled widely in Iraq and also crossed over to Iran, picking up more Arab dialects along the way as well as learning Kurdish and Persian. By chance he even visited the dusty little town near Baghdad where Yossi, as a very young bookkeeper, was to add up figures in a ledger after running across the desert every afternoon.

Tajar knew it was a life meant for him. Before the Second World War he served in different roles in Syria and Turkey and Lebanon. When the war came he was in Cairo, working with the British to organize Jewish commando operations in the Balkans and Jewish agents behind German lines in North Africa, but also serving Shai's interests all the while.

It was then that he had been in contact with Anna's brother, although Anna had never been aware of the connection. It was also then that he had come to know the one-eyed British officer with the disfigured face who was so helpful to Anna after her brother was killed. And Tajar had gone on many special operations himself during those years, in Greece and Turkey and as always in Arab countries, carrying out missions for the British while pursuing his own work.

When the Second World War ended Tajar was an important man in Jewish Palestine. No other native of the Middle East had more experience in intelligence than he did. He traveled in America arranging for arms to be smuggled to Palestine, then negotiated secretly in Arab countries during the struggle for independence. But when Israel was founded, Tajar was chief of its intelligence service for only a short time. His preeminence slipped and soon the son of another rabbi, from the Ukraine, became the head of the Mossad.

In a way it was precisely Tajar's brilliance with ideas that caused him to lose out. He was a superb agent but quite hopeless when it came to administering a government agency. His mind ranged in every direction at once and he tended to run his office out of his pocket and memory. Field work and improvising on the spot were what he understood, not budgets and committees and overseeing an arm of the civil service among competing bureaucracies.

There were also some who thought he might have lost the top Mossad position because he was an Oriental. Those in power in Israel were almost all from Eastern Europe, and perhaps they felt more comfortable with someone of their own background in charge of the country's intelligence service. But Tajar himself, with characteristic generosity, refused to see it that way. The man who replaced him, whom he along with everyone else respected, had worked entirely within the country over the years while Tajar had served mostly abroad. So Tajar felt it was a case of familiarity. Intimacy couldn't help but count within a small leadership. It was only human nature that it should, particularly when it came to the man who controlled the country's secret intelligence service. And of course

Tajar knew he had always had a reputation for being *out there* somewhere, alone, working by himself in the Arab world.

All the same he was deeply disappointed and there was no way he could deny his profound sense of failure, at least to himself. With others he made a great effort not to show his disappointment. Only Yossi would one day know the truth, and that was years later.

Not that Tajar's feeling of failure mattered, as it turned out.

Worry's useless because we always have the wrong thing in mind, he once said to Anna. That day, which was a fine spring day of sunshine, I was worrying about whether we'd get just a little more rain before the summer arrived for good. Because if not, would there be enough water for the tomatoes to grow? Tomatoes were on my mind, you see.

That day was the day a few years after independence when a decrepit vegetable truck wandered into the path of Tajar's oncoming car on a road near Tel Aviv, destroying the car and smashing Tajar below the waist. They had to cut him out of the wreck with an acetylene torch and for a time it was doubtful whether he would live. Then it was a question of what there would be left of him below the waist. But the doctors worked miracles and salvaged his legs, partially. While recuperating, he pursued a childhood dream by teaching himself ancient Greek in order to hear the words of Homer.

Eventually he was able to go back to work in the Mossad as an operations officer. But he moved with difficulty, a cripple who walked mostly with his arms, bent forward from the waist, supporting himself on aluminum crutches that he held with his hands. Thick braces reached up above the hand grips and encircled his forearms to balance his weight.

Now he trained and directed younger men in the Mossad to do what he had once done. His specialty was penetrating Arab countries and in that kind of operation no one could match his skill. Tajar had been there, after all, and knew exactly what his agents had to face. Without a second thought he could describe the street corners in a Syrian town or the cast of a remote stretch of hills in Iraq at twilight, or the homely manners of a farmer who kept an orchard on the outskirts of a village in Jordan. Because of his great knowledge he bred a special confidence in his men. Their reverence for him as a leader went beyond trust and was more like faith in a religious mystery, which led to exceptional daring on their part. Your mind is your weapon, Tajar told them, and with it you can do anything.

Tajar loved his agents and lived their dangers and fears as his own. His agents were truly extensions of him, part of his heart and part of that wrestling with life which for him was the only way a man could know he existed. And of course it was on the strength of his teaching that his men were able to cross borders and cultures and carry out his daring operations with so much success.

As for Anna, she knew nothing of Tajar's other life in espionage. She knew only that he had some quietly confidential role in the defense ministry which he never talked about, that he worked extremely long hours week after week and year after year, that he seemed conversant with everything under the sun, that he was often impish and playful and given to droll merriment, that he loved to laugh and was easily moved to tears, that he ate huge quantities of raw vegetables and fruit and leban with enormous gusto, that he revered the soups she had learned to make as a girl in Cairo, and that no matter how busy he might be he was always there if she needed him, with encouragement and strength and wisdom, with kind words and thoughtful smiles.

Being with Tajar was being with many men, because he was exuberant and sensitive and lived life to the fullest. Anna found him a rare and immensely lovable friend, simple and complex at the same time, a man who had learned to reach deep into his days and draw great riches from them. Oh yes, truly spectacular riches. The simplest things glittered in Tajar's hands.

TWO

The street where Anna grew up in Cairo was so crowded and narrow the roofs nearly touched overhead. The houses were also narrow and of the nineteenth century, their upper stories serving as living quarters for the families who ran the cavernous shops below, Egyptians and Greeks and Syrians side by side, and Armenians and Jews and an occasional Italian or Persian or Turk. During the day there was a constant clatter of donkeys and carts on the cobblestones, men shouting and hawking wares and a bustle of people poking and sniffing goods in the half-light of dust and raucous cries. But then at night the alley became a dark silent tunnel, where the shops were locked and the families retreated to their back courtyards and the shuttered upper rooms of their private lives.

Sounds that lived in the shadows were the memories of her childhood. Because it was Egypt, perhaps, where the sun never wavered and the sky was unchanging and featureless, forever a flat brilliant light without echoes which hid nothing and therefore gave nothing. In a land where rain never came and no cloud wandered there were hesitant scrapings beneath the eaves and the creak of shutters, a shuffle of wind and the distant whispers of corridors. Or the mysteries of a key stirring in an invisible lock.

So it was in Anna's world where shadowy clues rose like quiet footfalls from the corners of life, the restless sounds of other lives lived just out of sight, rich in suggestion yet beyond her grasp. Later this mood was inevitably deepened by her brother's clandestine life with its secret meetings and the secret names whispered at night in the darkness of their narrow Cairo courtyard—memories not quite from Anna's childhood but still early and unforgettable omens.

Her family's shop was one of many on the street that still displayed its original sign from the nineteenth century. It was an optical shop, opened by Anna's great-grandfather who had gone on to make a fortune speculating in cotton, which her grandfather later squandered in more speculation. Then her father, a soldier in the forces of General Allenby during the First World War, was killed in the British campaign to take Jerusalem from the Turks. Her brother David always thought he could remember their father but Anna had been born after his death, at home in the bedroom overlooking the courtyard.

What Anna and her brother did remember from those early years was being alone. Their mother went off to work each day and they were looked after by a succession of women who were even poorer than they were. When her brother was old enough he went to work after school as an apprentice to the elderly optician who rented the shop, learning their great-grandfather's trade. It was Anna's responsibility after school to keep the house and shop in order. She stood very straight and grew to be a tall handsome girl with long black hair, but it was her brother people noticed when their mother took them for walks along the Nile on holidays.

That's always the way, laughed their mother, buying them sunflower seeds to eat in the park. The son gets the beautiful eyelashes so he can learn they mean nothing, and the daughter is spared such illusions to help her find the true life within.

Their mother died before the Second World War. Anna's brother was still very young then but he was already secretly working for Shai. Cairo was an important center for their clandestine activities because British headquarters for the region were there, and Britain controlled Palestine under its

Mandate from the First World War. Anna helped her brother as best she could but the dangers grew much worse after the Germans invaded North Africa in 1941. Those were terrible days for two young Jews in Cairo, with the Germans advancing from victory to victory in the desert and refugees bringing ever new accounts of the horrors in Europe.

Four generations of her family's life on the narrow street came to an end on a June night in 1942, when her brother didn't return from one of his secret meetings. The next day she learned he had been killed, run down by a lorry in what the police described as an accident. Anna had no other family. She knew her brother's death wasn't an accident and for a time she thought she was losing her mind. She locked all the doors and shutters of the house and went around shrieking in the darkness.

The first person who came to help her was an utter stranger, an Englishman. Somehow he got into the house and found her crumpled on the stone floor beside the door to the courtyard. His voice gently called to her in the darkness, then he lit a candle and she saw he only had one eye. A bulky black patch covered his other eye and his twisted face was grotesquely shaped. It all seemed a monstrous dream to Anna, a nightmare of ugly shadows. But when the man put his arms around her to raise her, she knew how real it was. She had soiled herself on the stones where she lay, lost near the courtyard door in the house of her birth.

Years were to pass before she came to know this mysterious one-eyed man who was to be such an important part of her life. At the time she only wanted to escape from the house and from Cairo and the Englishman helped her in many ways, above all by providing her with papers for Palestine. She knew he must be connected to British intelligence and was helping her because of her brother, but she was too overwhelmed by grief and fear to make any sense out of what he was doing. Escape was all that mattered to her.

Anna was twenty-three when she left Egypt. The tanks of

the German Afrika Korps were little more than fifty miles from Alexandria. The British fleet had already sailed for the safety of Haifa and British military and civilian staffs were being evacuated from Cairo. Long columns of trucks wound away into the Sinai, an exodus heading north and east toward Palestine.

THREE

Palestine was a drastic change from Egypt, which made it easier for Anna. She was even grateful it was such a primitive place with nothing to remind her of the sophistication of Cairo, where different cultures had lived together for centuries. In Palestine every group distrusted every other: the Moslem and Christian Arabs, the Oriental and European Jews, the British. Only from the outside when faced by enemies did any one of them appear to be a community. As soon as she got to know them she saw how divisive they were among their own kind, with a hundred conflicting views about who they were and what they should be doing against the others. It was all a bewildering kind of confusion with turmoil everywhere.

A time of wandering and seeking, it seemed to Anna. Not unlike the way it must have been three thousand years ago, she thought, when Joshua led the twelve tribes out of the wilderness and they first caught sight of the plains of Jericho beyond the Jordan, and every man had his own vision of the promises to be found on the far side of the river.

She made no effort to find a place for herself during those first years in Palestine. Instead she wandered from the towns to the settlements and back again, a period here and an interval there, always moving even if it was only a few miles away, never staying long enough in one place to become part of a way of life. She had been trained as a teacher in Cairo, and it was easy enough to support herself with substitute and part-time work. In any case people came and went in the chaos of war and her restlessness was unremarkable.

Nor was it difficult for a young woman to find a room in some new place. There were many men in her life then, and perhaps what she liked most about those brief and intense affairs was lying in bed late at night and listening to her lovers talk about themselves, gaining what seemed to her a vast knowledge of the dreams and fears that haunted men's lives. To Anna, those intimate encounters so quickly come and gone were a way of avoiding intimacy with herself, a way of feeling close to life without opening herself to its dangers. For she was still fleeing, she knew, still trying to escape the narrow street in Cairo with its crowded memories.

The Russians advanced on Berlin and the world war drew to an end. More Jewish refugees arrived in Palestine from Europe and elsewhere in the Middle East, many on clandestine routes. After a period in Jerusalem Anna left the strife of the cities and towns, seeking smaller settlements. Her way led south to the desert and it was there in the Negev, not far from the Egyptian border, that she found herself when the fighting broke out between the Arabs and the Jews, even before the British left Palestine.

It was also there that she met Yossi, one of the handful of Palmach soldiers sent by the central Jewish command to help them defend their isolated settlement. Everyone in the settlement dug trenches and learned to stand guard duty, but the young Palmach commandos were the elite among them because they had received real training in warfare.

Yossi was a handsome man whose lean dark body glistened in the desert sun. To her he looked more like an Arab than a Jew, and she wasn't surprised to learn he was from Iraq. When they were alone he spoke Arabic with her. His beautiful smiles burst upon her with a flash of teeth and she laughed at that, recalling the ways of her Arab friends in Cairo.

The little ones don't understand, Yossi said to her one day, referring to the settlers who were from Europe. They want to be good Jewish farmers but that won't help us when the British leave and the Arab armies attack. With only twenty-five defenders, women and men, and the roads controlled by the Arabs, we haven't a chance out here. We're too far away.

What then? she asked. What will become of us?

Oh we'll use our few rifles and throw some bottles of petrol and then we'll try to get out at night. It's the resistance itself that's important, you know they think Jews never fight. They're out for plunder and picking grapes and we've got to show them it's not like that here. The Egyptian soldiers have a mad idea of the good times ahead, so resistance of any kind will frighten them. They'll take our sandy little hilltop but then they'll look around at these makeshift desert huts and say, Why in the name of God are the Jews fighting over this? And if they fight like that here, how will it be farther north when they're defending real land, real houses? Have the Jews all gone crazy?

And that's how we'll win with a few old rifles and some bottles of petrol, said Yossi, confident and strong with his radiant smile.

Yossi's knowledge of the Egyptian soldiers was firsthand. One of his duties for the Palmach was intelligence and he often disappeared at night, disguised as an Arab, going off toward Gaza where the main Egyptian forces were quartered on the coast near the border. A few days later he would turn up again at the settlement, exhausted and exhilarated from his secret journeys through the desert, and go to work sending his information north on the settlement radio.

On the evenings of his return Anna rearranged her guard duty and she and Yossi were alone in one of the huts. He was younger than she was and perhaps it was the remoteness of her life there, or the knowledge that the settlement would soon fall, but it seemed to her she had never known a man quite like Yossi, so sure of himself in his gentle way and so at ease in the wind-driven desert nights that brought fear to everyone else. Then too, there was no need to think of ending anything with

Yossi because in a day or two he would be gone again anyway, off on another secret mission across the desert.

In the morning sun they sometimes had a moment to sit on a rise of sand and enjoy the silence of a new day coming to the magnificent desert landscapes. Yossi would be thoughtful, gazing at the sand sifting through his fingers.

Just imagine, he said. Some of these glittering particles come all the way from the upper Nile. The river carries the sand three thousand miles to the sea, then the currents bring it to the eastern shores of the Mediterranean and the winds carry it over here. So seldom do we know the worlds we walk. Isn't it true, Anna?

That winter and spring they beat off attacks by Arab irregulars. At the end of spring the British withdrew from Palestine and Israel declared itself a nation. The armies of five Arab countries invaded, with the Egyptian army advancing into the Negev and up the coast from Gaza. When the settlement was attacked, Yossi and the others used up all their ammunition in a single day of fighting. After dark they abandoned the settlement, dragging the wounded, and set out north across the Negev with Yossi acting as guide for the little band of survivors. Before dawn he hid them at the foot of a cliff and went off alone disguised as an Arab in the direction of the Egyptian forces in Beersheva. That night Anna and the others traveled again, without Yossi, and reached the safety of a larger settlement in the northern Negev.

A month later, when there was a lull in the fighting, Yossi was able to find Anna.

It's working, he said. The Egyptians have stopped advancing and are digging in. Soon we'll hit back between their positions and even things up a bit.

Yossi laughed and rushed back to the front and the war for independence went better, against all odds. When she saw him that summer he was bursting with success and exuberant plans. He wanted to marry her and it was also what she wanted. She was six or seven years older than he was and sometimes she worried about that, but she loved him and she also knew her old life was behind her now, as much a part of the past as the Palestine of British days. She was used to more sudden changes in life but these feelings had come to her slowly, over time in the isolation of the Negev, beginning even before she met Yossi.

Nor was it because of their child that she was choosing a life with Yossi. She had already decided to have the child if she could, no matter what happened to Yossi. So when he came to her in the summer and their love was more intense than ever, it all seemed clear to Anna. Still, only after the decisions were made did she tell him she was carrying his child. Yossi listened to her and smiled and smiled, overwhelmed with pride and wonder.

My mysterious and lovely Anna, he kept whispering late at night. My infinitely mysterious Anna. . . .

He whispered in Arabic as they often did when making love. In a way it seemed strange and they laughed at it sometimes. But there was also no denying the sounds had an intimacy that was precious to both of them, recalling their first nights together in the desert as well as more distant bonds from both their childhoods.

◆◆◆◆◆◆◆◆

Yossi was twenty-two when their son was born toward the end of 1948. After the war they lived on the coast in the south in order to be near the Negev, which they both loved. Yossi took courses at night and tried several different jobs. He was good at mathematics and physics and for a time he thought he might become an engineer, but nothing seemed to work out for him and eventually he went back into the army, training as a paratrooper. He was away for periods of time at one post or another and Anna returned to teaching when the baby was old enough. Yossi seemed unsure of himself, preoccupied and moody. His silences deepened when he was home and a distance grew between them.

At first Anna told herself it was simply because of his age

that he was finding it difficult to adjust to a settled life. But as time passed she had to admit there was more to it than that, for she also knew Yossi was a solitary man who had always lived inside himself.

Yossi had grown up in a village near Baghdad, the only child to live beyond infancy in a family with little money. Being poor meant assuming responsibilities, and Yossi had cared for the family's animals while going to school, along with working outside the house from an early age, first in his father's small shop and later as an apprentice bookkeeper in the nearest town. He was studious and reserved and devout, and for several years he thought he wanted to become a rabbi when he grew up. Since he was always busy going from one responsibility to another, he could only find time for himself by constructing an inner world. His classmates liked him but they also recognized his strangeness, the differences that set him apart. At school he retreated to the edge of the yard between classes and read while the other children played, then worked in his father's shop in the afternoon with a book propped open on the counter. Even as a young child he never had the luxury of doing only one thing at a time, so he learned early to treasure the secret adventures of imagination.

When he was older there were the daily cross-country trips to the town where he bent over a ledger for hours in a dusty little office, writing figures in columns and methodically making sense of them. How he loved those long private journeys through the countryside on unmarked paths which he alone understood. No matter how many times he made the trip, he told Anna, it was always a landscape of make-believe and the great joy of his youth. Out there in the deserts and fields, at last, he was free and there was nothing to hold him back. On the way to the town he ran and ran, memorizing a thousand details as the panorama flashed by in the sun, running and running until his chest ached and his heart tore at him, for no other reason than the joy of feeling himself. Then later, going home after the long quiet hours at the ledger, he traveled slowly in the twilight to spy out what he had missed in the land and to see what had changed, a boyish game of learning to sense the world which strengthened his already profound imagination and gathered it around him like a cloak, against the cool darkness of stars and night.

Yet despite these early experiences of aloneness and duty and secret escape, or perhaps because of them, Yossi was a man of great charm, as no one knew better than Anna. He was often withdrawn and quiet, even shy in manner, but when he spoke it was with the passion of true feelings. And he acted with the dignity of his solitude, and of course he was handsome. So one way or another, everyone took to Yossi. Anna had never known a man or a woman who wasn't attracted to him. But unhappily she now knew he would have to make many more journeys alone before he found a way to live with himself and others. She wasn't angry with what had happened, only sad. In the chaos of war, she realized, some things had seemed clearer than they were.

She was also reluctant to admit that Yossi's strength and courage at the little desert settlement during the war had probably made her think of her brother, and that in turning to Yossi then she had been seeking a kind of shelter she had known in childhood. This saddened her even more because it meant she hadn't traveled as far as she thought during those first restless years in Palestine. Even now when she was in her thirties, the shadows from the house on the narrow street in Cairo were still with her.

Before it ended with Yossi she had long talks with their closest friend—Tajar, who was several years older than Anna and who had helped Yossi get back into the army when his various jobs had come to nothing. Tajar listened to her and shook his head. Once, briefly, he and Anna had been lovers in Jerusalem before she went south to the Negev and met Yossi, but now Tajar's friendship was equally strong with both of them. To Yossi, in fact, he had become almost an older brother. Tajar was a practical man, blunt and unmarried, dedicated to his work for the government.

It's not your fault, Anna, said Tajar. It's no one's fault and you shouldn't take it on yourself. Of course you feel you've failed, so does Yossi. But it was an understandable mistake and you're both still young. You can do other things, start again, make a new life. I love and admire Yossi, you know that, but I also suspect he's not a man to be a regular husband and father. Not now anyway, and maybe never. We both know there's a part of him that lives alone and he knows it too. No one's to blame but that's the way it is and we have to recognize what is in life. You fell in love with a man who was strong and laughed and ran free in the desert, and that's still what he is so you weren't wrong. You weren't then and you aren't now and you shouldn't blame yourself.

It's not that easy, said Anna.

No of course it's not, replied Tajar. You have a son and everything I've said is no more than words. Living life day in and day out is something else.

Day in, day out, thought Anna. Finally she and Yossi decided on a divorce. He was very tender with her then, with that wistful manner that often came over him.

I know you're right, he said. I know it's no good like this for either of us, or for our child. Maybe I was just too young. We tried but . . . well, it just hasn't worked.

We didn't try hard enough, said Anna, tears running down her face. No one ever tries hard enough and so many beautiful things are lost. Irreplaceable things . . . the treasures of our lives.

◆◆◆◆◆◆◆◆

All during those years there was enormous turmoil in the Middle East, with huge displacements of population. After the First World War it had been Greeks and Turks who were displaced and now it was the turn of Jews and Arabs. Nearly a million Jews left Moslem countries, about 700,000 of them going to Israel, and 600,000 Arabs left Israel for Moslem countries.

There were also constant bombings and murders carried out by Arab infiltrators crossing over from the Egyptian positions in the Gaza strip on the coast. In the autumn of 1956, Israeli tanks struck across the border and raced into the desert against the Egyptian army. During the eight days of the Sinai campaign the Israeli armored columns conquered the entire Sinai peninsula, but they soon had to withdraw because of combined American and Russian pressure at the United Nations.

Anna and Yossi's son was then almost eight. It was a clear autumn afternoon when Anna took him for a walk along the beach to tell him what she had learned from Tajar that morning.

Yossi was among the fallen. He had been killed while serving with the paratroop battalion in the western Sinai, caught in the crossfire of an Egyptian ambush at the Mitla Pass.

Yossi had died a hero's death and Anna took their son to the funeral. Tajar, ever loyal and strong, arranged everything and stood beside the two of them. But a part of Anna could never accept the fact that Yossi was dead. In her dreams she still saw him as he had been when they first met, a handsome young man with a beautiful smile, laughing, disappearing into the desert disguised as an Arab.

She said nothing about this to anyone, not even Tajar. But it didn't really surprise her years later when she learned that Yossi hadn't actually died in the Sinai, that instead he had gone away to pursue a secret and solitary life in the most ancient of all Arab capitals. For by then, through herself as well as her son, Anna knew much more about the strange ways the past can go on living in other lives, reworking destinies through dream and memory with those same soft echoes of time she herself had once heard in the shadows of childhood.

FOUR

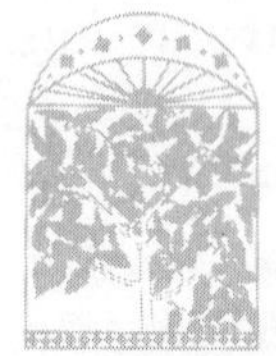

From the moment Tajar met Yossi, he suspected Yossi would one day become the most unusual agent he would ever know. Everything about Yossi suggested it.

Yossi had an astonishing visual memory that went far beyond the photographic. It was the atmosphere of a scene that he remembered, almost its shape in time. Details of objects and movement all flowed from this unique sense of moment, a configuration which time never repeated. It was a way of observing the world that Tajar worked hard to instill in his agents, but with Yossi it was simply the way he saw things.

Tajar thought of Yossi as a boy running across the fields to the town where he worked in the afternoons, recording every scene to the rhythm of his heart, free at last to play his own childhood game of recognition.

Yossi also had a touch of self-denial about him, an abstemious quality. He felt very strongly the allure of the world's colors and sounds and textures but he always kept them at a slight distance, so as not to be seduced by them. If anything, this heightened his perceptions. He grasped the essentials of a moment but was not quite a part of them.

Tajar thought of Yossi on the edge of the schoolyard as a child, reading while the other children played. Of Yossi in his father's shop with a book propped open on the counter, one eye for himself as the customers milled and gossiped. Of Yossi's religious inclinations as a boy when he had thought of becoming a rabbi.

And Yossi was quick and alert and intelligent, and above all he was a secret adventurer. *The happiest moments of my childhood* were what Yossi called those times when he had run free across the desert in the glaring sun of the afternoon, to return home more slowly as the twilight turned to stars and still night. And of course there were his experiences as a young man in the Palmach during the war for independence, when he had crossed the Negev disguised as a bedouin, to penetrate the Egyptian positions along the coast and mix with the Egyptian soldiers in Gaza.

How did you feel when you made those trips? Tajar asked him. And Yossi laughed merrily in reply as Anna listened to the conversation between her husband and their friend.

That's exactly how he felt, she said to Tajar with a smile, as she chopped vegetables for their dinner. He was always laughing because it was always a game to him, more of the running game from his childhood with the added excitement of a costume and a secret purpose to it all, a tattered keffiyeh and a filthy bedouin's cloak and some new accent he was trying out. A different tribe every time because it was more fun that way, more challenging and dangerous. Admit that you loved the thrill of it, Yossi.

Oh I did, said Yossi, still laughing as he leapt to his feet and put his arms around Anna from behind. It *was* a game and *of course* I loved it and the only thing I loved more was coming back to you. Admit that you never had a wink of sleep the nights I got back.

The wildly romantic sheik, shrieked Anna as he tickled her, stealing into my tent at dusk straight from the exotic delights of dusty Gaza. That's enough now from the two of you or we'll never have any dinner to eat. . . .

Anna had been reluctant to admit that the Yossi she loved wasn't fitted for a settled life as a husband and father, but Tajar had been aware of it from the very beginning. It was no surprise to him that Yossi could find nothing for himself once the war was over and he was a civilian trying to live with the concerns of an everyday life. Yossi simply didn't have the temperament for that. His talents were elsewhere and he couldn't help but fail in the regular world.

Unlike Tajar, Yossi was a genuine solitary and his inner needs could only become more demanding as he grew older. Tajar needed to be with others and loved communing with people he felt close to. Without that, life was drab to him and he lacked peace of mind. But it wasn't that way for Yossi. In Yossi's heart there were vast landscapes where he would always roam alone, no matter what kind of life he lived outwardly.

Tajar saw this in Yossi. Born in different circumstances, in another era, Yossi might have adopted a life of religious seclusion, or perhaps some secular version of it, if that had been more in keeping with the age. Tajar could easily imagine Yossi as an explorer in the nineteenth century, one of those driven men who had gone off to march alone through deserts and jungles in search of the source of the Nile or the remnants of a lost civilization. Or in the Middle Ages he could have been one of those itinerant men who called themselves merchants and turned up with caravans from time to time at the barbarous outposts in Central Asia, while pursuing an interminable journey on the ancient silk route to China. Or earlier still, in the first centuries of the common era, he might have been one of those visionaries who took themselves off to the Egyptian desert to live alone for decades in a tiny cave, after the manner of St. Anthony, to sound the dimensions of their souls and ostensibly give shape to a new religion—the desert fathers, as they were known to a millennium of Christian scholars.

So circumstances and eras changed but Yossi was still an authentic solitary. And Tajar, with his special knowledge of the secret ways of secret worlds, was quick to recognize it long before Anna or even Yossi suspected the truth.

A decrepit vegetable truck had ended Tajar's days as a master of disguise, but in Yossi he had found a man who could do more than he ever had. With Tajar planning for him and supporting him, Yossi could in fact live the dream that Tajar had only imagined as a boy running through the bazaars and courtyards of the Holy City, listening to the stones of Jerusalem.

◆◆◆◆◆◆◆◆◆

Tajar was patient.

When he and Yossi met in the early 1950s, after Tajar had learned to walk again and had gone back to work in the Mossad, Yossi was still a young man in his middle twenties, about ten years younger than Tajar. For other young men that would have been the right age to begin training for a deep-cover role, but Tajar thought Yossi was so exceptional that only a very special career could match his talents. And for that he needed maturity, Tajar decided. Tajar wanted Yossi to know himself well, to be sure of himself.

Yossi had always wanted to go back into intelligence, but in those days a young man couldn't choose the Mossad, the Mossad chose him. When Yossi's efforts at civilian work came to nothing, Tajar found him a job with the army, translating Arabic documents, which Yossi was able to combine with service in the paratroopers to keep himself active. Yossi was deeply dissatisfied with his life and he and Anna drifted apart. More than ever Yossi wanted to get into covert operations but still Tajar hesitated, waiting for the right moment, some final break in Yossi's life.

Tajar didn't know what form it would take but he was sure it would come and it did, after Yossi and Anna were divorced. One evening he was sitting alone with Yossi by the shore, talking and looking out to sea, when Yossi confessed he didn't want to go on living in Israel. He was a devout Jew and believed in the state and its destiny, but it wasn't a place where he felt at home. Yossi tried to explain his reasons for wanting to leave, which had to do with the strangeness of the society and the ways of the country being foreign to him, by which he meant Western. Most of what he said Tajar already knew, as did Anna, for Yossi had always been frank with both of them. But the idea of not living in Israel was new and momentous.

What do all these feelings of mine come down to? said Yossi. That I was born in a different place, that's all. That I learned to live differently when I was young.

Among Arabs, said Tajar.

If you want to put it that way, replied Yossi.

As a Jew among Arabs, added Tajar. As a person who is different and doesn't belong, who can never belong. Of course being different and not belonging can also be an adventure to young men, just as having a secret identity is an adventure. There's power and a sense of power in secret knowledge. But how long would it be before you decided you wanted to come home?

That's just it, replied Yossi. I'm almost thirty, old enough to know who I am, and I don't feel this is home. I can't find any work that interests me. I can't settle down. Of course I know it's impossible to live in an Arab country now. The antagonism is too great. But I also know I don't want to live here, so I feel lost. I don't know what to do.

I understand, said Tajar, and I think we can find a solution that's not only interesting and challenging but useful. Extremely useful. What I have in mind is working for an ideal. When we have an ideal we strive for, it never has to fail, does it? It can live pure and real in our hearts, beyond change and decay, and what could be finer in a man's life than that? Think of how Jerusalem appears to those who imagine it from afar. It shines and it shines through the ages, an exquisite dream of redemption and hope off on top of its mountain . . . our Holy City.

Tajar laughed.

And more, he added, not just ours. *Everyone's* Holy City. Certainly that complicates life but it also makes life fascinating. We'll have to talk more about it, Yossi. In fact, just tonight all at once, we seem to have a great deal of talking to do.

Tajar had been refining his plan for several years. It was extraordinarily complex but by laboring over its details he was able to make it appear an unremarkable sequence for a deep-cover penetration, its steps straightforward and logical and the inevitability of its true goal still far in the future.

True, Yossi's training lasted much longer than usual, well over two years. He had to learn the regular techniques of espionage. He had to learn Spanish. He had to learn the intricacies of Islam so that he could appear to have been born and reared a Moslem. And he had to learn all the other attributes that went with the past life Tajar had constructed for him. There were also lengthy training missions abroad, in Beirut and Cairo and Europe, for the passage of time itself was a secret instrument in Tajar's plan. Yossi's adjustment to his new life had to be complete because the transition was to be permanent.

Of course Tajar kept this ultimate truth strictly to himself. Yossi suspected it and hoped it would be so, but certainly no one else in the Mossad could have foreseen such a future for an Israeli: an agent who was to penetrate Arab culture so deeply he would never come back.

Near the end of Yossi's training by the Mossad, the 1956 war broke out in the Sinai. Yossi's death, while he was on a special mission with the paratroopers, was documented and announced and surprised no one who had known him in civilian life or in the army, or even in the Mossad. Only Anna had her wistful dreams which she kept to herself. In the Mossad itself Yossi no longer existed and the secret identity of *the Runner*, as he was to be known henceforth in reports, was now limited to Tajar as his operations officer and the man Tajar reported to directly, the chief of the Mossad.

Early the following year Tajar began to receive progress reports from Buenos Aires where the Runner was living quietly, perfecting his Argentine accent and his knowledge of the city and its large Arab community. After about six months in Buenos Aires, the Runner was at last ready to emerge in the new persona Tajar had so elaborately planned for him over the years.

Yossi's name was now Halim and he was a young Syrian businessman. In the following weeks he went about meeting people and making new contacts in Buenos Aires in a natural way, in the course of expanding the small export-import concern he had recently inherited.

The business itself was well established, having been founded by a cousin of Halim's before the Second World War. Halim's family had left Syria when he was three and moved to Iraq, where they made a bare living as petty tradesmen. The cousin in Argentina, related to Halim's mother, wrote to the family of the opportunities to be found in Buenos Aires and offered to help. When he was fifteen Halim traveled alone to Buenos Aires, paid for by the cousin, and went to work as an apprentice bookkeeper in the cousin's small company. The cousin was an elderly widower, thoughtful and kind, a second father to Halim. He had many ideas for expanding his trade to North America but felt he was too old to get them going. Halim learned the business and inherited the company upon the cousin's death. He put the old man's ideas to work and in time began to make a great deal of money.

Poverty and hard work, family loyalty, crossing oceans at an early age and faithfully serving one's elders—these things were well understood in the Syrian community in Buenos Aires. So Halim came to be admired and respected and not just for his success in business. He was a man of great charm and people took to him instinctively because of his modesty and sincerity and goodwill. He was reticent about his accomplishments, even shy, and when people praised his success he always spoke with passion of the wise and kindly cousin who had given him his start and been a second father to him, and whose ideas he had used in building his business.

There was no guile or arrogance in Halim, only a quiet self-assurance and a direct open way of speaking which inevitably invited confidence. And he was always generous in his friendships in many thoughtful ways, and he was also a patriot. He even talked of returning to Syria one day and helping to build a better country, now that he had succeeded so well in the new world.

Ah Halim, his friends said affectionately, you're a true idealist who'll put the rest of us to shame. But if you go back to Syria what will you export? All they have is politics and people, there's no pampas and no beef. What could you find to sell?

These conversations often came over games of shesh-besh, the Arab name for backgammon, which the Arabs of Buenos Aires played incessantly in their clubs and cafés, as addicted to it as their cousins in the Middle East. In answer Halim flashed his handsome smile. He threw the dice and laughed.

Why not shesh-besh? he asked. I'll export sets to Europe and make it the pastime of all the little old ladies. Why not? It's an Arab game they ought to know about. Skill and chance in equal measure, just like life. . . .

Older people, in particular, were struck by Halim's tact and understanding of human character, which were very impressive for a man his age. According to the biography Tajar had constructed for Halim, he was five years younger than Yossi had been, or only about twenty-seven when he began to move around in Buenos Aires and become well-known in the Syrian community. Yossi had always had a youthful appearance and Halim's age seemed exactly right for him: a handsome young man who wore an attractive moustache in the Arab manner to give his youthful face a touch of maturity, which was helpful in business.

In fact there were several reasons why Tajar had made Halim younger than Yossi. For one, it explained why Halim hadn't appeared earlier in the Arab men's clubs and cafés in Buenos Aires, since that wasn't acceptable until a certain age. And for another, it gave Halim fewer years to account for in his life, especially the years when he had been in the army and in training for the Mossad. But there was also a more subtle reason.

Tajar had learned that a young man with knowledge beyond his years had a natural appeal to men with more experience, who were also the men with power and influence. Somehow there was a slight psychological shift on the older man's part, perhaps caused by a sense of flattery. In any case it tended to enhance communion and lead to a sharing of personal beliefs by the older man, as Tajar had discovered on his secret missions for the British during the war. Tajar had learned this psychological device from none other than Anna's benefactor in Cairo, the one-eyed British officer who had taught him so many clever truths about the details of espionage, techniques for which Tajar himself was famous in the Mossad. And now this small detail that Tajar had learned years ago from the one-eyed Englishman, in Cairo, was to give Halim a stunning opportunity for entering Damascus with important connections.

One of Halim's shesh-besh partners was the general who was Syria's military attaché in Buenos Aires, a position of no significance. The general had been shipped into exile because his political faction was out of favor in Damascus. Disgruntled and restless, the general found Halim a sympathetic listener to all his troubles. And when Halim began to talk about taking an exploratory business trip to Syria to see if he could find a place for himself, the general naturally offered letters of introduction.

Thus a year and a half after his arrival in Argentina, the Runner was on his way to Damascus for the first time.

Tajar flew to Geneva to meet him.

◆◆◆◆◆◆◆◆

Tajar and Yossi were overjoyed to see each other and to be together again. They hugged when they met and parted at the safehouse near Geneva, where they talked and talked for hours every day.

I've never seen you looking so well, said Tajar. The moustache gives you a most distinguished air, very proper and very purposeful. But how do you *feel* now that you're finally on your way?

The way I did when I was a boy, replied Yossi, bursting with smiles. It's like those times when I used to set out after school to go to work in the next town, and I ran and ran across the fields and the desert knowing it was all there waiting for me to discover it, running alone as fast as the wind until my chest ached and wanting it to ache so I could feel myself more, seeing life and breathing it and gulping down all of creation. *Alive.* That's how I feel.

Ah yes, murmured Tajar, adjusting his stiff painful legs in front of his chair. Just so, my friend, and may it always be so, *insh'allah.* God willing.

⬥⬥⬥⬥⬥⬥⬥⬥

The patriot Halim, successful in the new world and absent from his native land since the age of three, found Damascus very much to his liking. The friends of the general were helpful and Halim decided to move to Damascus and establish an export-import business. In Europe he had already made some promising business contacts. He returned to Argentina to close out his affairs and to transfer his funds to Switzerland. The general in Buenos Aires was pleased with his young friend's decision.

May I follow you soon, said the general, raising a toast at the farewell party he gave for Halim.

And for the good of our country, replied Halim, may it be very soon, *insh'allah.*

⬥⬥⬥⬥⬥⬥⬥⬥⬥

The general's faction was the Baath or Arab Renaissance party, which combined radical nationalism with a policy of social reform. It was influential in the Syrian army but still far from power.

So you mustn't be too closely identified with your friend the general, warned Tajar, when he met Yossi again in Europe. There's no way of knowing how the Baath will fare, and if the general loses out you don't want to lose out with him.

In fact there's only one way for you to survive in a thieves' den like Damascus, Tajar went on, and that's not only to be incorruptible, but to be *known* as incorruptible. You're in business, you're a practical man and a patriot and you must never be associated with any political group. The Arab renaissance? Good. That's exactly what you want and you want nothing more and nothing for yourself. You're the conscience of the revolution and you live for an ideal and politics is for others. It's your country you serve, Syria, and of that there can be no doubt. Will it help Syria? That's the question you must always ask yourself, and them, when friends want you to do something or ask for advice or support or money. Is it in the cause of the Arab revolution? Does it serve the real Arab renaissance? And always at the same moment—is it *right?* Is it true? Is it the Arab way? A conscience, my friend, that's what you must be: strong and incorruptible. The rest is for the others who will come and go in Damascus, gaining power for a time and losing it as the captains become colonels and overthrow the generals and are overthrown in turn by new captains becoming colonels, the way it always is when the military schemes and runs things. But a conscience doesn't scheme. It *feels.* And that's how you will last in a den of thieves and connivers and money makers and power seekers. As a vision, an idea in the heart. Indefinable. Like our fathers, Yossi, with their dream of Zion and their vision of Jerusalem. And there's nothing foreign about that to any man. Secretly, all human beings dream. Even thieves and connivers have that hidden place in their hearts.

◆◆◆◆◆◆◆◆

Halim set up his business in Damascus and began exporting leather goods and jewelry to Europe. Soon he added sheshbesh sets and tables, which became his most profitable product. His new friends in Damascus were helpful and he had good contacts in Europe, especially in Belgium. His business flourished and once or twice a year he traveled to Europe.

At home in Damascus, meanwhile, Halim continued to live quietly, an unassuming and charming and modest man, a patriot with a growing circle of acquaintances. In Syria it was a time of rampant instability as the country broke out of its union with Egypt. There was one coup d'etat after another and the Baath party gradually strengthened its hold on the army. Then in 1963 the Baath seized power outright and the new ruler of Syria was the general who had once been a military attaché in Buenos Aires, Halim's former shesh-besh partner.

FIVE

During that time the most important struggles over the Runner's fate didn't take place in Syria but in the headquarters of the Mossad, between Tajar and his superior, the only two men who knew the identity of the Runner and the details of the Runner operation. Their disagreements were fundamental and unresolvable and concerned the very nature of the operation. Tajar saw the Runner as a long-term asset who would acquire his worth only after years of being in place, while the chief of the Mossad felt there was more use to be made of the Runner now. *Long-term* and *now* were terms that constantly changed and their arguments took many forms.

The argument might have seemed to be simply the traditional one between an operations officer and the man above him who paid the bureaucratic bills: the operations officer wanted to protect his agent and keep him from danger, and his superior wanted more immediate results from investments made in time and money. But Tajar's great experience, and the fact that he himself had once briefly been chief of the Mossad, made the issue far more complex than that, as both men recognized. Not only careers and roles and self-respect were involved, but history and philosophies.

The son of the rabbi from the Ukraine who was the chief of the Mossad had acquired his intelligence experience inside Israel, unlike Tajar. Little Aharon, as he was called, was a short stocky man of immense energy who did nothing in life but work at his job. He had made his start as a policeman and become a counterintelligence expert for Shai during the British Mandate, later expanding this position to counterespionage against the Jewish Revisionists and their right-wing cells. After independence, on orders from the prime minister, he disarmed the right-wing Jewish underground and became even more powerful in the government. He was a brilliant, ruthless man who knew how to run an organization and get things done.

His first serious clash with Tajar over the Runner operation came when it was time for the Runner to take up residency in Damascus. Tajar insisted that the Runner shouldn't report by secret radio, which was standard procedure for agents then and also their greatest risk. Instead, Tajar wanted the Runner to use false bottoms in the shesh-besh tables he sent to Europe for his reports. An agent who didn't use a radio was in a different category, by definition, with different goals. Tajar won that round of *long-term* over *now*, as he won several others. But in 1963 when the Runner's former shesh-besh partner from Buenos Aires became the president of Syria, Little Aharon exploded.

This is preposterous, he shouted at Tajar. The Runner's in a position to tell us almost anything. Why won't you put him on the general and let him tell us what is going on?

But what happens when there's another coup? replied Tajar. Even if the Baath stays in power, it's almost certain the general won't. He's just the first man out of their pack. Who comes next?

And what if there's going to be a war tomorrow? shouted Little Aharon. The Runner can't even tell us. It's madness.

No, it's wisdom, replied Tajar. If there's going to be a war tomorrow someone else can tell us. We have other people for that. The Runner's time will come but it's not yet. I want him to last.

Little Aharon frowned. *To last,* he thought. Yes, of course you want him to last. He's your hope and your dream, all you've got.

Tajar sat facing him, adamant, using his hands to rearrange his crippled legs. In a way Little Aharon pitied Tajar, and Tajar knew that. Little Aharon, after all, had captured Eichmann in Argentina and obtained, for the West, Khrushchev's secret speech denouncing the crimes of the Stalin era in the Soviet Union. He had an international reputation in intelligence and was famous among the powerful. When professionals in other capitals thought of the Mossad, they thought of Little Aharon, who *was* the Mossad to them. Yet at the end of the war it was Tajar who had been the one with fame and power and promise. Why shouldn't Little Aharon give in to him now over one agent? One operation?

Look, said Little Aharon, if you won't have the Runner jumping into bed with the general, at least give me something new. Some way I can tell myself the operation is going forward.

Two things, replied Tajar at once. I'll have him move closer to Syrian armaments and also to the Palestinian refugees.

Little Aharon looked down at his desk and at the crippled legs stretched out on the far side of it. Syria's armaments came from the Soviet Union, so that offer was something. But the activities of the Palestinian refugees were close to nonexistent, so that amounted to nothing at all. One offer of hard facts, another of the Runner skulking around in the desert disguised as an Arab. Sadly, he thought, Tajar was a prisoner of his own past. What had worked for him once he went on dreaming would work for him again. He was an idealist and a romantic who didn't understand change. He kept trying to do the same things over and over again, living in ideas and hope and cut off from change by his own imagination—and by an automobile accident. No one was better at the mechanics of infiltrating agents into Arab countries and supporting them once they were there. But when it came to goals, he kept slipping back into the past.

Little Aharon did some more shouting but his heart wasn't in it. In the end he decided to let Tajar have his way with the Runner.

All right, Little Aharon said finally. The Runner concentrates on Syrian armaments and Palestinian refugees and not the president . . . for the time being.

◆◆◆◆◆◆◆◆

Tajar was triumphant. He knew it was the most important decision ever made in the Runner operation. It would take still more time but slowly, methodically, he was giving the operation the shape he wanted. Not even Little Aharon could suspect how long-term his goals really were. And except for the Runner himself, no one else knew enough about the operation to be able to judge it.

What Tajar had been planning for so long was no less than the ultimate penetration of an enemy nation. The Runner would go on for years acquiring power and influence in Syria until one day he would be one of the most important men in the country. But at the same time he would never be simply an agent, a Syrian who worked for a foreign country. Foreign agents worked for money or power or out of faith or ideology, but they were always still *foreign* agents and the Runner would never be that. The Runner would be a Syrian who was also secretly an Israeli, his motivation and devotion forever beyond question. And that ultimate achievement in espionage, to Tajar's knowledge, had never been accomplished anywhere before, by anyone.

◆◆◆◆◆◆◆◆

We have two new directions to explore, Tajar said to Yossi when next they met in Europe. The first is the armaments business. It would be useful if you could think of a way to get into repair work. In a very small way to begin with, you understand. Nothing glamorous or dramatic but something quite ordinary, such as armored personnel carriers. They're always being modified this way or that, not the heavy work but little things. Rods and gadgets, the seats or the exhaust system, anything. I've looked at the work our people do and it doesn't require an engineer, just some competent machinists and a man overseeing them. Most of it is regular business. You call in a technician to design a fitting or a tool when you need to, give your customers good service and make sense of the books. The army supply officers get used to dealing with you, they know they can count on you and ask you to take on a little more, perhaps. In time it can grow.

And I know you like that sort of thing, added Tajar, because once you thought of being an engineer.

Yossi laughed. It sounds easy enough, he said. And the other new direction?

The Palestinian refugee camps, replied Tajar. Now that the Syrians are starting to organize and arm a few Palestinian groups, it would probably be wise for you to get started with them. It's patriotic and it's in the Arab cause and it would give you a chance to get out of Damascus and taste some desert air. There's that side to you too and you can't spend all your time over ledgers and talking to people in cafés or on strolls by the river.

And the general? asked Yossi.

After this general there will be another general, replied Tajar, and then another and another. But armaments and Palestinians, I suspect, will be with us much longer than any of them.

He always beat me at shesh-besh anyway, said Yossi.

I don't believe that.

Out of design, of course.

Ah, now that I do believe, replied Tajar, smiling, and went on to other matters.

◆◆◆◆◆◆◆◆

A Syrian army officer asked Halim to say a few words to the president about a personal matter. Others approached him with propositions for smuggling or special contracts or to serve as an intermediary with more senior officers who were Halim's friends. But with honesty and gentleness Halim always turned aside these opportunities for making men indebted to him.

Only ideals will sway him, it was said in Damascus as his reputation grew and he became known as a man of vision—the incorruptible one.

◆◆◆◆◆◆◆◆

As a boy growing up with Arab ways, long before he became Halim, Yossi had dreamed of the fabled place known as Damascus, a source of myth and wonder from his childhood which would always exist beyond time and stone. An imaginary city to him, like Jerusalem.

Damascus the fair, city of many pillars, the pearl of the East and the gateway to Mecca, where for centuries the caravans of the faithful had set out on the haj to cross the desert. A city of many moods but known above all as el Fayha, *the fragrant*, from its innumerable gardens and orchards.

Astride its river at the foot of a mountain where it nestled against a harsh landscape, a transdesert route from antiquity at the confluence of Asia and Europe and Africa, which was unique even in the ancient Middle East. For unlike any other city on earth, Damascus had never known obscurity in all its four thousand years of history. Instead, it had been preeminent to every empire that had ever held sway in the Fertile Crescent, Egyptian and Hittite and Babylonian and Assyrian, Persian and Greek and Roman and Arab, Seljuk and Mongol and Mameluke and Turkish.

Always important, forever destroyed and rebuilt, famous for its apricots and grapes and melons, its damask silk which was brought to Europe by the Crusaders and its figs and pistachios which the Romans transplanted around the Mediterranean as a far-flung gift from the Damascenes, worshipper once of Adad the storm-god and later a flourishing center of Christianity and Islam, holy to Christians because of the conversion of St. Paul and holy to Moslems as the burial site of Salah al-din, the great Kurdish warrior who defeated the Crusaders. With its luxuriant gardens and orchards, its old walled city to the south of the river and its new quarters to the north along shady avenues, the ancient beauty of Damascus reached back in history to the very birth of towns, recalling man's earliest dreams of an earthly paradise on the edge of the desert.

Halim loved the city and always felt these past worlds adding new dimensions to his life in Damascus, where the inhabitant's subtle sense of time also allowed him to find a place in his days for the distant persona of Yossi. Thus when Halim wished to strengthen himself by giving voice to his attachment to Tajar and the present, he talked to some Syrian friend about the kindly, thoughtful widower-cousin in Argentina who had given him his start in life and had taught him so much.

I owe everything to that man. His ideas, his very being, run in my veins and sustain me, Halim said truthfully, with complete conviction.

And when he met with his new Palestinian contacts and talked about their humiliation and anger and their national destiny, their fight for a homeland, his own childhood dreams fired his words with a passion no one could mistake. I know *exactly* how you feel, Halim told them, and the depth of his feelings could not help but make a powerful impression upon his listeners. Indeed, it was the intensity of Halim's vision that set him apart.

All this Tajar had foreseen. All this Tajar had carefully planned and made part of Yossi's training when the two of them were transforming Yossi into the patriot Halim, whose success would always depend on the sincerity of his feelings. For that was the heart of the Runner operation, although only Tajar and Halim truly understood it: the Runner would succeed because Halim was genuine.

Having been in Damascus a half-dozen years, Halim was completely at ease with his life there. It was then that Tajar decided it might be useful to add another dimension to the Runner's life. He discussed it with Yossi when they met in Belgium and told him something about the man he wanted Yossi to meet—an Englishman. Tajar was suggesting the connection, he said, not for any professional reasons, for the Englishman would never be of use to Yossi in an operational way. Rather, it was strictly for personal reasons.

To give you a different dimension of time, perhaps, said Tajar with a smile.

Yossi was intrigued. Then you know this man yourself? he asked.

Oh yes, replied Tajar. Once upon a time, in fact, he taught me much of what I know about our business. And oddly enough, he also knew Anna briefly, long ago.

Yossi turned serious. That *is* another dimension of time, he said. And what's the name of this mysterious Englishman?

He calls himself Bell, replied Tajar.

The man in Jericho?

Yes.

Yossi nodded thoughtfully. I've heard of him, he said.

SIX

In the early morning stillness of what he liked to call his north verandah, actually a warped wooden platform with a tin roof outside the front door of his dilapidated bungalow, the one-eyed English hermit of Jericho sat gazing at the luxuriant shade beneath his orange trees, studying the patterns of sunlight glaring on the hard mud. Ants worked busily moving bits of straw in and out of the small patches of brightness, so diligent in their unending tasks he sometimes imagined he could hear them. But in fact the whirring hum of early mornings came from higher up in the trees where thousands of tiny insects were beating their wings in joy at having found an oasis of paradise, an intoxicating garden of orange fragrance in the middle of the lifeless desert around Jericho.

The orange grove spread out on all sides of his bungalow, guarding his privacy. There was an open space near the back door where he could sit at night if he wanted to look at the stars, and next to it a grape arbor, the south patio as he called it, where he could sit during the day if he wanted to see no one at all. But generally he spent his mornings on the front porch —the north verandah—with its view of the dirt road beyond the orange grove. He had some benches and his most comfortable reading chair on the porch, and a table with its customary piles of fruit and books and two identical decanters of what looked like water to prevent dehydration, one decanter filled with water and the other with arak.

So for Bell, a man with a horribly disfigured face who had long ago retired from the devious world of espionage, mornings on his north verandah contained the essentials of life.

The bungalow itself, like most houses in Jericho, was a rambling one-story affair of mud-brick covered by plaster, painted with some faint color which had quickly faded away to indeterminate pastel. A rainstorm would have washed the whole place away in an hour, but of course it never really rained in Jericho. Instead, once or twice a winter, the sky clouded over and a vague misty substance brushed against people's faces, causing no end of wonder and a solemn rearrangement of greetings for several days.

Rain, a man would gravely say upon meeting his neighbor. *Rain, by the will of God*, came the equally grave reply.

Bell's rooms were sparsely furnished. There were some tables and benches and chairs, a cot here and there and bookcases fashioned from wooden crates hanging on the walls. The ceilings were high and it was always breezy inside the house because the fierce sun ate up the air it touched, causing turbulences where it didn't reach. From the road, beneath the thick foliage of the orange trees, only small children and donkeys could see Bell on his front porch. Callers, jingling the bell at the rusty wrought-iron gate, he came to recognize by the lower halves of their bodies and particularly by their sandaled feet.

What arcane arts we arrive at in life, thought Bell, inwardly smiling as he grew familiar over time with the idiosyncrasies of his friends' feet planted inside the gate.

Bell could never smile in a normal way because his face was a mask built by surgeons. A bullet had once shattered a spyglass he was looking through, driving metal and glass fragments into his face and ripping away an eye and most of his features. So in a way he was fortunate to have anything at all resembling a face.

The shattering spyglass had also torn apart his hand that was holding it. The best the surgeons had been able to do with that, using grafted skin and metal inserts, was to reconstruct a permanently rigid claw which was half-closed and half-open, a kind of tool for holding things. Bell made use of this ugly claw of a hand by wrapping it around a glass of arak, which was also a more or less permanent fixture with him.

No one in Jericho and few people anywhere knew that Bell had been a man of great power in the Middle East during the Second World War, when he had headed an elite British intelligence unit in Egypt, mysteriously known as the Monastery because its headquarters were hidden away in an ancient abandoned monastery in the desert. Bell's agents, inevitably referred to as Monks and famous for their elaborate disguises, had operated behind German lines and among German sympathizers in many Arab countries. So effective were the Monks that their anonymous leader had become an awesome legend to intelligence experts in London. Yet Bell himself, who had gone by another name then, had managed to keep his identity secret even within his own organization. Most of the Monks had thought the withdrawn man with the claw and the war-blasted face was no more than a minor aide to the ruthless colonel who apparently ran the Monastery—actually Bell's second-in-command.

No sooner had the North African campaign ended than the Monastery was disbanded by order of the highest authority in London, partly out of professional jealousy and competitive maneuverings within the War Office, partly because of an unspoken fear that the Monastery's uncanny ability to penetrate almost any target was considered too dangerous in all but the most extreme of wartime emergencies. For by then, justifiably or not, the Monks had acquired a reputation for being able to go almost anywhere and do almost anything.

The brilliant leader of the Monastery was offered an important staff position in London which he firmly refused, arguing that he was emotionally exhausted and not equipped in any case for the usual promotions of government. Instead, he offered to work in a lesser role in Cairo until the end of the war, when he would retire in the Middle East on disability pay. With a tired voice and his customary self-irony, Bell gestured at his bulging black eye patch with his twisted claw.

Some of us are never meant to be more than field hands, he said. And an empire, no doubt, always has forgotten corners for its honored cripples.

To his superiors in the War Office, Bell seemed much too young to be ending such a successful career. But the fact that he had been born and brought up in India and had never really lived in England, together with his face, was enough to convince even the most skeptical generals in the War Office that they had to respect his wishes and not bring him back to London. Indeed, Bell's face had always been indisputable proof of his sincerity. There was simply no arguing with that grotesque misshapen affliction with which he looked upon the world, the most terrible face anyone had ever seen.

Bell took advantage of his free time in Cairo by studying Arabic. When the war was over in Europe he retired on disability pay and changed his name and moved to Jerusalem, where he continued to improve his Arabic. Of course he knew his former colleagues in British intelligence were keeping an eye on him. That was only to be expected. One of the reasons he had chosen British Palestine was to make it easier for them to watch him. For the same reason he later decided to move to Jordan when the British Mandate in Palestine was coming to an end, since the British had created the country of Jordan out of the larger, eastern part of Palestine and operated quite freely there. Because of his face Bell had always been extremely sensitive to the feelings of others and he felt certain he couldn't cause anyone trouble in that little bedouin kingdom: a war-torn English expatriate quietly going to seed in some out-of-the-way place on the edge of the desert.

Bell found his forgotten corner of empire on a journey east one blustery winter day when he set out from the heights of Jerusalem to walk down through the wilderness of the Judean hills, down and down through the dry barren wastes. And then he caught sight of Jericho deep in the Jordan rift. With its flaring tropical flowers overhanging silent dusty lanes, its tall stately date-palms and cascading jasmine and tumbling walls of bougainvillea, its waterways and gurgling springs and fiery flamboyants bursting against a sun-washed sky, the little Arab village seemed no less than a miracle on the lifeless plain north of the Dead Sea. So small and intensely green in the haze, the lush oasis of Jericho struck Bell as the very mirage of his dreams, truly the Prophet's vision of paradise in a desert of eternal summer. From the lookout claimed by tradition to be the Mount of Temptation on which the devil had spread before Jesus the good things of the earth, Bell feasted his single eye upon Jericho. Later that same week, with an excitement unknown to him since the loss of his face, he moved his few belongings down the cold windy mountain from Jerusalem.

◆◆◆◆◆◆◆◆

In Jericho Bell walked and read and kept to himself, sipped arak and learned about orange trees. He also learned more about the town.

Presented long ago as a love-token to Cleopatra, as a gift from Mark Antony to his Egyptian queen of infinite variety who had then turned around and rented it to Herod for a good price, famous in antiquity for its balsam and henna and myrrh and saffron and balm of Gilead, *the town of palms* of the ancients was fed by water that went underground on the ridge of Jerusalem and found its way down beneath the desolate sweep of the Judean wilderness to gush forth in springs, miraculously, on the spot where Jericho had existed for ten thousand years, far longer than any other town ever built by man.

Because of the heat Bell got into the habit of always wearing white in Jericho, white cotton trousers and loose white blouses which he washed out every day and hung beside his grape arbor. As a foreigner he was an object of curiosity, but not overly so. With the Mount of Temptation standing nearby, and also the stretch of the Jordan River where John the Baptist had wandered and listened to God—and taken up the ancient

Eastern practice of purifying his friends and others by dunking them in the tepid river water, including his cousin Jesus—there had been Christian monks around Jericho for the last two millennia, desert outcroppings of poor Greeks and Copts and Syrians and Ethiopians tending their holy concerns.

Bell was different because of his face, and at first the villagers shunned him out of fear of his single eye—the evil eye to them —turning away when he passed and hiding their children and refusing to look at him. But he was used to this and made no effort to impose himself, having long ago acquired a profound inner solitude. In fact he went out of his way to shield the villagers from the ruin of his face and the single eye, always wearing a drooping straw hat when he left his orange grove and keeping his head down when he walked in town, even addressing the floor in shops so that his face would remain covered.

These were the ways of a humble man, people realized, and in time the villagers came to accept Bell as part of their shade and sunlight and flowers—the foreign hermit with the terrible God-inflicted face, thin and silent and withdrawn, an apparition in white quietly passing the days behind his orange trees.

◆◆◆◆◆◆◆◆

Bell had been in Jericho about a dozen years when his dramatic transfiguration took place. Before that time he had gradually become part of the unfathomable landscape of life, but then all at once a startling revelation gripped the villagers: Bell hadn't aged a day in twelve years. The austere one-eyed hermit looked exactly the same as when he first set foot in Jericho.

It took some time to grasp the magnitude of this discovery in a place where eternal summer caused all things to age more quickly than elsewhere. The flowers never stopped blooming in Jericho and the fruit trees never stopped bearing, but it was also true that the fierce sun took what it gave and decay was every bit as rampant as growth. In a matter of months a new house or a new dusty lane looked as if it had already been standing in neglect for half a century. And people, burning dark and wrinkled in the desert sun, moved rapidly through the stages of life to become slow-moving ancients at an early age, retiring to sit in the shade of memory while directing their grandchildren to open the water channels and flood the fruit trees, when the time was right and memory spoke.

But unlike every other thing in Jericho, Bell didn't age. His erect thin body was still the same and his drooping straw hat was the same and he still went for the same long walks in the desert at dawn and at twilight, a silent white figure off in the distance, alone with his thoughts. Above all, what everyone now talked about was the unchanging state of Bell's terrible face.

Bell's face couldn't change because the shattered bone and muscle had long ago been worked into a rigid mask by surgeons. Those were the medical facts of the matter. But the villagers understood growth and decay much better than surgery, and to them Bell's face never changed because it bore the special mark of God, a sign of that profound inner peace which was the ultimate treasure of every man's soul.

Thus subtly, in time, horror was transformed into beauty and Bell's monstrous affliction became a cause for reverence in Jericho. The idea shaped itself slowly in the shade of the village but eventually everyone sensed the unmistakable truth. The austere foreign hermit was touched by God and immutable, beyond the fingers of decay that turned even the rocks of the desert to dust. The white he wore signified purity of heart and his round single eye, once feared as evil, was now recognized as a sign of the divine presence that penetrated men's souls, the all-seeing eye of heaven.

In the minds of the villagers Bell had become a holy man, in other words, and from then on his gaze and his greeting were revered as blessings.

Beyond Jericho the myth of the one-eyed English hermit continued to acquire ever more fantastic dimensions through the years. No rumor was too extreme to find its way into the fanciful legends that foreign travelers heard repeated with awe in Amman, the desert capital of Jordan.

Nor was official interest in Bell at an end. Two decades after the world war an officer from the British embassy in Amman still journeyed down to Jericho once a year to spend a day at Bell's cottage, ostensibly to inquire after his welfare but in fact to write a detailed report on his state of mind and his habits. For it seemed there were still those in London who were curious about the recluse who had once been the brilliant leader of the anonymous Monks in Egypt.

Bell accepted these official intrusions gracefully, answering questions as best as he could and withholding nothing he felt might be of interest. As the years passed these visits were made by younger men who were unaware of Bell's role in the world war and knew only the mythical Bell of the stories told in Amman—the eccentric English recluse with the appalling wreckage of a face who lived a life of asceticism and alcohol eight hundred feet below sea level, in a town that was ten thousand years old, reading and drinking and refining his soul in the heavy sun of Jericho. So perhaps it was only to be expected that these young officials occasionally let slip some wild piece of hearsay while eliciting information on Bell's front porch, blurting out the latest rumor then making the rounds in the capital of Jordan:

> And is it also true, sir, that you've existed on nothing but mangoes and arak for the last ten years?

Bell's guest would be sitting poised on the bench beside the front door, notebook and pen in hand, hopelessly mesmerized by the inhuman mask of Bell's face. On the table were Bell's customary two decanters and the usual piles of fruit and books. Bell listened to the insects humming in the orange trees and a twisted look of conspiracy came over his face, an expression Abu Musa or Moses the Ethiopian would have recognized as a gentle smile.

No, it's not true, replied Bell. In fact I've revived the ancient Gnostic rite of eating fresh figs on the night of each new moon. Ripe, sticky, juicy fresh figs, a great basket of them for ceremonial reasons. More than enough to keep a man in visions of ecstasy for an entire month.

SEVEN

No one in Jericho was happier with Bell's miraculous transfiguration than his great friend and admirer, Abu Musa, a patriarch of the village who had innumerable cousins and nephews and nieces, and great-nephews and great-nieces, scattered around the Middle East. Although a grower of fruit trees in Jericho for many decades, Abu Musa was a man with another past. Early in the century he had ridden with the forces of Lawrence of Arabia, triumphantly blowing up Turkish trains in the deserts between Damascus and Medina, and he had never forgotten his spectacular adventures with that famous Englishman. Through some strange quirk of the years the old Arab still associated the English with romantic destruction, with dynamite exploding in barren places in a noble cause, and thus Bell's ruined face to him was a guide to heroic memories and the glories of his own extravagant youth.

Or at least that was the way Abu Musa explained his feelings of friendship for Bell, conjuring up a chaotic imagery which was typical of the old Arab's abstruse mixtures of time and nostalgia and fact, an airy heartfelt exuberance that was as inaccessible to reason as the shifting patterns of sunlight beneath the orange trees in Bell's front yard. For the truth was simply that Abu Musa enjoyed Bell's company. Like Bell, he was a thoughtful man who pondered the world from a distance, and so the two men had much in common.

Abu Musa had discovered Jericho in much the same way as Bell. After his own world war, the first one, like Bell but journeying in the opposite direction, heading west from the deserts on the other side of the Jordan River, Abu Musa had glimpsed Jericho from the heights of Moab one winter and decided it was the place where he should spend his life. When Bell turned up in the village three decades later, Abu Musa sold him a house and under the pretense of giving advice on orange trees, which required lengthy discussions in the shade, he became a regular visitor to Bell's north verandah. Their friendship flourished and Abu Musa soon became Bell's advocate and protector in Jericho.

It was Abu Musa, not surprisingly, who planted the first suggestions around the village as to the secret meaning of Bell's face, when he thought it was time for that miracle to be revealed. Abu Musa believed divine revelation sometimes needed a human nudge, perhaps as a railway in the desert sometimes needed dynamite, so he had gone around delicately placing hints in coffeeshops in order to acquire for Bell the status he felt his friend deserved—that of holy man. This he admitted to Bell only after his secret campaign was well under way. As usual the two of them were sitting on Bell's front porch that day, Bell sipping arak while Abu Musa puffed away on the nargileh he kept there.

A shameless deception, said Bell, with a sneer of contempt, which was the way his face showed affection.

Abu Musa nodded happily, his thick white moustache rising and falling as his waterpipe gurgled and bubbled. He was a tall heavy man whose voluminous, light-blue galabieh made him look even larger than he was, as massive as a bank of faded morning glories spread over Bell's front porch, where he half-reclined on a bench propped against the wall of the house. In answer Abu Musa waved the mouthpiece of his nargileh in the air, composing an indecipherable script from the whiffs of smoke, perhaps a quotation from the Koran or an obscure reference from the *Thousand and One Nights.* Sometimes the smoke had the smell of tobacco and sometimes of hashish, depending on Abu Musa's mood.

No deception on my part, mused Abu Musa. I was just tired of seeing you hide behind that tattered straw hat of yours. At a certain age a man must step out in the open and declare himself, and there was no question in my mind that you'd been hiding long enough. So I asked myself, Who is Bell really? What are we to make of him in Jericho? And the answer I heard in my heart was as clear as the peaks of the Moabite hills at sunrise. Surely he's a holy man. Doesn't he have all the attributes? And if that's the situation, I thought, wouldn't it be better for people to recognize the truth? So I whispered a suggestion here and there and now people are beginning to grasp the truth, God willing.

Bell laughed, sensing more devious schemes at work. A holy man who drinks all day? he asked.

Once more Abu Musa majestically scattered smoke, wafting aloft the mouthpiece of his nargileh as if he were a magician dispensing illusions with a wand.

My friend, he murmured, we live in the lowest and oldest town on earth, far below sea level where facts and the air lie heavy and have done so for ten millennia, much nearer the core of the world than people elsewhere. Who can be concerned with a little sipping in such an ancient dry hot place? And anyway, no one's claiming you're a saint, just holy. Of course while I was thinking my thoughts back then I also asked myself why I spend so much time on your porch talking and talking and talking, and listening. According to Jericho time I'm nearly three hundred years old, counting four summers and therefore four years for each one on a normal calendar, and it's inconceivable I should be a fool at such an advanced age. No, impossible, surely I should be wise with so many years behind me, God willing. And so? And so I considered these flowers within my head and decided the reason I like to sit here and talk and talk with you, and listen, is because I'm in the company of a holy man with whom such things are right and good and the one true way of the one true God. Don't you see? It's all very clear when you think about it.

Bell laughed again. Well it was clear enough, he thought, given Jericho time and his friend's logic. Why shouldn't a three-hundred-year-old patriarch assign himself grand motives for his everyday habits?

But Bell also sensed the old Arab was only partly joking and that disturbed him, because Bell knew there was nothing admirable about his retreat from the world, which was caused solely by his unbearable ugliness. *He* knew he was a drunkard and a coward who was terrified by the horror of his own face, which to him was a brutal cause for shame, a mark of his utter uselessness as a human being. Indeed, Bell sometimes felt he wasn't even qualified to be called human. Others might think he acted out of humility, but to Bell his ways weren't those of humility but of abject humiliation. No one could ever know what the horror of his face meant—to him.

For a time, it was true, he had tried to hide reality from himself in the secret conceits of espionage. But all of that clever subterfuge had ended long ago in the Monastery in Egypt. By becoming a recluse in Jericho he had intended to render his soul naked through a life without visible purpose, and the reverence he now saw in people's eyes was causing him a new agony of self-doubt, because he felt he was slipping back into deception. Even the respect shown him by Abu Musa was painful in a way it had never been before.

Bell abhorred deception because of his face. But he also loved Abu Musa and was always careful to hide his pain, for the simple reason that he felt it was his to bear and shouldn't be inflicted on others.

◆◆◆◆◆◆◆◆

Besides Abu Musa, the only regular visitor to Bell's north verandah was his neighbor from the adjoining orange grove, a eunuch and monk who was the biggest man anyone had ever seen. Even Abu Musa looked small when standing next to the great chocolate bulk of Moses the Ethiopian, a resident of Jericho since Turkish times.

The giant had arrived in Palestine early in the century, a retainer to an elderly Ethiopian princess who had come to the Holy Land to live out her last days in pious Christian seclusion. After a few winters on the windy heights of Jerusalem the princess had drifted down to Jericho, where the perpetual warmth was more to her liking. She built a small bungalow and a private chapel in the middle of an orange grove and there devoted her days to prayer and contemplation. Her royal retinue, a half-dozen monks and nuns, had their tasks to perform and saw to her needs. Moses was the youngest among them and it was his duty to sit by the gate of the orange grove and guard the solitude of her tiny estate. This he did from first light to last, wearing the brilliant yellow robes of his native land while positioned beneath a royal poinciana or flamboyant tree. The combination of colors thereby presented to passing villagers was startling even for Jericho—bright yellow and gleaming chocolate, flaming orange-red and deep green. Moses took his role as gatekeeper seriously and managed never to smile while the princess lived, but he also utterly failed to look fierce because he was such a gentle young man by nature.

Once a week the princess had gone into town to select the hot peppers that were used in such abundance in her dishes. She did this with great care, feeling and sniffing each pepper, accompanied on her shopping excursions by a nun-in-waiting and by Moses, who towered along behind the two elderly women delicately holding a parasol over their heads, by his sheer size enforcing an air of decorum where they passed.

On one such occasion a camel in the marketplace had suddenly taken a manic turn and come charging toward the princess, legs flailing, dangerously out of control. *Moses,* murmured the little princess. Whereupon the giant, without lowering the parasol that shaded his mistress, stepped in front of the crazed beast and reached an arm over its neck and shoulders and gave the camel a heave that spun it up and over and dropped it on its back in the dust. The frothing camel was so surprised it lay with all four legs churning busily in the air, as if it thought it had broken free from the earth and was flying. At the same moment the camel's heavy upper lip fell back to produce a demented upside-down grin, quite friendly. The giant smiled in return and the noble procession proceeded on its way, and thereafter the fearsome strength of Moses was public knowledge.

When the princess finally died she left her property in Jericho to the Ethiopian church in Jerusalem, to serve as a monastery. Naturally Moses stayed on in monastic retirement in the orange grove next to Bell's, a soft-spoken man of kindly humor given to wide smiles now that he no longer had to perform duties as a gatekeeper. He and Abu Musa had gotten into the habit of playing shesh-besh every day, either in the late afternoon or early evening, and when Bell became their friend they moved their game to his front porch, which was convenient for everyone. Bell himself never played, preferring to relax in his chair as he sipped arak and listened to their conversations.

These leisurely sessions over the shesh-besh board, Bell noticed, had a peculiar way of exploring the universe without appearing to do so. Each of the two players, the elderly Arab and the elderly Ethiopian, merely related his thoughts of the day between throws of the dice, without apparently commenting on what the other said. The shesh-besh games had been going on for forty years, however, and Bell was forever amazed at this unsurpassed method of friendship the two men had devised for themselves. Moses the Ethiopian tended to talk about God and the river Jordan and his departed princess, while Moses the Arab talked about flowers and fruit trees and hashish. But somehow, in one guise or another, most of human experience seemed to find its way into their rambling monologues, which for Bell were thereby transformed into comprehensive philosophies of the highest order.

In addition to the small estate next to Bell's orange grove, the princess had owned a bungalow down beside the Jordan where she retired on certain Christian feast days, to pray on the banks of the river and wade in the water in the spirit of John the Baptist. When she died this property was also bequeathed to the church. An ancient Ethiopian monk lived alone in the bungalow as an anchorite, a tiny frail man, mostly deaf, who had shrunk with the years until he was little bigger than a child. One of Moses's duties was to go down to the river every few weeks to visit the anchorite, to bring the man the few vegetables he required and keep the place in good repair.

For these excursions Moses made use of the dead princess's elegant steam coach, an open touring vehicle from the experimental days of the automobile, specially built in Italy for the princess early in the century. She had chosen a steam-driven automobile after having been advised that gasoline, then rare, might be hard to come by in the Middle East. Wood fired the steamer's boiler and Moses preferred olive wood, following the tradition of professional bakers of bread in the Middle East who always used olive wood in their ovens, because of its superior scent and slow even heat.

The coach was a baroque masterpiece. Despite its great age it appeared almost new, for in all its many decades it had made only one crosscountry jaunt of consequence, the triumphant journey from its point of delivery at the port of Jaffa up the hills to Jerusalem, and from Jerusalem down the hills to Jericho. Thereafter it had only been used for the occasional trip over to the Jordan River and back, a matter of a few miles, and the fiercely dry air of Jericho had preserved it as easily as if it were just another paleolithic artifact.

Reflecting its era and an Italian concept of Ethiopian princessly grandeur, the steamer resembled a huge horseless carriage fit for a coronation. A gigantic wooden statue of the Lion of Judah, symbol of the Ethiopian royal house, reared at the front of the coach. The carriage itself was all polished woodwork and shiny black leather with gleaming brass fittings, standing on wooden-spoked wheels half as tall as a man. Fold-down steps gave access to the lofty perch in front for the driver and the spacious cockpit in back for the passengers. An array of thick leather belts strapped down the barrel-shaped hood over the steam engine, as if the forces hidden beneath the hood were so dangerous they might try to break out at any moment. And a long menacing whip stood in a holder beside the driver's seat, on guard and ready to beat back any beast of the field or jungle which foolishly got in the way of the steamer.

To have some company and make a day of the outings, Moses took Abu Musa and Bell with him on his trips down to the river. The day began before first light with the sound of wood being chopped—Moses preparing his fuel for the excursion. In due time he fired up the boiler and the magnificent coach came rolling around the corner to Bell's front gate, where Abu Musa and Bell were waiting. Moses always wore racing goggles when he was at the wheel, his bright yellow robes gusting dramatically in the early morning sun.

All three men waved in greeting and Abu Musa and Bell climbed aboard. Moses filled the entire front seat so his two friends sat in back. Bell, thin and austere in white, pressed himself into a corner and held down his floppy straw hat with the claw of his bad hand. Abu Musa spread himself and his pale blue galabieh over the rest of the seat, a dazzling white keffiyeh on his head for the occasion, set at a rakish angle above his hawklike face.

Are we ready? boomed Moses, studying the gauges in front of him.

Check, replied Bell. *Onward*, roared Abu Musa.

Moses turned valves and pulled levers and with a *whoosh* they glided away. Driving was a solemn concern to Moses and he peered intently through his goggles at the road ahead, maneuvering with care and continually tooting the rubber bulb of the hand-horn to alert stray goats and children. Bell sat stiffly erect in his corner but Abu Musa swayed from side to side and merrily waved to everyone they passed, in the manner of some benign desert chieftain reviewing his slaves.

After a stately turn around the dusty central square, where they scattered chickens and raised a chorus of ululations, they headed out of town past the fruit trees and the banana plantations to the edge of the cultivated lands. Once civilization was behind them Moses let fly with the valves and the levers and the coach shot forward, gaining speed on the flat wastes of the plains of Jericho, the expanse of the Dead Sea shimmering deep blue off to the right, the high ridge of the Moabite hills looming up in the distance in front of them, the thin line of green which marked the banks of the river directly ahead.

An advantage of the steamer's engine was its lack of noise, so they floated across the desolate landscape in near-silence, not even disturbing the gazelles in the desert where they passed. It was a sensation of flying, thought Bell, of swooping along a few yards above the earth with all the carefree grace of a bird.

A journey on a magic carpet, Abu Musa called the trip, and the silence of the smooth ride was so eerie Bell sometimes wondered if he hadn't been transported across the centuries to some ageless tale from the *Thousand and One Nights.*

They floated up to the banks of the river and came to rest near the bungalow. Moses went to find the anchorite and to see to his duties around the place, while Abu Musa and Bell sought out a shady grove beside the water. Bell usually brought a book with him as cover for the hours of daydreaming ahead. But Abu Musa, decisively shameless in old age, at once hoisted up the skirts of his galabieh and went wading boldly into the shallows to amble away the entire morning, playing with sticks and squealing and launching toy rafts on the currents, as delighted in the miracle of flowing water as the youngest of his great-nephews would have been.

Toward noon, his labors done, Moses joined them on the river bank with the picnic hamper packed by Abu Musa. With their feet dangling in the water they feasted in the shade, devouring pots of thick goat's cheese flavored with pepper and olive oil, whole onions and tomatoes and cucumbers and ragged hunks of coarse chewy bread, the rich fare washed down with quantities of fiery arak. After lunch Abu Musa and Bell slept, to awake much later to the haunting strains of an Ethiopian chant and the thump of an African drum drifting down from upstream, where Moses and the shy anchorite were conducting an impromptu service of prayer on the shores of their holy river, far from home.

All too soon came the silent journey back to Jericho, across the stark somber valley in the spreading twilight. Their magic carpet flew west toward the purple Judean hills and the orange-red sky glowing with memories of the fast-falling sun, the moon and the evening star already fixed in their places for the long night ahead. To Bell that was always the magical time in the desert, when the sun finally sank beneath the hills and the land softened into a thousand colors for a few brief moments, as the sands and the dark sea prepared to receive the full might of another vast starry night over Jericho.

On the evenings of their excursions to the river there was never a shesh-besh game on Bell's front porch. The friends were exhausted from their day's journey and retired early to their separate concerns. Moses to chant prayers in his monastery chapel for the soul of the anchorite who dwelled by the river. Abu Musa to recount his splendid knee-deep adventures with rafts and currents to a crowd of sleepy children. And Bell to sit beside his grape arbor and gaze for hours at the night sky from his still point in eternity, once more a witness to the entire universe laid bare to the eye of man in all its incomprehensible glory, utter joy in his heart at the beauty of the world.

EIGHT

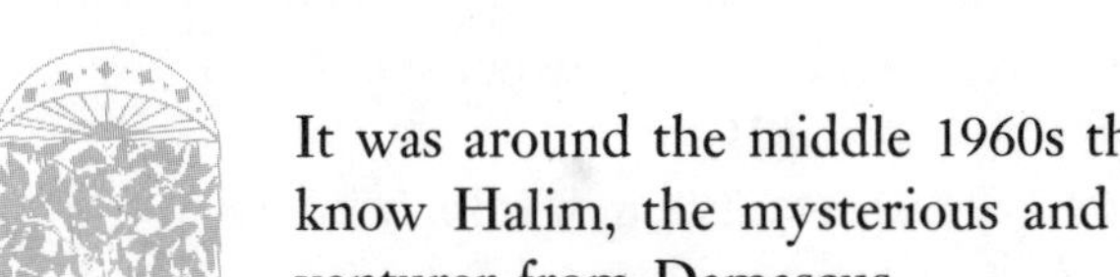

It was around the middle 1960s that Bell got to know Halim, the mysterious and appealing adventurer from Damascus.

When strangers turned up in Jericho and wanted to see Bell, it was common practice for them to pay a call first on the man known locally as his protector, Abu Musa. Without an introduction from Abu Musa the hermit generally remained inaccessible, not for a passing word or two but certainly for a more meaningful visit. Abu Musa took his role seriously and guarded his friend's privacy with vigor, turning away the merely curious with consolatory tales of antique Turkish trains blowing up in the wastes. So Bell was surprised when Abu Musa suddenly began insisting he meet this man called Halim whom Abu Musa didn't really seem to know.

At first I thought he was a Palestinian with Syrian connections, said Abu Musa, but then I decided he must be a Syrian with Palestinian connections. His accent and manner tend to move back and forth as it suits him, now Palestinian, now Syrian. He is Syrian after all, as it turns out, but he's also much more, a kind of conscience for the Arab world, a visionary and a man of ideas who's above any one nation or cause. A remarkable man for one so young, great things will come of him. Men look to him instinctively and perhaps he's already a secret leader, who can say.

Bell laughed. It didn't make any sense to him. And how do you know him? he asked.

Through a cousin in Damascus, replied Abu Musa, puffing his waterpipe. Oh he comes very highly recommended, but that's not the point. The way he talks is the point, and his eyes and his smile and his grasp of people and events. Men like Halim are rare, as rare in their way as you are.

Why does he come to Jericho? asked Bell.

To visit the refugee camps outside of town, replied Abu Musa. He has contacts there, naturally. Such a man would have contacts everywhere, it's only to be expected.

Is he political then? asked Bell.

In some manner, I suspect, although I don't know anything about that, nor do I care. I would say, rather, that he's very deep into the affairs of men in all ways.

This time Bell didn't laugh. Instead he nodded, thoughtful, perplexed by Abu Musa's enthusiasm. It was true that Abu Musa had no interest in politics and usually avoided men who were involved in politics.

I turn my back on all of them, Abu Musa often said. They disgust me because they haven't learned the simplest truths yet. Having lived for three hundred years in our Jericho time, I know man's political endeavors are devious and futile and completely without merit when compared to even one flowering fruit tree, which is truly a boundless philosophical subject. . . .

Yet somehow the stranger from Syria had made a powerful impression on Abu Musa. Why did he so much want Bell to meet the man? Was it because he felt the Syrian was a visionary, and therefore perhaps a seeker on his way to becoming holy? Was the purpose of their meeting in order for the man to be instructed in some unknown way in the shadowy and undefined vocation Abu Musa had conjured up for Bell?

These thoughts made Bell uneasy as he was always made uneasy by any reference, other than in jest, to Abu Musa's belief that Bell actually was a holy man. Abu Musa's faith in

Bell wounded him because he knew he wasn't worthy of it. But at the same time he couldn't ignore Abu Musa's request, no matter how much it discomforted him. They were too close for that and the old Arab's friendship was too precious.

Bell spoke directly. And why must I meet this Halim? he asked.

Above all because he wants it so much, replied Abu Musa. He's heard about you and feels he must meet you. He needs that, he says. And why? Ah, but the why is not for me to know and perhaps not even for you to know. What is true is that a holy man sometimes has special obligations, to others even more than to himself.

Bell nodded. So it was as he had suspected, he thought. The meeting did have to do with Abu Musa's belief that Bell was a holy man.

Abruptly Abu Musa leaned forward, his face grave as he gazed at Bell.

My friend, murmured Abu Musa. We leave only one thing behind in the world and that is love. This Halim is a serious man and he says he needs to meet you, so just meet him once for my sake. Then, if you don't care for him . . . but of course you will. No one can help but like Halim. A rare man, like you.

Perhaps a secret leader, Abu Musa had said. Halim was a generation younger than Bell in appearance. Abu Musa obviously knew nothing about it but Bell suspected from the beginning that the Syrian was involved in espionage, an easy assumption for Bell given Halim's self-assurance and knowledge and his frequent trips from Damascus to the Palestinian refugee camps in Jordan. What Bell couldn't understand was why a Syrian agent had sought him out. What use could he be to Halim? What could Halim possibly need from a recluse who saw almost no one?

Still, he enjoyed Halim's company every bit as much as Abu

Musa said he would. When Halim was in Jericho he took to joining Bell on Bell's long walks in the desert at dawn or at twilight. At dawn they walked east, down through the wastes to the Jordan River and back. At twilight they were apt to go in the other direction, over to the western foothills where the wadis began winding up through the Judean wilderness toward the heights of Jerusalem. The ruins of Herod's winter palace lay at the foot of one of the wadis, and Bell often went there to watch the last of the day's light linger on the Moabite hills across the valley. Or they might find their way to the ruins of the other winter palace to be found on the outskirts of Jericho, the one built by the Omayyad caliphs of Damascus some seven centuries after Herod's time. Bell had long been in the habit of wandering among these ruins at sunset and finding a perch where he could watch the darkness descend over the plains of Jericho and the Dead Sea in the distance.

Why in these ruins? asked Halim.

Because they suggest humility, replied Bell in answer to the question about his feelings.

And so it went for much of the time when they were together. Halim asked questions about why Bell did what he did, even the simplest things, much as if he were a disciple who had come to learn. That was the impression Bell had and it was close to the truth, as Bell discovered one night when they were sitting together in the ruins of the Omayyad palace. Halim was smoking and Bell was sipping from the small flask he always carried on his walks, when Halim happened to observe that old Abu Musa actually did believe Bell was a holy man. Bell laughed harshly, mocking himself. With a gesture of despair, he held up his flask in the moonlight.

Oh I know nothing's that simple, said Halim. I know because I once met a man in Damascus, a man about your age, dead now, who was in the Monastery in Egypt during the world war.

And so? murmured Bell, suddenly alert at this unexpected reference to long-dead, secret information.

Well that's all, replied Halim. But naturally I'm curious about what happens to a man after he gives up the monastic life. How he goes on, if he does.

Oh I see, said Bell. Well I suppose what often happens is that such a man merely adds more vows to those he has already made.

Halim smiled at the cryptic answer and they both fell silent as if a great deal had already been said, which of course it had. The Monastery in Egypt during the world war and Bell a part of it? How could Halim have learned about that?

Bell was intrigued and more. He put away his flask and got to his feet. It was time to return to the village but someday, he suspected, he would come to know much more about this visionary from Damascus with his mysteriously appealing manner.

NINE

When Anna looked back over the years when her son was growing up, it was easy to see how much time she had squandered dreaming of worlds that didn't exist. It was a habit that had been with her since childhood, a will to find comfort in the shadowy echoes of imaginary worlds where time was kindly and took nothing, only gave, and there was no need to face the losses of life, that stark Egyptian sun of regret whose glare never wavered.

Echoes, time passing, years gone. . . . It terrified her how life crept by for whole months and years in meaningless routines, only to be cut short by some pitiless insight which shattered the rhythms and revealed them to be no more than a pathetic escape from lost moments. Season after season, day after day, there was always so much to do. Yet suddenly Assaf was five, suddenly Yossi was dead, suddenly she was forty and more and Assaf at thirteen was reading the words from the books of Moses that announced the symbolic coming of his manhood, his turning away from her. So quickly they came, these abrupt moments that pierced her heart and wrenched her out of a kind of time that she preferred to think was everlasting, much as she had felt life's echoes on the narrow street in Cairo—in her childhood—would be everlasting.

She had always thought she would remarry someday, at least vaguely she had thought so. Certainly she had nothing against the idea, and it seemed a natural thing for a woman her age with a young son. Her friends had assumed she would remarry and Tajar, ever loyal, had brought along suitable men on his visits from time to time, or contrived to have them turn up when he and Anna were meeting somewhere. She had affairs with some of them and others became friends, but somehow it never got around to marriage. For a while her memory of Yossi was the reason she gave herself, and later of course there was Assaf and his upbringing and her busy life as a teacher and mother. But Tajar in his blunt way would have none of these excuses. Although committed to living alone himself—I've always been a misplaced bedouin tracker, he liked to say—he didn't feel it was a life for Anna, and every so often he put his hand on hers and spoke his heart.

My lovely Anna, he said, time is passing and I fear God is sad. Don't you sense it?

Anna smiled. And why is that? she asked.

For the simplest of reasons, said Tajar. God has a very big heart, but there is one thing that gnaws even at Him and that is when a woman withholds her beauty from the world. I know because a wise old Arab told me. Not only is it a waste of God's bounty, it leads to disharmony. Men go crazy when there is a beautiful widow around, women go crazy too. Everyone is uneasy and has to stop beside the road to see what might happen next. Nothing can get done and there's turmoil everywhere and God is sad and even I am sad. Shouldn't there be just a hint of a permanent man in your life by now?

Anna laughed and mentioned the usual things.

No no no, replied Tajar. Forgive me, but even though everything you say is true and real, what does it matter? Yossi always hoped you would remarry someday, he told both of us that long ago. And Assaf, like any boy, would be better off with a father, even a makeshift step-father. And you would be helping society enormously by not causing these terrible disruptions every time we walk into a café. People look at me with loathing and disgust, don't you see it? How can it be, they ask themselves, that this crippled old pervert has such a handsome young woman in his grasp? Is nothing as it should be in the world? That's what they think as they seethe with secret discontent, and why, Anna? Because you haven't met the right man yet? No, I don't believe it. You have to risk life and take the chance and seize it, as frightening and disappointing as it is. It's foolish to let the years go by like a dream, always living in the shadows and echoes of things. Life is disappointment and only dreams are not, but it's the very tension in that, in those failed longings of ours, that becomes the music of the human soul. What use can there be in denying time's counterpoint? . . .

So Tajar went on in jest and eloquence over the years. He was always a wise and loyal friend to Anna, forever helping her in countless ways. He even became a kind of uncle to Assaf. Yet somehow Anna's moments of reflections slipped by and she didn't remarry. Instead time slipped away and she turned forty.

◆◆◆◆◆◆◆◆

One important thing she did do during those years was move to Jerusalem soon after Yossi's death. Thus Assaf grew up in a city divided between its Arab and Jewish neighbors, between its old and new parts, and that was to have far-reaching effects on his life.

Even as a girl in Egypt, Anna had dreamed of living in Jerusalem. Her brother had always talked of going there someday and her father, after all, had been killed in the campaign to take the city, fighting with the British forces against the Turks in the First World War.

Anna first saw Jerusalem when she was moving restlessly from place to place in Palestine during the Second World War, when the city was undivided and its various quarters were open to every wanderer. From the very first moment she was captivated by the ancient walled city with its sense of mystical hope and its haunting beauty: the clarity of the light on its domes and minarets, the subtle colors of its living stone, the mysteries of a glorious past which could never be obscured by the ruins of time. To her it was a vibrant silent dream of a city, its narrow alleys a maze of man's strivings through the ages where even the smallest corner guarded a hoard of secret history, a treasure of secret tales only fitfully at rest in the dust of millennia. For Anna it was a city like no other, and she resolved when first she saw it to live there someday.

Not the sad end of her marriage but Yossi's death in the Sinai was what decided Anna that *someday* had come. When she told Tajar of her decision to move to Jerusalem he was naturally enthusiastic, since he had grown up there and loved the city more than any place on earth.

At last, said Tajar happily. Of course, my dear Anna, what could be better? It's as if you've been circling Jerusalem all these years the way a bird in the desert circles an oasis before swooping down to the life-giving water. A city of sunlit stones, Anna, and there are faces in the stones of Jerusalem which you will learn to see as you walk its worn gentle hills. The faces of many races and believers, make no mistake, but especially of our people who went up there so long ago to seek what has no end. And there our prophets looked into their hearts to glimpse the unseeable, diviners for the entire race of man and seers of all time on those ancient slopes. Oh yes, Anna, there are faces in the stones of Jerusalem and Assaf will grow up carrying them in his heart. A wise decision. It's so right, so very good. . . .

Tajar helped her find a place to live on a short narrow road called Ethiopia Street, a twisting secluded lane which he claimed was the most beautiful street in Jerusalem. The solid old stone houses with their red-tiled roofs, built by wealthy Arab effendis in the nineteenth century, were set at odd angles in courtyards amidst cypress and fruit trees, behind high stone walls running the length of Ethiopia Street. Flowers and arches cascaded everywhere. Anna had the second floor of a large stone house, reached through an echoing stone corridor that led in from the street to an outside stone stairway which then climbed and turned in the sunlight through banks of bougainvillea, a light and airy place of tall windows and window-doors opening onto wrought-iron balconies, overlooking her courtyard. It was an enchanting house to Anna. Every turn and window proffered an unexpected view, never failing to surprise her with its beauty, with great gusts of warm sunlight swirling through the rooms and deep corners of cool shade.

The winding little street was not far from a slope that led down to the barren, blasted strip of no-man's-land which had divided the city into east and west since 1948, separating Arab and Jewish Jerusalem. She could see the Old City to the east from her house, but not the valley where no-man's-land ran. Yet in fact the border was so near there were bullet marks in the dome of the Ethiopian Church across the street from her house, left over from the 1948 war.

All the better that it's so close to the border, Tajar had said when first he took her to see the house. The call of the muezzin from Damascus Gate in the Old City will float up to you on still afternoons, the bells of the Holy Sepulchre will sound in the darkness, and little Assaf will hear all the wondrous sounds of our Holy City, even in his sleep. . . .

Anna loved her old stone house with its courtyard and flowers and fruit trees and balconies, hidden away behind high stone walls. She loved it so much she wanted to express the beauty she felt, and it was there, on those balconies, that she first began to paint the scenes of Jerusalem which would one day make her famous.

Assaf, too, felt the beauty of Ethiopia Street. But it was its closeness to the mystery of the Old City, as Tajar had foreseen, that was to be particularly important in his young life.

TEN

For Assaf, the image he held of his father never flared or dimmed with the seasons of a boy's growth, never tumbled through the reflections cast by life's day-to-day mirrors, never blurred in the bewildering confusions of childhood. Instead, unshadowed by age and untouched by a human voice or hand, the vision shined pure and immutable, a presence forever shaping his life in unseen ways.

In the visible world of Ethiopia Street and the new world for him of Jerusalem, Assaf clung close to Anna at first. He missed Yossi's warmth and love and the wound never quite healed despite the passage of time. Inevitably, life seemed incomplete to him and he was always looking for something he couldn't find in the airy rooms of the old stone house, or off on a balcony where the boughs of the cypress trees sighed, or deep in a corner of the courtyard amidst the vines and bright flowers.

His father's death as a hero in battle marked Assaf as special among his classmates at school, as it did for their parents and also for the neighbors on Ethiopia Street. In games and on school outings and in the homes of others, Assaf was always given a central role and an added measure of sympathy, out of honor to his father's place among the fallen. Aware of this special concern for her son, Anna reacted by sometimes being too strict with him. She wanted to provide the discipline he needed but then, feeling remorse, she would relent and let him have his way. In retrospect, she thought herself too strict on unimportant things and too lenient in bigger matters. Somehow it seemed impossible to achieve a sensible balance that would work for both her and Assaf.

Still, she made a great effort to speak frankly with Assaf and explain her actions. He never complained when she did that. Sometimes she wished he would. But instead he seemed to accept what she said as a far more mature person might, because he understood she could only do what she was capable of doing, or perhaps because he was so close to her in his heart that he sensed the helplessness she felt in wanting to do more and be more, to be both mother and father to him and, indeed, to be all those other family members which some boys had and he didn't.

This intense closeness between them had always been evident to Anna, and the divorce and Yossi's death had only deepened what was already there. There were times when Anna truly regretted how much they were alike in temperament, in manner, in feeling. Because it led to a great sharing between them, even when it was unspoken, and she feared in some obscure way that by sharing so much with her son she might be depriving him of his childhood, burdening him with a knowledge beyond his years and denying him childhood's richest gift, that bounty of glowing, joyful memories which could forever be cherished later in life. But Anna's own childhood had been neither lighthearted nor carefree, with her brother her only companion for much of it, and there was no way to know how Assaf's life on Ethiopia Street would have been different had Yossi lived and been part of it, even if only from a distance.

At home Assaf tended to be a quiet, dreamy boy whose fingers worked restlessly while his mind wandered elsewhere. When Anna went out to paint in the afternoons, Assaf sometimes went with her. She would find some peaceful spot in an olive grove and quickly fall under the spell of her work, while

Assaf roamed the hillside and explored the crevices in the parched stony land. For hours he would play alone and amuse himself, much as she had done as a child, but it pleased her immensely that he had the sunlit slopes of Jerusalem for his playing fields, rather than the dark narrow rooms on a crowded street which she had known in Cairo.

Assaf gathered rocks and built strange structures, imagining castles and moats and causeways. Or he returned proudly with slivers of pottery to show her, a curved surface or broken handle for her to admire, some secret remnant of Jerusalem's long history which he had recovered from its hiding place in the rocks and crevices.

But if there were a view of the Old City from the hillside where she had led him, Assaf often sat down and did nothing. Then, for an entire afternoon, he would be content merely to sit and gaze through the silver-green leaves of the olive trees at the massive walls in the distance, entranced by the majestic splendors of that ancient mirage which floated so mysteriously on the far side of the valleys, the domes and towers and minarets of Jerusalem lightly adrift in the heavens on the haze of a summer day.

Assaf could also see the Old City from the balcony of his room. When she came to put him to bed in the evening, Anna sometimes found him sitting out there in the shadows, gazing east at the yearning nighttide fingers of the Old City, those same towers and minarets now darkly set against the stars. Anna sat down beside him and held him.

It's beautiful, isn't it, she whispered. So exquisitely beautiful. Nothing in the world can compare to it.

And it's so very close, whispered Assaf. How long would it take us to walk there, if we could?

Ten minutes, no more. Out to the end of Ethiopia Street and down the Street of the Prophets and across a flat space and there we would be right in front of Damascus Gate, which has that name because the ancient road to Damascus begins there. The great golden dome rising above Damascus Gate, beyond it really, is the Mosque of the Dome of the Rock, the rock which was called the threshing-floor of Araunah the Jebusite when King David first came to Jerusalem and made it his capital, the place where Abraham went to sacrifice Isaac and where Solomon raised the Temple and where Mohammed is said to have mounted his horse to ascend to heaven, a great broad rock which is the heart of the Temple Mount. And on one side of the Temple Mount is the retaining wall known as the Western Wall where our people have prayed for two thousand years, since the Second Temple was destroyed. And to the right of Damascus Gate are the two domes of the Church of the Holy Sepulchre, and in between and all around are the minarets and spires of the other churches and mosques.

Assaf nodded. He knew all this by heart but never tired of hearing it repeated.

And are the alleys of the Old City the way Tajar describes them? he asked. Are there really so many different peoples speaking so many different languages and living in a dozen different eras? Two dozen different eras?

Anna smiled at these words of Tajar repeated so exactly by her son.

Oh yes, she said, it never really changes. It was still like that when I went there before the city was divided.

Someday I'll go to the Old City, said Assaf.

I hope so, sweet one. When there's peace you'll go. But what do you think when you look at it now?

I think of father, said Assaf. I want to go there for him because he never could. I want to stand at the Wall and say his name and repeat his name so God will know I came for him. To the Wall, the place, for him.

◆◆◆◆◆◆◆

Surely it's good, Anna, said Tajar. It's right for him to think of Yossi as he longs for our City of Peace. It's only as it should be. Nothing could be better for Assaf than to be growing up in Jerusalem. And peace will come, you know. There won't always be a divided Jerusalem and an ugly no-man's-land between us and the Old City. We've negotiated with the Jordanians before and it will happen again. A little time is all we need. You'll see. . . .

When Assaf was growing up he heard many stories about his father, lovingly retold by Anna and Tajar.

Yossi as a boy in Iraq, for one. Yossi leaving his village every afternoon to run across the fields and the desert to the town where he had worked as a bookkeeper, running and running as fast as the wind, seeing and feeling everything. This memory from his father's life became so deeply embedded in Assaf that he himself had to live it out in some way, which was how his dangerous trek to Petra came about.

A strange dream, the ruins of Petra, and Assaf wasn't alone in feeling its lure.

◆◆◆◆◆◆◆◆

The desert capital of the vanished people known as the Nabataeans lay in the biblical land of Edom south of the Dead Sea, about fifteen miles east of the Israeli border near the Wadi Musa, one of the traditional sites where Moses struck the rock and water gushed forth. From Petra, some two millennia ago, the Nabataeans controlled the trade which brought spices from India and Africa to the Gulf of Aqaba, and thence by caravan up the Great Rift to Damascus in the north, and across the Negev in the west to Gaza, on the old route of frankincense and myrrh to the shores of the Mediterranean.

Herod's mother was a noblewoman of Petra. Both accessible and secluded in ancient times, its valley was enclosed by cliffs of red and purple sandstone eroded into fantastic shapes and displaying towering rock-cut temples and tombs with columned façades, so huge they appeared to be deserted palaces fashioned by a forgotten race of giants. It was an eerily romantic place which was lost to history before the Middle Ages and only rediscovered when the Swiss explorer Burckhardt passed that way in the nineteenth century and wrote his famous description of Petra: *a rose-red city half as old as time.*

For Assaf as for other young Israelis, the dream of seeing forbidden Petra became one of those symbolic journeys that can haunt the youthful adventurers of a generation, a way of breaking out of history's confines through a near-mystical trial of courage and daring.

The journey through enemy territory could only be made at night. During the day the intruder had to hide in caves or crevices. Jordanian army patrols roamed near the border, and there were wandering bedouin who would report a hiding place or a footprint. The land was stark and lifeless, deeply cut by the erosions of thousands of years. If there was enough moonlight to illuminate the jagged terrain, then there was also enough light for a lone figure to be visible from a great distance.

There was no easy way to reach Petra. Even if the route hadn't traversed enemy territory it would have been an arduous desert crossing in darkness. And with Jordanian patrols and hostile bedouin out hunting and waiting in ambush, the dangers of the journey were extreme.

Nor was any practical purpose served. It was an act of pure bravado to cover that dangerous distance merely to gaze down on the ruins of Petra for a minute or two, from some crag, before turning back. But of course the appeal of the adventure was precisely its purity.

Some never found the ruins and others never came back, but for those who reached Petra and did return there was a singular sense of triumph. *He's been to Petra,* people whispered. A young aspirant to the Mossad, those elite of the elite, was sometimes casually asked by an interviewer: Have you been to Petra? Before long a popular song about the forbidden journey to Petra was banned by the Israeli government, so seductive was the lure of this lost city to the young.

Assaf was one of the lucky ones who succeeded. He was

only fifteen at the time, younger than most. An Israeli army patrol picked him up when he crossed back over the border just before dawn. Anna was severely shaken by the news and turned to Tajar, who left at once to drive down to the army post in the Negev where Assaf was being held. During the drive Tajar thought of many things he could say to Assaf but rejected them all. In the end, when he arrived at the army post, he led Assaf to the side of a hill and sat with him in silence, looking out over the desert in the direction of Petra.

At fifteen, Assaf was already as tall as Yossi and as darkly handsome. He had a quiet and thoughtful manner which resembled his father's reticent charm, but he was less spontaneous with his feelings and given to a kind of solemnity unusual in one so young. Tajar saw aspects of Yossi in his son, but the boy's reserved nature also reminded him of Assaf's uncle, David, Anna's dead brother. Assaf's dignity mixed with melancholy, in fact, was exactly what Tajar recalled of David when he had known him in Cairo during the world war.

Anna also recognized this resemblance and had spoken of it to Tajar, who accepted what she said without mentioning that he readily saw the similarities himself. For Anna was still unaware that Tajar had once known her dead brother. When Tajar met Anna after the world war he didn't say anything about her brother, because he didn't want to cause her pain by reopening the past. Then later there seemed no reason to bring up the matter. Now Tajar was sorry he lacked this additional bond of kinship with Anna and her son. It might be especially helpful to Assaf, he thought, and he decided to speak with Anna about it as soon as he could. But that was for the future, when the shock of the Petra adventure was behind her.

After sitting with Assaf in silence for a time, Tajar found he didn't want to say anything so much as to listen. As for Assaf, he was more frightened in a way of Tajar, the known, than he had been of the unknown during his days and nights on the journey to Petra. Finally, nervously, Assaf spoke up and admitted as much. He also mentioned Anna.

She's deeply disturbed, said Tajar. Show her as much love as you can when you see her, and remember, she takes no pride in what you've done. She can't. You're her only child and to her the trip was dangerous and pointless and nothing else.

Assaf gazed down at the sand, sifting it through his fingers.

And you, Tajar? How do you feel about it? he asked softly in Arabic, a form of intimacy between them since Assaf's earliest childhood.

I feel it was dangerous and pointless and also that what's done is done, replied Tajar. So what I want now is for you to tell me about the trip. What and where and how, and the ruins, and everything you saw and felt from the moment you crossed the border until the moment you returned. I want to hear it all so I can tell you what you might have done better. The ancient, colossal ruins of Petra glimpsed for a moment beneath the stars? What are they, Assaf, but an exquisite fantasy? An illusion and a dream and a way station of the soul? Of course the journey is always what counts, sweet one, the journey and nothing more. You know that now and it's an impressive piece of wisdom to have learned at your age. So tell me about it, every detail.

Solemnly Assaf did as he was asked. He had always felt close to Tajar but never closer than that afternoon when they sat together on a hill in the Negev, gazing across the desert, and Assaf talked of his secret journey into his heart to see the mysterious ruins of Petra by starlight, to behold the ancient wonders of that unforgotten lost city of caravans somewhere to the east—a dream and an illusion which Tajar knew from the very beginning could only be connected in Assaf's mind to the Old City of Jerusalem, always so close to Assaf when he was growing up yet always just *over there* beyond reach, a dream on the other side of the valley.

◆◆◆◆◆◆◆◆

A few years later Tajar sat with Anna on her balcony one cold winter day in Jerusalem, the two of them bundled up against the weather. The heavy sky was gray and threatening but even when it rained they often sat on the balcony, looking down on the courtyard with its lemon and cypress and fig trees. It was December 1966, the month of Assaf's eighteenth birthday when he would go off to begin his military service. That morning he had told Anna he was volunteering for the paratroop brigade, an elite unit which took the most casualties in time of war.

Tajar rose when Anna told him the news and hobbled inside and returned to the balcony with a framed photograph, which he placed on the table. It was a photograph of Yossi at the age of twenty-nine, in a paratrooper's uniform somewhere in the desert, taken a month before the 1956 war broke out and Yossi was supposedly killed in the Mitla Pass in the Sinai. A photograph of a handsome and dashing young officer who would never age, who always smiled and was eternally a hero—the image of his father that Assaf had lived with since the age of eight.

Tajar looked at the photograph and sighed.

Ah yes, he said. All these years this has been sitting on your desk, Anna, so how could we have expected anything else?

ELEVEN

The Runner operation grew significantly in the middle 1960s. More and more information flowed into the Mossad from Damascus. Equally important from Tajar's point of view, there was now a back-up team supporting the Runner from Beirut and even in Damascus itself. The team eased Tajar's tasks and greatly strengthened the security of the operation. Tajar had always hoped to have such a team someday. Communicating with a deep-cover agent and receiving his material was by far the greatest danger to any long-term penetration. With a back-up team of professionals handling communications, while the identity of the Runner remained unknown to them, everything was simpler and safer. Of course putting such a team in the field was expensive and difficult in itself, and the operation had to justify the additional support it entailed. Tajar had made plans for such a team long ago, but the opportunity for setting it up came sooner than he expected with the downfall of Little Aharon.

For more than a dozen years the rabbi's son from the Ukraine had run the Mossad as his own private fiefdom. Except for the few months right at the beginning when Tajar was in charge, the Mossad had never known another director. Through hard work and an emphasis on personal loyalty, Little Aharon had taken over a small country's intelligence effort and built an international reputation for the Mossad. His successes were legendary. And because the Mossad was small, Little Aharon had always been able to run it as a family. There was no real command structure and little in the way of operational procedures. Instead there were Little Aharon and those who worked for him.

But as admired and powerful as Little Aharon was, and as ruthless, he was unable to survive the political upheavals that came with the decline in fortune of the country's founding prime minister, David Ben-Gurion, who had often used Little Aharon as a troubleshooter in domestic affairs. Over the years Little Aharon had made many enemies. As Ben-Gurion faltered and finally went off to retirement in the Negev, those opposed to Little Aharon eased him out of the Mossad. For the Mossad without Little Aharon, as for the country without Ben-Gurion, it was the end of an era.

Military intelligence had always been the junior partner in Israeli intelligence. The director of military intelligence reported to the army chief of staff while the director of the Mossad reported directly to the prime minister. After Little Aharon's downfall, the man picked to replace him at the Mossad was the army officer who ran military intelligence, General Dror, once a flamboyant battlefield commander.

General Dror had been the army's second-ranking officer during the Sinai war in 1956, and he might have become chief of staff had he not believed so strongly that a general's place was with his men. He took a paratroop refresher course after the 1956 war, and his parachute failed to open all the way on a jump. General Dror survived, barely, and spent eighteen months in a hospital. His days as a field commander were over but eventually he was brought back into the army as chief of military intelligence. Subsequently he became the focal point for those in the government, particularly those in the army, who were opposed to Little Aharon's power and the way he used it.

As director of the Mossad, Dror began to make changes to tighten it as an organization. Immediately he was faced with a revolt. Many of the Mossad's senior members threatened to resign and others withheld information from him. The father figure had gone and the family was angry. Inevitably, Little Aharon's men saw General Dror's appointment as a takeover by the military.

To Tajar, the whole affair was deeply ironic. Years ago he himself had lost out as chief of the Mossad because he wasn't considered as capable as Little Aharon of administering a government agency, because he took too personal an interest in his agents, because he ran operations in an old-fashioned way out of his pocket. Now Little Aharon was being accused of these same faults by the more efficient and better organized men Dror had brought with him from the army. A further irony was Dror's near-fatal parachute accident. But for that accident Dror would still be an army field commander, probably chief of staff. And but for his own near-fatal automobile accident years ago, Tajar himself would still be in operations in the field, not overseeing them.

One of the criticisms of Little Aharon was that he had ignored day-to-day intelligence from the neighboring Arab states, which the army needed, in favor of more glamorous operations in Europe and elsewhere. Dror meant to correct this by reshaping the Mossad and redefining its priorities. As it happened, Tajar was the Mossad's leading expert on penetrating Arab countries. He also ran one of the Mossad's most effective Arab penetrations, and against its most militant neighbor: the Runner operation in Damascus. Lastly, Tajar was an old hand from Little Aharon's generation. His experience went back even farther than Little Aharon's and his expertise was impeccable. No one was more respected among the senior executives of the Mossad.

For a variety of reasons, then, Tajar was a natural ally for Dror to turn to in his new job. Tajar recognized this and decided to make use of the circumstances that had come his way.

Suddenly I seem to be back in favor at work, Tajar told

Anna. Is it possible that if you survive long enough your ideas come back into fashion, the way old clothes do?

Anna laughed. She knew Tajar worked for the ministry of defense, perhaps in military planning, but she wasn't aware he was connected specifically with intelligence. Or at least that's what she told herself. Tajar never talked about the nature of his work and she preferred not to speculate on it. Since the death of her brother long ago in Cairo, intelligence had always been a painful subject to her. Tajar knew this and avoided it.

Well I suppose it's possible, said Anna. It happens in other things, why not in ideas?

It's an odd one for me all the same, said Tajar. I'm much more used to being considered an old crank who was born before the flood. I'll have to be careful not to let it go to my head. It's almost enough to make me feel young again.

They were sitting on Anna's balcony watching a fierce spring downpour soak the flowers in the courtyard, the sweep of the rain softened by thousands of tiny fingers on the cypress trees. Tajar hummed his way through an old song and Anna smiled wistfully, her eyes far away. The song had been popular when she first met Yossi on the little settlement in the Negev, during the war for independence.

Another world, she reminded herself. Another world that's gone and no longer exists except in memory.

◆◆◆◆◆◆◆◆

Dror sensed at once that Tajar's support for him within the Mossad hinged on the Runner operation, because it was the only important operation Dror had no trouble getting his hands on. Elsewhere, in other cases, essential details were withheld or buried and Dror had to dig to uncover them. But Tajar was lucid and straightforward when he briefed Dror on the Runner operation. Obviously Tajar wanted the new director to appreciate the value of the operation, to invest in it and make it his own.

It was also apparent to Dror that Tajar was almost alone among the senior Mossad executives in not feeling threatened by the appointment of an army officer as director. Tajar made this clear by always referring to Dror in an easy manner as *the general,* to his face, the only senior executive who did so. To others Dror was a general only behind his back. Given the atmosphere of the Mossad after Little Aharon's downfall, this habit of Tajar's never seemed to emphasize Dror's seniority but rather, in some subtle way, had the opposite effect of expressing an equality of feeling between the two men. Dror knew that Tajar had always stood alone, that he was unattached to any particular doctrine and without ambitions for himself. His concerns revolved entirely around the Runner operation.

In any case, Dror had a high opinion of the Runner operation from the very beginning. It was an extremely clever long-range penetration, meticulously planned at every stage, each aspect of its development exactly fitted to the personality and character of the Runner himself. Dror admired this careful planning and was quick to tell Tajar that he did. It was the kind of planning that won wars, he said.

In particular, Dror was struck by the Runner's recent involvement in the repair of Syrian armored vehicles. It was nuts-and-bolts work, but to a military man the opportunities inherent in it were intriguing. And at that point in his briefing, curiously enough, Tajar all at once lost his place in his files and began rummaging through papers, giving Dror a chance to let his imagination roam.

For years the Syrians with the help of the Soviet Union had been constructing a vast series of fortifications on the Golan Heights, most of them underground and invulnerable to air attack. These self-sustaining concrete bunkers and gun emplacements went on for miles surrounded by hidden tank traps, a massive in-depth defense that was a kind of modern Maginot Line. But in Israel's case there was no question of ever being able to go around the fortifications, the way German panzer divisions had swept around the flanks of the Maginot line during the invasion of France in the Second World War. The nature of the terrain in the upper Galilee denied that possibility. It was direct shelling from the Golan that continually caused Israeli casualties in the settlements of the Galilee. In any future war against Syria the Golan Heights could only be assaulted directly, from the bottom straight up the steep slopes and then on and on through those miles of buried emplacements. Most military planners, and not only in Israel, thought a direct assault was impossible. To get through the maze without being cut to pieces, an assault force would have to have extraordinarily detailed information on the exact location and strength of the entire network of in-depth fortifications.

When Dror finally mentioned the Golan, Tajar stopped shuffling papers. He looked up and nodded. The two men were alone in Dror's office.

What we're talking about now, said Tajar, is a very great quantity of information. First the Runner would have to get his hands on it, then he would have to ship it to us. The task would take several years, with the Runner concentrating on one section of the front after another, or however he could manage it, and all the while the flow of physical material would be enormous. He'd have to map out the entire complex because the Golan's a mosaic, integrated, and even a number of pieces wouldn't provide what's needed.

Could he get the information? asked Dror.

I think he could, replied Tajar. Both the commander of the Syrian paratroop brigade and the Syrian minister of information are personal friends. The nephew of the Syrian chief of staff, a junior officer who spends a lot of time on the Golan, is a close personal friend. And there are others. The Runner has the right military connections and the repair work he does increases his access. But he'd need a back-up team to move the material for him, so he could devote himself to acquiring it. He can't do both. No one working alone, in a place as hostile as Damascus, could move that much material. And anyway, communicating via Europe the way we've been doing was never meant to accommodate an assignment such as this.

What kind of a team? asked Dror.

Professionals with experience in Arab countries, replied Tajar. Mostly working out of Beirut but with several of them resident in Damascus. They won't know who the Runner is and he won't know who they are, and they'll never meet. It's the only secure way to move so much material.

Dror nodded, smiling. Do you have some people in mind? he asked.

By chance I do, replied Tajar. Several other operations will have to be readjusted because some of the men are already on assignment abroad, but that can be worked out. As soon as the men are back here I'll begin training them for exactly what's required. They should be Runner specialists from now on and the Runner operation should take priority for them.

Do you have a timetable? asked Dror.

And a tentative cost sheet, replied Tajar, pulling out papers and putting them on the table. We should begin by bringing the future members of the team in from the field immediately. Later this month I'll see the Runner in Belgium and he and I, together, will work out the functioning of the team. In less than six months you can expect to see results. The Runner's fast, General, as you'll discover. In fact he works miracles. . . .

Dror was known for his daring as well as his careful planning. Tajar was given his hand-picked team. As before, only Tajar and the director of the Mossad knew the true identity of the Runner. The members of the back-up team were led to believe the Runner was an Arab but not a Syrian national, perhaps a military attaché or a diplomat on assignment in Damascus, in any case a man in an extremely sensitive position. Security would be complete, with Tajar himself overseeing every detail.

♦♦♦♦♦♦♦♦

When Tajar told Yossi the news in Belgium, they both took pride in the moment. Yossi knew the significance of the Golan Heights and was deeply pleased their work was taking this specific course. Mapping the Golan would be an immense undertaking, of enormous value to Israel and precisely the kind of task for which they had waited so long.

This is it, isn't it, said Yossi with enthusiasm. Now at last—this is it. Everything we've always prepared for.

Yes, this is it, replied Tajar. And with a team behind you to take care of all the logistics, now at last you can raise your eyes to the horizon and truly fly like the wind.

Yossi nodded. And remember every detail where I pass, he said, just as I did when I was a boy running across the desert.

Just so. The Runner even then, mused Tajar. But I suspect life is often like that, secretly. Finding our true way is perhaps no more than being what we have always been . . . but with eyes that see. And in that you're fortunate, Yossi, because you go much farther than most people ever can. Few people see as much of where they pass in life as you do. I know, because I once lived that way myself. Often it can seem isolating, and it is, but the isolation is no greater than anyone else's, really. It's just that other people aren't so aware of it, the way they're not aware of so many things. But intensity, eyes that see . . . well, it's exhilarating beyond all else and once you taste the drug you can never give it up because it's the ultimate addiction in life. . . . Living. Now. Knowing it.

You miss it so much, don't you, said Yossi.

I do, replied Tajar. But I also have you and that's a great gift. It's true these two legs of mine are ugly and stiff and awkward, twisted pieces of smashed flesh and bone that barely carry me from one place to another, but in my mind I can run with you and see what you see and feel what you feel and that's a very grand thing. So do it all, Yossi. Do it for yourself and that will also be doing it for me, and more. Every bird that flies is a joy for God to behold. . . .

◆◆◆◆◆◆◆◆

He's confident, Tajar told Dror upon his return from Belgium. He doesn't see any insurmountable difficulties. The next step is for me to work with the team, then move them into place as soon as we're ready.

In the beginning Tajar often brought back the members of the team from Beirut, and once or twice from Damascus, in order to question them at length in person. He wanted to know exactly what they saw and felt and suspected, and what he learned encouraged him. The Runner was protected, safe as never before. The operation was proceeding smoothly on its new course.

As for Dror, he was discovering that the Runner could indeed work miracles.

TWELVE

In 1966 there was another army coup in Syria and a more extremist military government took power. In the spring of 1967 Syria began pushing Egypt toward a new war with Israel. The Egyptian leader Nasser, the hero of the Arab world, asked the United Nations to withdraw its troops from the Sinai and the United Nations did so. Swept along by his own and other Arab propaganda, Nasser lost control of events and massed a thousand tanks in the Sinai near the Egyptian border with Israel, then blockaded the Gulf of Aqaba, closing Israel's outlet to the Red Sea and the east. Syria and Jordan and Iraq were on a war footing and military units arrived from Algeria and Kuwait and Saudi Arabia.

Israel faced an Arab force of two thousand tanks, seven hundred frontline aircraft, and two hundred and fifty thousand troops. The leader of the Palestine Liberation Organization made his famous statement that the Arabs would throw Israel into the sea.

On the morning of June 5, 1967, Israeli planes destroyed most of the Egyptian air force on the ground and the Six-Day War began.

◆◆◆◆◆◆◆◆

On the morning of June 5, Assaf's paratroop battalion was waiting in an orange grove near an airfield in the south. The rumor was that they would be dropped that night on el Arish, the Egyptian town not far from the border on the Mediterranean, to gain a bridgehead and await Israeli tanks striking across the border into the Sinai. But by early afternoon their orders had changed. The breakthrough toward el Arish was going so swiftly there was no need of a paratroop drop behind enemy lines. Instead they left their parachute gear and got on buses to go to the Jerusalem front, where the Jordanians, already on the attack, had taken United Nations headquarters and were shelling the coastal plain in the center of the country.

They were shelled all the way up the narrow corridor to Jerusalem, which had been the Israelis' only access to the city since 1948. The confusion on the road was enormous. Israeli units were fighting the Jordanians on both sides of the corridor while Israeli supply trucks and infantry wound up the road trying to reach the city. The bombardment was continuous. Night came, increasing the confusion. As they drew near Jerusalem after dark the shelling intensified. The Jordanians held the heights around the city and were bombarding Jewish Jerusalem with mortars and artillery.

Assaf's bus lost its way in the darkness and they arrived in the city late, after the paratroop battalions had already gone into battle a few hours after midnight. Assaf and the others left the bus and began running through the city in search of their units. The streets were deserted and no lights showed in the houses, but shells were dropping everywhere. They guessed where the fighting was from the intensity of the explosions and the tracers crossing the sky and headed in that direction.

The streets were familiar to Assaf because in fact the main fighting was not far from the old stone house where he had grown up on Ethiopia Street. The paratroop battalions, it turned out, had been sent on a night attack against the most heavily fortified Jordanian positions in the divided city, a complex of bunkers known as Ammunition Hill, which lay just to the north of no-man's-land and Assaf's house. At the same time another paratroop attack had been launched to the east directly across no-man's-land, toward the center of Arab Jerusalem in the valley below Assaf's house.

When the alleys became unfamiliar Assaf realized he was close to no-man's-land, but the fighting was still up ahead of him so he knew the paratroopers must have already opened a breach in the Jordanian lines. He stumbled around a wall and came upon a unit of recoilless guns mounted on jeeps which was supporting the breakthrough. They told him his battalion was in the breach up ahead. Many wounded paratroopers, some from his unit, lay in the street waiting to be evacuated.

Suddenly the area was lit up by tracers and a mortar shell fell between the jeeps, blowing one of them into the air and killing some men and wounding others and further wounding those who lay on the ground. He helped pull the wounded into buildings and helped bandage them and then moved on toward the sound of the heaviest firing, where he knew the breach had to be.

Men were rushing in every direction through the smoke and the flames and the darkness, trying to find their units and bringing up guns and ammunition and carrying back the wounded. He kept asking for his company but no one knew where it was. Shells exploded everywhere as the Jordanians poured out artillery fire from their positions along the ridges to the north and the east, trying to break the night attack on the low ground through no-man's-land.

Men were hit by shrapnel, fell, got up and ran again or lay still. It was a chaos of screams and shouts and explosions and shrapnel, of pulling back the wounded and rushing forward into more flames and explosions and shrapnel. Assaf never stopped running and crouching and running, pushing on toward the main fighting. He had passed dozens of dead and wounded paratroopers before he saw a Jordanian soldier for the first time, dead, lying beside a machine gun with two dead paratroopers a few yards away.

To open a breach, the assault units had to break through five lines of barbed-wire fences and mines before they reached the first Jordanian bunkers. Beyond that front line of bunkers were more bunkers and connecting trenches and fortified gun emplacements between stone houses and stone walls. The fighting went on in the trenches and alleys and houses, behind the walls and on the roofs and in the cellars. Bunkers and houses were taken two or three times as one paratroop platoon after another fought its way through the breach and the Jordanians moved back through the trenches into the houses, which came to have names of their own for the paratroopers: the house of the burning roof, the house with the pillars, the house of the yard.

More and more wounded paratroopers were being brought back from the area around the breach. By four o'clock in the morning dawn was beginning to break, but black clouds of smoke from the mortar barrages still covered the breakthrough area and kept out the daylight. This was a help to the paratroopers because they couldn't be seen from the Jordanian bunkers, and also a danger because it became more difficult to pinpoint enemy fire from the flashes the guns made in darkness.

Assaf was through the breach now, beyond the area of barbed wire and mines and the open fields of fire, among the squat stone houses of Arab Jerusalem which lay to the north of the Old City. He had fallen in with a platoon from another company in his battalion which was moving south along a narrow street, keeping close to the stone walls on each side of the road and fighting from house to house.

As they passed the gate to the house of the yard, which had already been cleaned out twice, firing burst out at them and two paratroopers near Assaf were hit. The platoon commander pulled one of the men back behind the wall. He seemed to be dead. The other man who had been hit managed to crawl through the gate to a hut just inside. He was spitting blood and appeared to be dying.

Assaf and another paratrooper ran through the gate into the

yard, throwing grenades and firing their Uzis to cover the man in the hut. A third paratrooper was firing into the yard from across the road.

There was a Jordanian soldier firing from a trench in the yard, another Jordanian firing from a corner of the house, and a third firing from the second story. A grenade exploded against the wall of the house and the soldier on the second story disappeared. A grenade exploded in the opening of the trench and the Jordanian there disappeared. The firing stopped from the corner of the house and they went back to the hut by the gate, where the wounded paratrooper was already dead.

The platoon moved on up the road in the darkness, shrinking in size as it advanced and men were wounded or left behind clearing out houses. The large YMCA building of Arab Jerusalem appeared on their right. Paratroop units had already passed it but now a machine gun was firing at them from the upper stories.

Assaf and some other paratroopers raced across to the door and went in. They passed a dying Jordanian soldier lying on the stairs. A burst came from somewhere and hit the paratrooper beside Assaf in the thigh. They went up the stairs and divided, two paratroopers down the right wing, Assaf down the left. They faced long dark passages with rooms opening onto them from both sides. They had to check each room, open the door, burst in.

Assaf burst into a room with his Uzi at his hip and caught a glimpse of a terrifying enemy facing him, features distorted and blackened, a weapon at his side, ready to kill. He fired a burst and a mirror shattered in front of him. Do I really look like that? he thought.

There was no one on the floor. They crept up the stairs to the next floor and a burst of automatic fire came down the stairwell from the attic, hitting one of the paratroopers in the shoulder and hand. Now there was only Assaf and one other paratrooper. They didn't dare throw a grenade up the stairs in case it rolled back down on them, and they didn't think just the two of them could go up the stairs against a man armed with a machine gun.

Assaf went to a window to see if he could signal for help and was immediately fired upon by paratroopers down below and by Jordanians farther up the street. Just then a tank shell shook the building, fired from one of the Israeli tanks that had finished on Ammunition Hill and had come down to join the paratroopers advancing toward the Old City.

Assaf and the other paratrooper decided not to try the attic alone. They took their wounded comrade and made their way back down the stairs to the ground floor. The paratrooper who had been wounded when they entered the building, near the front door, had already been carried away. When they came outside they saw their tank up the street, firing its cannon at the top of the building.

The advance was pinned down at the next strongpoint, a mosque which was right across the street from the American Consulate of East Jerusalem. The paratroopers were trying to fight their way past the mosque, along an alley that would come to be called the alley of death. Unknown to the paratroopers, a network of trenches and bunkers ran through the open area beside the mosque right up to the end of the alley, which also had a concrete bunker running along its entire length.

An anti-tank grenade knocked out the Jordanians who were firing from the top of the minaret. A makeshift squad of paratroopers, Assaf among them, was put together for another charge up the alley. As soon as they entered it they came under deadly fire. Grenades were thrown at them and splinters of rock flew through the air.

The officer leading the squad was killed, then the paratrooper behind the officer was killed. The whole line of paratroopers in front of Assaf was falling and dropping. Suddenly Assaf felt an intense burning in his chest and one of his legs went out from under him. He landed hard and men were running over him, continuing the attack, rushing up the alley through the smoke and the flames and explosions and shrapnel.

The burning sensation in Assaf's chest was overpowering. A boot drove into his back. Darkness came over him and he remembered nothing after that.

◆◆◆◆◆◆◆◆

Eventually Assaf had found his battalion but not his company. He had done all his fighting with another company, which had lost its way in the night assault. The company had fought its way up the wrong street in Arab Jerusalem, but it made little difference because the area was so small. They were supposed to be on the street that led to Herod's Gate in the Old City, while in fact they were on the street that led to Damascus Gate, a little to the south. The alley of death where Assaf was wounded was very close to the Old City, no more than four hundred yards from Damascus Gate.

By seven in the morning the assault was over and the paratroopers occupied all the buildings facing the walls of the Old City from the north. The fierce night attack had carried them the length of Arab Jerusalem. There were still Jordanian positions on the ridges east of the city, so another day was to pass before the colonel in command of the paratroopers led his men through Lion's Gate, the same northern approach that had been used by the Babylonians and Romans and Crusaders in taking Jerusalem. The Old City itself passed to the Israelis without any organized resistance within the walls.

The Old City was taken on the third day of the war. The Jordanians had been beaten back along the central front and were retreating to the east bank of the Jordan River. On the fourth day of the war Israeli armored units reached the Suez Canal, trapping what was left of the Egyptian army in the wastes of the Sinai. The paratroop battalions in Jerusalem were put on buses again and sent north, along with all other available troops from the southern and central fronts.

At noon on the fifth day the assault on the Golan Heights began. No surprise was possible and the Syrian army was fresh, having done no fighting, whereas the Israeli units were tired and worn. The assault forces rushed straight up the steep slopes with heavy losses, fighting their way through the massive Syrian fortifications which both the Russians and the Syrians had considered impregnable. In a little over twenty-four hours the Israelis accomplished the impossible and conquered the entire Golan.

And thus on the sixth day the new war came to an end.

THIRTEEN

Assaf's wounds were not as serious as Anna and Tajar had feared. He would have restricted movement of his left shoulder and perhaps a slight limp, but the rest of his body would mend with time, they were told. When Anna was with him in the hospital Assaf kept up a show of courage, but when Tajar was alone by the bedside Assaf let all his bitterness pour out.

It was *horrible*, he said. Even when we were succeeding it was horrible. Men are ripped apart and blown to pieces and you just keep pushing on trying to kill. It's brutal and ugly and there's no sense to any of it.

There was a family hiding in one of the Arab houses we went through, he said. We had to stay for a while because we were giving covering fire. The family was huddled in a corner watching us, as still as death except for a little girl who couldn't stop crying. It was a small room and they were just a few feet away. We were firing out the windows. While I was reloading I said something to the little girl, trying to comfort her. She wasn't surprised I was speaking to her in Arabic. Then it struck me. She was too young to know enemy soldiers don't usually speak in your tongue because enemy soldiers are always from another country or tribe or another something. Her father was surprised but not the little girl. We were ready to leave and I had a moment before crossing the yard. I knelt beside her, wanting to stop her terrible sobbing. It's going to be all right now, I said. The soldiers are moving up the street and you'll be safe in your house. She didn't stop crying but I knew she heard me. Then she choked out some words between the sobs, pathetic little words that were meant to explain her crying and justify herself in front of her family. I'm so frightened, she said. This is my first war.

Tajar leaned over the bed to hear Assaf, who had closed his eyes. A shudder ran through Assaf under the sheets. He opened his eyes and stared at the ceiling, speaking in an exhausted voice.

Her *first* war, repeated Assaf. That's what she said in that room where her family was huddled in the corner as silent as death. If this were the last war then *maybe* I could justify what I saw and did that night. But where is the *last* war? My mother conceived me in the first war and my father was killed in the second war and I was mangled in the third war and . . . what's the *matter* with people? What's wrong with their minds and their hearts? This isn't survival or life or anything at all a man can speak about. It's just horror. *War.*

Tajar sat with his hand resting on Assaf's arm, saying nothing, listening. Some of the exploits from Tajar's early life had become known to the public by then, not his intelligence work in Arab countries but his efforts to smuggle Jews into Palestine when it was still under British rule. Accounts had appeared in books and Assaf made reference now to these histories.

And I'll tell you something else, said Assaf. If I were asked to rescue people, I'd volunteer for every mission as long as I had the strength. Bringing people to safety and freedom? That's easy because there'd never be any doubt in what you were doing and never a fear in yourself. Who doesn't want to help people? It's right and it makes you feel good and that's the way it was when you were my age, Tajar. That's what you faced and you did it, but doing the right thing then was simple. Don't you see it's not that way now? You were lucky. You saved lives. But that's not what I'm called upon to do. I lie awake at night listening to a little girl cry. But when she's older and stronger and harder, when she knows hate better, maybe she'll no longer cry. . . .

Sadly, Tajar listened to Assaf pouring out his feelings. It was all understandable after what he had been through, with his body still in great pain. He was severly troubled and more time would have to pass before they could know how his experiences had changed him.

We can only wait, Tajar told Anna after describing what Assaf had said to him. The psyche adjusts to trauma in so many different ways, we just can't assume anything yet. But the resilience of the human spirit is a wondrous thing, truly limitless. Despair passes and anything can be born from it, anything at all. And Assaf is very young and he's strong inside, so we'll wait and watch and listen, and we'll see what we can do to help him regain his footing.

Tajar was a profound comfort to Anna that summer. She didn't know how she could have got through the first visits to the hospital without him, or the days and weeks that followed. Often in the evening he turned up after work at her house, unannounced, and the two of them would sit on her balcony until a late hour, talking quietly in the shadows beneath the stars, a heady fragrance of jasmine drifting up from the courtyard on the night breezes. Anna was now aware that Tajar had once known her dead brother David, in Cairo during the world war, so their conversations carried even further back into the past, spanning her entire life.

We try so very hard, she said to Tajar one night, but no matter how hard we try we never do very well. And people always seem to struggle for the same causes, wanting life to be a little better for their children than it was for them, but what comes of it?

Are you referring to your own life? Tajar asked after a moment.

Yes of course, she replied. Here I sit twenty-five years after the death of my brother, who was my only living family then, while my only child is lying in a hospital in pain, tormented by his terrible memories of a night in a place where I brought him, in that valley just below us. I thought I was trying when I brought him here. I meant to try and I did try as best I could, but what have I done? What have I done and why? Just look what's come of it.

Tajar knew there were tears in her eyes without being able to see her face. He could hear the tears in her voice and feel them in the darkness. He stirred and a match flared as he lit a cigarette.

What have I done and why? he murmured. It's a question that never gets answered and always has to be asked. And what, I wonder, did you do today, Anna?

I went out, she said simply.

And?

I was painting. I went out and painted.

Where?

On a hillside. Just on a hillside.

Just on a hillside in Jerusalem, you say. And why, Anna?

To forget, she replied. And to remember. And to know a moment of beauty in Jerusalem.

Tajar nodded in the shadows. And just so is life, he said. To forget and remember and know the beauty of one afternoon in Jerusalem. . . . Surely no sage has ever said it better.

FOURTEEN

The extent of Israel's victory in the Six-Day War astonished the world. A tiny new nation had triumphed against overwhelming odds. In America photographs of Israel's dashing, one-eyed military leader, General Moshe Dayan, appeared with the legend: We try harder. And in Israel itself the euphoria was complete. Everyone saw a new era. Security and prosperity and peace—the good things of life were only a matter of time.

The Mossad had played its part. Dror and Tajar had planned wisely and the Runner operation was a brilliant success. No one had done more for victory than the Runner himself.

Yet Tajar was profoundly disturbed, alone in the gloom he felt. It made him angry to drag around secretly grumbling when everyone else was ecstatic, but no matter how hard he tried he couldn't shake his depression. His gloom was inexplicable to others. He managed to hide it from Anna, or so he thought, but others sensed it readily enough and spoke to him about it. The young men he worked with at the Mossad were particularly incredulous.

What's the matter with celebrating a great victory? they asked him. It wasn't just some gift from heaven, so why plague yourself about whether we deserve it or not? And as a matter of fact, Tajar, we do deserve it. We earned it. Our boys did it, the whole country did it. We all made the sacrifices and made it happen. The Arabs were the ones who wanted war, not us.

They pushed and pushed for war and finally it came and we gave it to them, and they've learned their lesson. They're finished and now they'll have to make peace.

Tajar grumbled and shook his head and went shuffling off in his awkward gait. Nobody's just finished, he thought. It doesn't happen like that to a people. Doesn't our own history prove it doesn't? You can't just humiliate a people and expect good to come from it. Anyway, nations don't learn lessons the way a child does, history isn't as simple as that. People learn to hide and survive or hate and survive or dream and survive, but the one thing they do is survive and not with acceptance in their hearts for those who humiliate them. A million more Arabs under Israeli rule? It's impossible. It can't be, it won't work.

Behind his back his younger colleagues found reasons for Tajar's feelings. He's always been very close to the Arabs, they said. Naturally he understands how they feel and now when they've taken such a beating, when they've lost so much territory. . . .

But it wasn't territory Tajar was thinking about. It was people that haunted him. He had profound respect for the despair born of humiliation and what it could lead to. And of course it was also true that he had been intimate his whole life with Arabs and Arab ways, unlike so many of the men he worked with, who were of European descent and oriented toward a European past.

Or maybe it's those other things they say, thought Tajar. Maybe it's just that I'm from another generation, an old Jew, *the* old Jew. Perhaps I worry and fret when things go well because I'm too used to things not going well. The old Jew? Well I am old. Fifty-one is old when you first risked your life on a mission thirty years ago and have gone through a world war and three other wars since then. But can there really be an old and a new man in that respect? Do the inner ways of a people change so suddenly from one generation to another? Can feelings and perceptions become obsolete in only a decade or two and be discarded, like some weapon from the battlefield that doesn't fire as rapidly as a newer model? Is human nature like that? Are people like that? Is there something wrong with me because I can't accept our generals as heroes and our little country as invincible?

A mere two decades after the holocaust, thought Tajar, and the nation of two million Jews defeats their enemy nations of eighty million and the whole world applauds as if history had suddenly reversed the evil of the holocaust, easing everyone's conscience a bit, while even we applaud the wonder of our new selves, the new Jew inside us who's proud and young and strong and says never again.

Well it's true I must be from another time and place, thought Tajar, because something deep inside me doesn't like any of it. The Arabs wanted war and we had no choice, but I fear what's happened. We're out of balance, the proportions are wrong. War isn't our strength as a people and generals shouldn't be our heroes. Those are foreign gods, for others. Nor are the Arabs Nazis, nor is Israel in Europe, nor should anyone pretend we're settling history's scores. Israel is here and we're not of Europe or the West. We're a people of the far more ancient Middle East, one of many, who have wandered and come home, where all our neighbors are Arabs and always will be Arabs. True, they don't have to accept us, but if we're going to live here we have to accept them. And even to begin to imagine we can remake the world here in six days and rest on the seventh? It frightens me. In that presumption lies arrogance, the hubris of the ancient Greeks, the insupportable pride from which all human tragedy flows. . . .

Tajar tried to keep his gloomy fears to himself. In any case there was no one he could really talk to about the feelings that had come over him. The men he knew professionally all had other views, and Anna had Assaf and her own concerns. What she needed from him then was confidence and assurance and strength, the same qualities he had always been known for in the Mossad.

Tajar's house was very near Anna's, just around the corner and up the Street of the Prophets, for it was a part of Jerusalem he dearly loved. When he left her on her balcony in the evening he took a long time going home, hobbling slowly through the shadows and stopping to gaze at the noble old buildings dark against the stars.

Finally he reached his turn off the Street of the Prophets, a collapsed gateway with a giant cactus rearing inside it. The scarred ancient cactus, taller than a man and many yards across, gave an appearance of desolation to the gateway, as if the desert had crept into Jerusalem and taken over an abandoned lot. But in fact the cactus merely guarded the gateway and hid what lay beyond it from the curious eyes of passers-by.

Once around the cactus a large compound opened up, unkempt and seemingly impenetrable, the silver leaves of thick-trunked olive trees shimmering above a solid tangle of flowering rosebushes gone wild with the years. A giant cactus and gnarled olive trees and roses blooming in confusion—for Tajar, it was a Jerusalem kind of splendor.

The compound was enclosed by a high wall. Beyond the cactus a narrow path wound its way into the tangle. There were glimpses of three or four small stone houses sheltering off to the sides near the wall, but houses and wall alike were mostly obscured by the bushes and trees. Sometimes the houses were occupied and sometimes not. They were tumble-down little places left over from the nineteenth century, as was the compound, and people seemed to move in and out of the houses as it suited them, without any particular notice to anyone, staying for a while and leaving when they found something better.

Tajar had bought his house years ago when he was recuperating from his automobile accident. Here he had learned to read Homer and also to walk again. The path wound through a final maze of rosebushes and all at once there was an open space and his low stone house standing beside it, at the very end of the walled compound.

It was a tight little cottage built close to the ground, no bigger than the others in the compound but in good repair. An English painter of Jerusalem in the nineteenth century, William Holman Hunt, had once lived in the house and Tajar enjoyed the associations of paintings having been created there.

He had a hammock strung between a corner of the cottage and an olive tree. Often in the summer he brought a blanket from inside and lay down out there, unable to tear himself away from the vast beauty of a starry night over Jerusalem. Often, too, he fell asleep in the hammock without even closing his eyes, it seemed, for one moment he was gazing up at the stars in a perfect stillness and the next moment he was stirring stiffly, a faint light of dawn gently nudging him awake.

I sleep in the yard like an old horse, he thought with a smile, gathering up his blanket to go inside for another hour or two of rest before it was time to begin the day. But there was so much to see in a Jerusalem night, how could he possibly close his eyes on such exquisite beauty?

Still, he wished there were someone he could talk to who understood his work, not the everyday details but what it meant to him, the scope and direction of his life and especially the new concerns that troubled him as a result of the June war. And then all at once he thought of just such a man, the man he had sent Yossi to see a few years earlier for that very reason, so Yossi in his isolation in Damascus could have someone to talk to who understood.

Bell. The one-eyed hermit of Jericho whom Tajar had worked for in Cairo during the world war. Just the other day Anna had mentioned Bell, recalling his mysterious connection to her brother David and the way he had helped her in Egypt long ago.

Bell? Naturally Tajar had kept himself current with Bell's situation in Jericho over the years, for professional reasons and also out of curiosity. Jericho was a small place and it was easy enough to come by reliable information, and of course he would never have sent Yossi to see Bell if he hadn't been sure of Bell's circumstances.

And now as chance would have it, Jericho was in Israeli hands and Bell was living only fifteen miles from Jerusalem, in the same place where he had been living for the last twenty years. And what might that mean for me? wondered Tajar.

In a world of secrecy and fury and chaos, it was astonishing how short distances were and how quickly things changed. Indeed, how near an unexpected friend could be.

FIFTEEN

In Jericho on the morning the June war began, Abu Musa and Moses the Ethiopian came drifting over to Bell's front porch and positioned themselves on their benches, there to remain most of the time during the next days, taking comfort in the company of friends and keeping a kind of vigil. As the hours of light passed into darkness and the darkness passed back into light, Abu Musa and Moses brooded over the shesh-besh board on the table between them, playing game after game and saying little. As usual Bell reclined in his tattered chair to the side, sipping arak and saying even less.

At first the Arab bulletins on the radio spoke only of victory. But the noise of heavy fighting came echoing down the hills from Jerusalem, and since the Arabs had begun with positions of strength surrounding the city on three sides, with the Israelis holding only their narrow corridor up to Jerusalem from the coastal plain, it seemed likely to Bell that the fighting was in fact going the other way. Perhaps in the excitement of going to war against the Jews, he thought, the Arabs were once more indulging that profound Levantine trait of preferring the mirage in the distance to the dreary stretch of desert at hand, the rich prospects of fantasy rather than the gritty facts of everyday life.

This seemed even more likely to Bell when the bombardments on the heights of Jerusalem all but ceased at the end of the second day of the war. By then Jordanian troops were moving through Jericho but they were all heading east across the river, away from the fighting. From time to time Abu Musa rose and went inside the bungalow to pick up the latest news on Bell's old radio, which he relayed to his two friends when he returned to the porch.

Total Arab victories everywhere, announced Abu Musa the first day.

Total Arab victories continuing in a glorious manner on all fronts, he announced on the second day. It sounds bad, he added. They must be losing.

Total Arab victories everywhere in the most glorious of manners and the Jews are being thrown into the sea, he announced on the morning of the third day, when the bombardments had stopped in Jerusalem.

You don't sound pleased, said Moses. What does it mean? Can you decode the bulletin for me?

I can, replied Abu Musa. In such a situation, when the mirage recedes in the distance and the desert track is long, our brothers generally mean the opposite of what they say. So the truth is probably that the Arabs are being defeated everywhere in the most ignominious of manners, while the Jews are advancing away from the sea on all fronts. Moreover, the silence we hear with our own ears from Jerusalem is ominous. Perhaps the Jews have already taken east Jerusalem and the Old City and are at this moment on their way down to Jericho? Perhaps we'll see them this very afternoon in Jericho? That's what the bulletin means, decoded.

The two men went back to their shesh-besh game. That afternoon an Israeli mechanized battalion came rolling down from the western hills and sped through Jericho. There were no defensive positions in the town or on the plains of Jericho, so after some sporadic firing around the police station the battalion left a few jeeps and soldiers in the central square and moved on north up the valley. The Jordanian troops had already retreated across the river and all was quiet in Jericho once more.

It's a second coming, mused Moses, studying the shesh-besh board. Three millennia ago there was the first coming when Joshua crossed the river from the east and had seven ram's horns sounded seven times while walking around the oasis of Jericho seven times. And so the walls fell, and the conquest of Jericho was Israel's first act in the promised land.

For me it was the Turks first, observed Abu Musa, also studying the shesh-besh board. Then after the Turks came the English and then the Hashemites and now the Israelis. In my three hundred years I have seen several proud conquerors come to Jericho in search of oranges in the lowest and oldest town on earth, but I suppose that's the nature of living in a desirable place. Rulers in Jerusalem and Damascus have traditionally turned their eyes this way, longing to escape those blustery cold winters they have up there. Didn't Herod and the Omayyad caliphs choose Jericho for their winter palaces? Further, Jericho is a crossing of history. To the east one thing, to the west another, to the north or south a third. Ideas and armies and caravans of believers have always passed this way on their relentless journeys to wherever it is they're going. We sit but fifteen miles from Jerusalem and a little more from Amman, and Jerusalem is midway between Amman, the ancient Greek city of Philadelphia, and the sea. Jerusalem is holy and biblical Rabbat Ammon or Amman is where King David put Uriah the Hittite in the forefront of battle to be killed, so he might enjoy the dead man's wife Bathsheba, who gave the king a son called Solomon. Thus the mountains and the valley, the deserts and the sea, lust and wisdom and murder and empire, these various profane and sacred causes of man all find their crossroads in Jericho, which is why we grow oranges here. To refresh those who are forever passing through.

And yet nothing that happens today changes our yesterdays, mused Moses. The Mount of Temptation still rises above us to the west, the river where John the Baptist renewed souls still flows beside us to the east. We are as well-situated today as ever for shesh-besh and holy matters. . . .

The dice clattered as the two men bent over the board,

making their moves. Bell sipped arak and gazed through the bottom of his glass at his orange grove.

War gets no better with age, said Bell. My own war was fought mostly in the desert, away from towns and villages and innocent people, but that's the only good thing that can be said about it.

Also my war, observed Abu Musa. My part of it, at least, was fought entirely in the desert. We blew up trains amidst the sand dunes, little snorting trains puffing steam at an empty azure sky, quaint little antique trains chugging from nowhere to nowhere across an immensity of desolate wastes. In retrospect that can seem romantic, but in fact there's not a glimmer of romance in blowing things up.

True, said Bell. I have only to look in the mirror to be aware of that.

Now now, said Moses the Ethiopian, it won't do to have you two brooding over your dark pasts on such a warm and sunny June day. All of that was long ago for both of you, as was the stroke of a knife when I was a boy, making me into a eunuch. Once I yearned for a different kind of manhood, the usual kind, but as destiny would have it I've never taken part in war, nor could I. I'm just not warlike. So I ask myself, isn't that a goodness God has given me?

Abu Musa grinned across the board at Moses. Whatever your status as a warrior, he said, you're still an African giant who plays a fiendishly clever game of shesh-besh. And in any case the ceaseless conquest of the soul is a far more demanding campaign than that waged by any general, as we all know. So, O gentle giant, as two seasoned players in God's scheme let us now roll the dice in order that our friend the resident holy man can feel whatever it is he feels, and immortalize us with his thoughts. Bell? Immortalize away. Moses the Ethiopian and his partner Moses the Arab have returned to their eternal game. . . .

Bell smiled as the dice clattered and his two friends bent over the board. Several times that afternoon Bell saw boots approach his front gate. Then a man would crouch there—a young Israeli soldier—and peer into the yard beneath the branches of the orange trees. As the young man gaped, his expression turned from curiosity to amazed disbelief. The first time it happened Bell quietly cleared his throat so his two friends would notice. They both looked up from the board and, along with Bell, pondered the soldier.

The conqueror looks stunned, observed Abu Musa.

Jericho has always been a strange place, mused Moses.

And less a conqueror than a frightened boy, said Bell. Like all conquerors, he wears the too-old face of a boy who has had to endure the unspeakable.

Bell raised his glass, toasting the startled young soldier, who stared a moment longer in wonder before disappearing. Certainly for the soldier they made a bizarre trio sitting on the dilapidated porch in the orange grove: a lean one-eyed European dressed in white with a glass of what looked like water in the air, while positioned over a shesh-besh board sat a huge elderly Arab in a pale blue galabieh, and an even more enormous chocolate-skinned giant in bright yellow robes.

And all three of these benign apparitions were gazing thoughtfully down at the soldier as if he were a petitioner come to call in heaven on the day of judgment, heaven that fateful day having taken on the appearance of a sweet-smelling stand of fruit trees where God had chosen to take His ease in a tripartite guise of diverse Selves, a threefold manner of presentation, the better to convey His pleasure at the handiwork of differing races He had created for His human family . . . light and dark and darker, dressed in white and pale blue and bright yellow to add a measure of gentle variety to His dream of an orange grove.

Ah yes, thought Bell. Races and wars and caravans of believers from the deserts and seas, with their armies of chance and their games of skill . . . all come to meet in an orange grove at the crossroads of Jericho.

The Holy Land, in other words. And also a fair enough assessment of the lowest and oldest town on earth, it seemed to him. Workable and adequate for the time being, at least until God *did* show His hand.

Part 2

ONE

The Arab village of el Azariya faces the rising sun from the eastern slopes of the Mount of Olives, away from Jerusalem on the Jericho road, clinging to the last patches of green where the Mediterranean finally loses hold of the land and the desert begins its eastern march to the Persian Gulf and the Hindu Kush. The village is small, perched on the very edge of the barren vistas that drop away to the plains of Jericho and the Dead Sea valley.

Two thousand years ago a poor religious teacher from the Galilee, Yeshua, was in the habit of staying with friends in the village when he journeyed south to visit Jerusalem. The friends he stayed with were two sisters and a brother called Mary and Martha and Lazarus. The present name of the village echoes in Arabic the name of this brother, a memory of the evening when Yeshua turned up to stay with his friends and was told by Mary and Martha that their brother had died four days before then, whereupon the visitor raised Lazarus from the dead in a miracle of guesthood.

In the time of Yeshua, or Jesus as he was later called by the Greeks, el Azariya was a Jewish village known as *the encampment*, Beit Haniya in Hebrew, from which its Western name of Bethany is derived.

Place is the beginning of memory. In both Hebrew and Arabic, Christians are called *Nazarenes*, people of Nazareth, after the village in the Galilee where Yeshua lived in obscurity until the age of thirty, before he became a wandering teacher during the last three years of his life. Thus near Jerusalem an encampment or outpost, a brother and a guest and a miracle, a mix of Greek and Hebrew and later Arabic . . . and the passage of two thousand years. As so often in the ancient Holy Land, even the name of the village of el Azariya resonates complexly in time, recalling how deep is the well of the past in a land where the voices of history forever call out with different memories for different peoples, memories which have become known as cultures or traditions, and thenceforth enshrined as religions.

With its lack of water el Azariya has always been a poor place, which is perhaps why Jesus preferred to spend his nights there or in the open on the Mount of Olives, rather than within the gates of Herod's grand city on the other side of the hill. The winter rains from the Mediterranean reach as far as Jerusalem but no farther, and to the east beyond el Azariya come the descending rock-hard fissures of crumbling time and relentless sun known as the Judean wilderness, which ends in the multicolored grandeur of the Dead Sea valley.

The Judean wilderness is no more than fifteen miles wide as the hawk flies, but because of its bleak and terrible landscape it has always been a place of refuge for those seeking safety or solitude. A few centuries after Jesus, ascetics living in its caves evolved the beginnings of the Christian monastic movement which was to become so powerful in the West. Before then Jews hid from Roman persecution in its caves while preparing their revolt, and a thousand years earlier King David fled into this same wilderness to escape the murderous designs of his son Absalom. Throughout the millennia, outlaws and prophets and kings and the wretched have all known the fiery chasms of its summers and the icy cold crevices of its winters.

Small though it is, in the midwifery of time the Judean wilderness has been one of the great birthing places of man's spirit. Out of its stark and stony reaches, through the mysteries of creation, vast events have been given to history. And the destiny of this particular desert has always been coupled to the dream of Jerusalem, joined at the Mount of Olives, as if men could not contemplate the idea of a Holy City without also facing a harsh wilderness of the soul hard beside it, the existence of one inexorably a part of the other.

◆◆◆◆◆◆◆◆

Abu Musa had two great-nephews who were born and grew up in el Azariya, sons of a nephew who had been killed fighting the Jews in the 1948 war. At the time of their father's death the older boy was four and the other was still a baby. Their mother, alone, couldn't raise them both, so the older boy was taken in by the Greek monks who ran an orphanage in the village, connected to their monastery which honored the miracle of Lazarus. The older brother, Yousef, thus grew up as a Christian while the younger brother, Ali, remained a Moslem.

The chance separation caused other differences in their upbringing. Yousef became studious under the guidance of the Greek monks and learned Greek and English, eventually training as a schoolteacher. Ali lived the more traditional life of a village youth, working outdoors with his hands and his back, and would probably have ended as a laborer had not Yousef argued with their mother that more could be done. Because of his older brother's insistence, Ali became an electrician's helper for almost no pay. But in a few years, being a clever boy, he too was learning things and their mother was proud that her younger son also had the beginnings of a trade. Yousef, serious in manner, had taught himself early to seek out responsibility.

From the time they were children, Bell knew the boys as well as Abu Musa did, perhaps even better. All during their youths they were brought to Jericho at least once a season to stay with the family patriarch, Abu Musa, in order to listen to his wisdom and hear tales of cousins and uncles and ancestors, to experience the story of history and learn of their own place in it.

Abu Musa's method of passing on knowledge to the boys was in the wandering oral tradition, as befitted a man of the desert turned grower of fruit trees. Like a philosopher-king, Abu Musa ambled through his regular Jericho days with the two little boys at his heels, wide-eyed and silent, the smaller Ali clutching the older Yousef's hand for safety.

First thing every morning they visited Abu Musa's orange groves, where they examined the soil and the fruit and the blossoms while Abu Musa chatted on about the adventures of this or that relative who had lived in some distant era before the boys were born, in far-off Damascus or Beirut or Aqaba. Following Abu Musa's example, they dipped their fingers in the gurgling channels of water and found it sweet. Then it was time for a leisurely stroll around the central square with a stop for syrupy coffee and gossip for Abu Musa and sticky sweets for the boys, sitting at a little table in front of a coffeeshop under a towering sycamore tree, where the owner of the shop circled their table in an ancient ceremony of welcome, sprinkling water with his hand to lay the dust.

Camels and donkeys came by laden with bananas. The important men of the village salaamed up to Abu Musa to ask their questions of the day and receive advice. A baker brought an offering of hot sesame wafers for the boys. After holding court for an hour or more Abu Musa graciously distributed smiles all around and swayed off home to eat. Then he slept and the boys were free to explore his sheds and play in his water channels. When Abu Musa awoke there was more chatting under the trees before it was time to head for Bell's front porch and Abu Musa's afternoon shesh-besh session with the African giant in bright yellow robes, gentle Moses, who slipped the boys chunks of sugar cane when he embraced them. Sometimes the boys listened to the men on the porch and sometimes they wandered around the orange grove with Bell and ended up sitting under the grape arbor in back, where Bell told them tales of Egypt and India.

And at least once a year they were taken on those wondrous

journeys down to the river in the magnificent steam coach driven by Moses. The boys stood in the rear compartment where Bell and Abu Musa sat, fearfully high above the ground and breathless with excitement, two sets of small eager hands gripping the polished woodwork and two solemn little faces peering over the side of the coach, dark eyes round and staring, silently watching the desert fly by.

Since the boys had always known Bell, they never thought his face ugly. As with the other wonders of their visits to Jericho, Bell was merely part of Abu Musa's mysterious domain, the timeless oasis of the family patriarch where brown-skinned genies and flying carpets and one-eyed holy men, where bubbling water and banana trees and sugar cane, where eternal rivers and fleet gazelles and the barren desert all had stately roles to play in the enchanting visions of a child's imagination.

When the boys were older they had more serious talks with Bell under his grape arbor, wide-ranging discussions on many things. Because Bell wasn't kin and also because he was a foreigner, they could be intimate with him in a way that was unthinkable with Abu Musa. Since the boys had no father they felt the need for this kind of friendship and Bell was always ready to give them his ear and his counsel, modestly as was his habit, speaking in a manner they could understand but without any trace of condescension. Abu Musa, for his part, was overjoyed at the boys' great love for his friend and Bell's love for them. When little Ali hugged Bell in some moment of passion, or when the older Yousef gravely made a comment in English and Bell replied in English with equal gravity, the old man's eyes brimmed with tears of pride.

How *rich* life is, he whispered to Moses across the shesh-besh board, watching the boys wander away with Bell on their roundabout route to the grape arbor.

Truly, murmured Moses. For God is ever-present if we but open our hearts to His grace.

Ali grew into a forceful young man, active and passionate

with an ability to do anything with his hands. His dark eyes glittered when a problem was set before him, some object in need of repair. Quietly he studied the task, turning the object over and over in his hands, then flew at it and quickly made everything right, laughing happily as he finished the work with a triumphant flourish. Electricity was his trade, but for him it was just a way of feeling the world with his hands and making himself one with it.

Yousef's interests were more in a theoretical vein, less given to tangible matters than to speculation. He enjoyed his work as a schoolteacher and spent most of his free time reading in English, seeking Bell's advice for direction and discussing everything he read with him.

As if to emphasize the differences between the two brothers, Ali grew to be tall and thin and bony while Yousef was shorter and thicker in body, the one face lean and the other full. My son of the desert and my son of the town, as Abu Musa fondly described Ali and Yousef when they sat with him under the sycamore tree in the central square of Jericho, the two of them no longer boys but handsome young men ready to make their way in the world.

And then came the aftermath of the Six-Day War and it was Ali who was killed in a town and Yousef who went into the desert, a reversal of fate which would reach far into the future and change the lives of Assaf and Anna and Tajar in Jerusalem, of Abu Musa and Bell in Jericho, and even of Halim in Damascus.

TWO

The Palestine Liberation Organization was founded in 1964 under the patronage of Nasser of Egypt. In 1965 a sack with an explosive charge was found floating down a canal in northern Israel by an Israeli water engineer, having been placed in the canal by saboteurs who crossed over from Jordan on horseback. In Damascus a militant wing of the PLO calling itself el Fatah, *the victorious*, took credit for the sack in the waterway and announced it was the beginning of another kind of war against Israel.

A month after the Six-Day War the leaders of el Fatah moved into the territories lost by Jordan west of the river to begin a popular war of liberation. From the marketplace of the Arab city of Nablus, in biblical Samaria, they directed sabotage operations in Israel and tried to organize civil disobedience in the occupied territories. But the PLO wasn't accepted then by the local Arabs. Its followers were unable to move through the villages as Mao Tse-tung said resistance fighters should move, as fish in water.

By the end of the year the attempt at popular resistance had failed and the PLO left the land and moved back into Jordan. There they set up bases near the border to strike across the river. When these bases were destroyed by Israeli raids, the PLO moved more deeply into Jordan and dispersed its forces in refugee camps and in Jordanian villages and towns, where they couldn't be easily targeted without causing heavy civilian casualties. This increased the PLO's safety but made it less effective for fighting. Having failed at a popular war in Palestine and at a war of attrition from neighboring Arab countries, the PLO turned to bombings and terror in Europe, in particular to hijacking planes in Europe.

At first the PLO concentrated on Israeli airliners. But when armed men were put on Israeli flights, the PLO began hijacking European and American airliners. The campaign culminated in September 1970, when three hundred hostages from Swiss and American flights were taken to an airfield held by the PLO in Jordan.

King Hussein of Jordan had steadily been losing control of his country to the PLO. After the three hundred Swiss and American hostages were freed, the Jordanian army attacked the PLO bases in Jordan—Black September to the PLO—and drove their armed units out of the country into southern Lebanon. Syrian forces invaded Jordan but then pulled back when Israel made it clear it would oppose a Syrian attempt to overthrow Hussein.

Such was the course of history for the Palestinian national movement in the first years after the Six-Day War, a murky tale of violence and conflicting intrigues, of ruin and retreat and terror, made up of innumerable moments of hope and despair, disinterest and suffering.

◆◆◆◆◆◆◆◆

Ali was one of those young men who heard the call of idealism in the summer after the Six-Day War. Unknown to his brother, Ali joined a cell of el Fatah in east Jerusalem. The boys he dealt with were amateurs and their organization was inept. Ali at nineteen was among the older members of the cell. They met at night to design the acts that would lead to a better future, to plan liberation from the conqueror in passionate surges of commitment.

But Ali's role in history was over almost as soon as it began. His cell was raided one night and he tried to escape out the back of the building, firing a revolver which he didn't really know how to use. The exit was covered and he was shot, killed on the spot.

◆◆◆◆◆◆◆◆

Yousef was so stunned by the suddenness of Ali's death he didn't know how to react. After the interrogations ended he went to sit in the church of the Greek monks who had educated him, the church dedicated to the miracle of Lazarus raised from the dead. There, alone and undisturbed, he could weep like a child and experience his feelings of loss, above all his emptiness. Their mother had died several years before, and Youself had no one in the village to share his grief.

Yousef didn't pray in the church. He was too skeptical to be a follower of rites and rituals or a believer in divine mystery of any sort. The figure of Jesus had always been meaningful to him but in the simplicity of the Nazarene's life, not in the hierarchy of ceremony man had constructed from it. As with Mohammed or the Buddha or Moses, Jesus was to him a messenger and prophet of God, a bringer of the vision of man's better nature and a teacher of the great moral truths which would allow man to realize it. In this as in so many things, Yousef reflected the feelings of his own moral teacher—Bell.

For a long time Yousef was suspended in remembering. He hovered over his memories of Ali as a hummingbird hovers over a lemon tree and savors the mysteries of its blossoms, recalling his brother's passionate smiles and warm embraces and loving voice.

He could make no sense of Ali's death. Yousef believed in liberty and equality as much as anyone, and because of his reading in history he knew more about them than most people. But what did Ali's death, he kept asking himself, have to do with any of that? This pathetic attempt at conspiracy? These gestures of defiance and enthusiasm offered up in the company of some spellbound village boys beguiled by their own rhetoric? Ali had gone about reworking the future the way he would have gone about any childhood game, eyes glittering with confidence, ready to set things right with his very own hands and then exult in the triumph, as if history and wars and conflicting peoples, the whole enormity of memory, were no more complex than a little electric motor waiting to be undone and rewired by nimble fingers and a clever mind.

It was pathetic, futile. If only they had talked about it, thought Yousef. If only Ali had come to him and told him what he had in mind. Then they could have examined it together and Yousef could have helped his brother to see more, to grasp more, to do more.

The bell tolled above the church of Lazarus and the solemn Greek monks came and went leaving their trail of prayers and incense. The candles burned low and shadows flickered over the walls of the church as Yousef sat on in the half-darkness, remembering Ali.

He talked with the Greek fathers and heard their prayers, which brought him no solace. He raised his eyes and gazed at the painting of Jesus on the dome of the church, arms spread in hope in the role of the Paraclete, the comforter and intercessor. Jesus had walked in this village with friends. He had accepted their food and their water and even raised a brother among them from the dead. And it was in this poor place that Jesus had chosen to stay, not in glorious Jerusalem on the other side of the Mount of Olives.

Yousef left the church and took to wandering across the barren hills below el Azariya. All day and most of the night he sat out on the empty slopes in the fierce summer heat and the cool evenings looking down on the bare hills, watching some bird soar in the sunlight, alone in the still starry nights.

When he was able to face it he went down to Jericho to grieve with Abu Musa, with Bell, with Moses. Abu Musa burst into tears and gripped him tightly, holding him for long minutes.

Such a fine boy, sputtered Abu Musa. Such an excellent boy. So full of life and laughter and the good things of the earth, our passionate little Ali.

Bell, too, wept. Alone with Yousef under the grape arbor, he bowed his head and let the tears flow, his face a thousand years old in its grief, a timeless map of endurance as scarred and ravaged as the Judean wilderness itself.

Gentle Moses the Ethiopian also expressed his sorrow.

Each morning at four, said Moses, I sing the Psalms for our lost little brother. In my language the very act of prayer is known as *to repeat David*, to recite the Psalms, and this I do each morning in wonder and thanksgiving at the memory of our departed Ali.

Abu Musa sat hunched in his great bulk. To live, he murmured sadly, is to become expert in farewells.

I feel responsible for his death, said Yousef. I didn't talk with him enough and explore his concerns and help him consider what is and what might be done. It was all so pointless, so useless and to no end, but what can I do now? *What can I do?*

To each of the three men in Jericho, Yousef put this same question.

You can live honorably and according to your own inner voice, replied Abu Musa. Every man must do that and no man can do more.

I am a monk, said Moses, and I believe a man should seek God with all his heart and all his strength. Many are the ways to seek, but surely they all demand a broad-minded and merciful and humble spirit.

Words. Mere words to Yousef in his pain and suffering. But then Bell's reply seemed less elusive.

People only speak from what they know, said Bell, and we in turn only hear what is already shaping itself within us. Words are always pale reflections of what we feel, shallow and approximate, grossly inexact. At twenty-three you know farewells, but fortunately you haven't become expert in them yet. So for a while, Yousef, perhaps do nothing. I mean, make a point of doing nothing. Don't try to work things out or reach decisions. Let your feelings shift and your thoughts wander. Walk and sit and look at life going on around you. You can't join in it, I know that. So just watch and give yourself a period of doing nothing, three months or six months or whatever. Remind yourself that only regret gives nothing. It's always a sickly futile thing. You're strong, turn away from it. Then when the time comes go back to teaching school. Do it out of habit, the way you walk down the street. Eventually, things will shape themselves within you. We can talk whenever you like and eventually words will have some meaning for you again. . . .

At the end of the summer Yousef went back to el Azariya. His inattention was still too great to allow him to read when he wasn't at school, so instead he wandered over the hills, looking down on the Judean wilderness and doing nothing as Bell had advised, waiting for his emptiness to subside.

That autumn a young stranger moved into el Azariya, a Jew who spoke perfect Arabic, a former Israeli soldier recuperating from wounds received in the June war. The stranger limped with a cane and moved his shoulders stiffly. In a few months he would be nineteen, the same age Ali had been. The stranger's name was Assaf.

◆◆◆◆◆◆◆◆

The stranger was renting a small house at the end of the village. Each morning he limped over to the store to buy his food and each afternoon he went to sit alone in the coffeeshop. He was correct in his behavior and the villagers couldn't fault his manners. He greeted people when it was appropriate but waited for others to begin a conversation. When asked a question he answered directly.

He had been wounded in the night battle near Damascus Gate in east Jerusalem. A paratrooper. Shrapnel in his legs, his shoulder, his chest. His mother was from Egypt and his father, dead in the 1956 war, had been from Iraq. For his regular meals he ate olives and cheese and tomatoes and bread like everyone else, but he didn't eat much, perhaps because of his wounds. Once or twice a week he went off by bus to visit a hospital. He had grown up in west Jerusalem. At set hours he limped up and down in front of his house, exercising his legs. A village carpenter rigged bars on ropes in his house so he could exercise his torso. He was quiet and reserved and seldom smiled. He drank neither beer nor arak. In a village as small as el Azariya, Yousef knew all about the young stranger.

Yousef often passed the stranger's house on his walks out of the village in the evening. The first few times he nodded or waved from a distance, then he greeted the stranger and exchanged a few words in passing.

On Friday, his day off, Yousef set out early in the morning to wander across the hills. The sun was just above the Moabite mountains on the far side of the Jordan Valley, the wilderness golden in the first light of day. When Yousef went by that Friday the stranger was out in front of his house limping back and forth with his cane, exercising his legs.

The stranger smiled. Coffee for the traveler with the world at his feet? he offered.

Yousef accepted the offer and thanked the young man and walked ahead of him through the gate. Despite the early morning chill they sat in the front yard, where there was a sweeping view of the desert dropping away to the Jordan Valley.

It was the first of many visits Yousef made to Assaf's small house. In the beginning they were both careful not to talk about the war, but they couldn't ignore Assaf's wounds and soon Yousef had also spoken of Ali and his death. He had no idea what he was doing, concluded Yousef.

Nor did I that night on the road to Damascus Gate, said Assaf. You just keep pushing on until you're cut down. But now I have to make some sense of what happened, or not make sense of it but live with it anyway.

It was Assaf's wounds and Ali's death that made their friendship grow so quickly, so easily. They shared even more feelings than they knew. Both of them were desperate to reach out and be understood, to be forgiven, to find a way to go on. In their friendship they found the power of forgiveness, which was strengthened by the difference in their ages. Assaf became like a younger brother to Yousef. The need was great for both of them, and before the end of the year Yousef was brought to meet Anna in the old stone house on Ethiopia Street.

Anna liked Yousef. She found him thoughtful beyond his years, a serious young man who was having a beneficial effect on Assaf. She had been doubtful when Assaf said he wanted to live for a time in an Arab village near Jerusalem, while he was getting back the use of his arms and legs. But Tajar was strongly in favor of the idea and convinced Anna she should be too.

Right now, Tajar had said, anything he wants to do should be encouraged. Being on his own is good, living in a village is good. Of course you want to take care of him, but giving him encouragement is probably the best way to help.

Tajar stayed away when the two young men came to visit Anna. He felt it was important for her to be alone with Assaf and his friend. Anna came in from painting and served them one of her vegetable soups, which they gulped down, unused to such fine fare. Afterward, Yousef wandered around the room admiring Anna's landscapes.

They're wonderful, said Yousef. To me, such simplicity conveys great honesty. The hills around Jerusalem look exactly like that. The houses cling to the slopes and seem to grow right out of the rock, to be part of the hills.

Yousef stopped in front of a painting which showed some Arab women sitting under a tree, gathering olives. It was a monochrome rendered with severe economy, the only painting in the room with people in it.

You've just begun doing people? he asked.

Yes, said Anna. It's an experiment. I'm not really sure of them yet.

Yousef peered at the painting more closely. Landscape matters in ancient places, he said, but anyway, it's an experiment that's working. Your power of suggestion is truly extraordinary. Every line is specific but the effect is timeless.

He turned to Anna, smiling.

Someday your house will be a museum, he said. Cakes and coffee will be served on the balconies and people will come from far away to experience the beauty of Jerusalem through your eyes, the way it used to be. What a grand thing to be able to give so much, to leave so much behind you.

Anna smiled and Assaf laughed, the first time she had heard him laugh since the war. He's found a friend who helps him laugh, thought Anna. And we have Tajar to thank for seeing the good of his living alone.

After the visit to Anna there was a trip to Jericho, so Assaf could meet the formidable trio of wise men on Bell's front porch. Abu Musa was deeply pleased and showed it.

Nothing heals like love, he whispered to Moses over the shesh-besh board. How splendid that Yousef has found a brother when his heart aches. The two boys will make each other whole again. Each of them has much to give.

Bell agreed. After sitting with the young men under his grape arbor, he came away impressed with their devotion to one another.

They're unalike in many ways, Bell said later, but so were Ali and Yousef. In any case, I imagine their friendship will be lasting and profound because of the way it came about.

And because Assaf is a Jew, added Abu Musa. In times like these, that's also something special.

Oh yes, that too, said Bell.

Jesus was a Jew and I'm a Christian, murmured Moses, so naturally I rejoice in brotherly love that's both lasting and profound. But perhaps the two of you already suspected that?

THREE

All the while Yousef was watching life go on around him, waiting to discover what course his own life would take. Assaf's companionship hastened the healing of the wounds in Yousef's heart. And as Yousef grew stronger in spirit, Assaf walked with greater confidence, his limp less pronounced.

Yousef talked with Assaf more than he ever had with his brother, as if to make up for that failure he blamed on himself and its terrible outcome. No feeling was too intimate for Yousef to lay bare to Assaf, who was eager to listen. For Assaf, listening to Yousef and understanding him became a way of escape from the alley of death, a kind of absolution from the horror he had survived when so many others hadn't.

As time went on Assaf felt Yousef's resolution growing. From the way Yousef talked Assaf knew his friend was nearing some decision having to do with himself and his people and the Palestinian cause. Yet Assaf also knew his friend wasn't warlike or fit for conspiracy. Yousef was a scholarly man, a dreamer and a thinker incapable of aggression. Killing was abhorrent to him and he would never hate nor fear enough to set aside his abhorrence. Significantly, when Yousef talked about himself and the Palestinian people, his thoughts always returned to his village, the poor place on the edge of the Judean wilderness where Jesus had chosen to stay with friends.

Assaf also came to realize how important the austere one-eyed man in Jericho had always been to Yousef. Something in Bell's life, Bell's manner, Bell's ways, had an enormous hold on Yousef.

What is it exactly that appeals to you so much about Bell? Assaf once asked his friend. Yousef gave several answers, then admitted he had never been able to describe it adequately to himself.

It has to do with his calm, I suppose, said Yousef, and how he set about achieving it and did achieve it. To me, that seems a miraculous accomplishment. Of course I don't believe he's really a holy man the way Abu Musa does, but perhaps that's because we don't have that kind of faith today, Abu Musa's kind of faith, or at least I don't. There have been times when I wished I did, though. When I was a boy I used to marvel at the faith of the Greek fathers, and envy them for it, their absolute belief that what they were doing was the right thing to do. Bell has never had faith like that and he's not a religious man in that sense. Then too, there's his drinking and all it implies. Yet somehow despite all that, and despite his face or because of it, there's a grandeur to him. He denies it and always has, but you can't be around him without feeling it. As wise a man as Abu Musa senses it implicitly, and no one's shrewder than Abu Musa when it comes to human beings and what they're up to. Moses recognizes it too, and he's far more knowledgeable about people than you might suspect from being with him just once or twice. No, it's not a light matter, and the very fact that Bell has done what he's done, without a religious kind of faith, is what's so arresting about him. To me it's an astonishing mystery, intriguing and indefinable. Haunting, even. . . .

Assaf listened and nodded and felt he understood most of it. In his own manner Yousef was seeking Bell's way in life, and Yousef's period of doing nothing, as he called it, was the time needed to let that path reveal itself. As for Assaf, he was surprised by his own understanding. His grasp of Yousef's feelings was itself a step toward self-discovery, the sort of knowledge he might have expected to hear from Anna or Tajar in the past.

The winter turned blustery and cold. The sun was lost and the wind howled as thick clouds raced over the hills, bringing rain and more rain and an early darkness to the Mount of Olives. Yousef returned from his evening walks in the wastes laughing and stamping his feet, sweeping into Assaf's little outpost like some phantom from the wild desert night, his bulky shepherd's cloak heavy with rain and a pungent woolly smell of the sheepskins from which it was made. Together they huddled around Assaf's charcoal brazier where water steamed for coffee. Assaf dug chestnuts from the coals and they burned their fingers cracking them, then scooped up handfuls of fresh dates and drank more cups of syrupy sweet coffee, eating to keep warm as the wind blasted the slopes and screamed through the village. The door shook and the shutters rattled. They laughed and joked and told tales over the charcoal, facing each other in hats and scarves and sheepskins pulled tight against the icy drafts gusting through the room, their hands raised in front of them, warming at the fire.

A pair of open hands facing Assaf, facing Yousef. A palmist's indelible map of the lines of the heart, of the lines of the mind and destiny for the soothsayer in each of them to read by the firelight, one day to ponder.

And so without knowing it the two young friends came to memorize each other's fates down through those rainswept nights of midwinter where they escaped the darkness with warm words, sheltering in Assaf's house on the edge of the wilderness.

◆◆◆◆◆◆◆◆

The first *hamsin* appears in the Eastern Mediterranean in March, a sudden false summer drifting up from the vast African and Asian deserts to the south. Invisible sand weighs the air and a dry heavy heat grips the land. The sky turns thickly yellow, the sun is obscured, an unworldly glow suffuses the yellow heavens. After several days the hamsin lifts. The temperature tumbles back to March and the sky is cooly blue, only to be followed in a week or less by the unnatural heat, the stillness, the strange yellow glow of another hamsin.

Hamsin means *fifty* in Arabic, the number of days this season is said to last. Thus does the desert reassert its hold on the land and boldly lay claim to the sensuous habits of spring, vanquishing the stormy ways of a brief and foreign winter.

The Judean wilderness turns softly green in the spring and whole ranges are bright with wildflowers, gifts of the winter rains and a new sun. But the herbs and flowers and grasses have only a few weeks to complete their cycle of life and shed their seeds to another year, for in just such a time the earth is baked rock-hard once more as the sun hammers all growing things to dust.

The end of winter brought the end of the long evenings of communion between the two friends in Assaf's little house on the edge of el Azariya. Assaf now walked without a cane. When Yousef joined him in the evening they sat in front of Assaf's house, looking down on the desert. Yousef was both serene and excited, apparently having reached a decision about his future. But Yousef didn't speak of it and Assaf felt no need to question his friend. They both sensed it was something better left unsaid and instead they talked about Assaf's future. Yousef felt strongly that Assaf should go to university. As a wounded veteran his education would be paid for and Yousef thought it was too good an opportunity to miss.

They made more visits to Anna in the spring and also traveled down to Jericho. Anna didn't know it but Yousef was saying good-bye. Abu Musa sensed a farewell, but because the death of Ali was still too recent a loss to the old patriarch, he and Yousef didn't speak of it openly. With Bell, though, Assaf suspected that Yousef was more direct. When they were in Jericho, Yousef went off with Bell on his walks out of town at twilight while Assaf, using his leg as an excuse, stayed behind on Bell's front porch with the two shesh-besh players. Assaf knew without being told that Yousef was going away. It was just a question of when he was leaving and where he would go.

To the Eastern churches, Easter is alone in holiness. Christmas, unmentioned in the gospels and falling near the winter solstice, is to them perhaps a memory of some northern, pagan ceremony honoring the rebirth of the sun. But Easter, born of Jesus' trip to Jerusalem to celebrate Passover and forever linked to Passover through lunar calendars, celebrates the central mystery of Christianity, the resurrection to eternal life.

For the Greek fathers who maintain the church of Lazarus on the Mount of Olives, as for their brethren, forty days of fasting and prayer culminate in the midnight mass which welcomes Easter Sunday. Then, as the church bell tolls twelve in the deepness of the night, the bishop turns to face his congregation with a lighted candle and speaks the words *Christ is risen.* The church is dark. Each celebrant holds an unlit candle. From the one candle, the light and the promise spread.

When the words were spoken at midnight that Easter, Assaf was watching from the back of the Greek church in el Azariya. It was the first time he had attended a service in a church, and he went because Yousef asked him to come and he felt it was important to his friend. As it happened, it was also the last time he saw Yousef.

The chants and incense swirled for hours, then the church was darkened. The bell tolled, the words were said, the light spread until the whole dim church was flickering brightly. But when Assaf looked around for Yousef he could no longer see him. He waited outside while the church emptied but still there was no Yousef. In that most precious of moments to the Greek fathers who had raised him, Yousef had paid a silent farewell to his village and slipped away in the darkness to pursue his destiny, gone to live in the caves and crevices of the Judean wilderness as other refugees in the Holy Land had done before him.

Yousef wasn't a man to take up arms and he never did. His

cause was liberty and equality, rare facts in his part of the world and hardly known from the Eastern Mediterranean to the East China Sea, but no less desired for that. Yousef had become a member of the Palestine Liberation Organization and thereby a fugitive west of the Jordan River. During his early months in the wilderness he did provide tangible assistance to the PLO, acting as a guide to infiltrators and other fugitives. But soon his flight was too elusive even for that and he became simply a symbol of resistance, a solitary wanderer given to self-imposed exile in his own land.

As the months and years went by Yousef became the subject of stories, living alone as he did in the fiery chasms and icy caves of that desolate landscape, surviving in some meager way that only God could comprehend. Of course the wilderness wasn't truly deserted. Bedouin roamed the stark hills with their black tents and goatherd boys from the villages grazed their flocks deep in the wadis in all but the coldest weather. Tales were brought back by those who sometimes caught sight of Yousef, or thought they did. He was said to move with the speed of the wind, a sharp small figure disappearing on the horizon at twilight, so quickly gone in the fast-falling desert night that the bedouin and goatherd boys couldn't be sure they had seen a man or a phantom, a man or an eerie trick of last light playing a final echo in a corner of the stony wastes. But mostly he wasn't seen and his presence was only sensed, for to the bedouin and goatherd boys Yousef was more a spirit than a man, to be known through a sudden, distant whirl of sand or an abrupt and peculiar whisper of wind.

Among them it became a custom to leave food and water for the invisible wanderer in some protected place, a sharing offered up after the manner of a portion for the prophet Elijah, to remind God of the dream which forever stirs in the barren places of the human soul. By way of these secret friends and their secret wishes, Yousef somehow survived in the wilderness and became a legend to the Arab villagers of Palestine, a fugitive whose silent desert voice spoke clearly to the hearts of many, a witness to the life and death and yearnings of his brother, an exile who went on gathering his spirit around him as a cloak woven from the stuff of myths, unshakable even in the fiercest summers and cruelest winters.

When Assaf told Anna what had become of Yousef, she wept. Such a thoughtful young man, she said, and so dear a friend to you, sweet one. Why does it have to be like this? Why can't he have a better life, our Yousef?

Tajar, on the other hand, was somber. He listened carefully to Assaf and his eyes turned far away, deep in thought. And so now Yousef also runs in the wilderness, he murmured, hiding and watching and guiding himself as best he can.

While in Jericho, Abu Musa let out a great sigh and bowed his head. Farewells and more farewells, he said to Moses the Ethiopian. What's the use of being a patriarch if you outlive your descendants?

When Assaf talked with Bell, he said he had suspected something like this might happen. Bell agreed with him. But perhaps it's just for a time, added Bell. Yousef only has to slip across the river to live a normal life again. His exile may not be forever.

Assaf took heart from the words because he also suspected Yousef was still seeing Bell. One of the familiar routes of Bell's walks near Jericho at twilight was to the ruins of Herod's winter palace, which lay at the foot of the wadi bounding the Mount of Temptation. There the runoff of the winter rains from the heights of Jerusalem had once fed Herod's pools and baths. The deep wadi could provide hiding places for a man coming down from the wilderness. Where the wadi entered the plains there was a banana plantation, and its thick low foliage was also a hiding place, right next to the ruins. On certain moonless nights Bell made a point of visiting the ruins, and sometimes he heard Yousef's voice calling to him from the shadows.

In the beginning Yousef turned up almost every month to see Bell. Later his visits were far less frequent. The shesh-besh players on Bell's front porch knew of the secret meetings and Assaf suspected them, although he never said anything about it. So perhaps it might have gone on like that for years if Yousef hadn't become determined to meet an even more legendary figure, the great friend of the Palestinian cause who was known as the conscience of the Arab revolution—the mysterious Halim from Damascus.

FOUR

The Runner operation entered a period of quiet after the Six-Day War. Before then the Runner had produced an enormous quantity of information on the fortifications of the Golan Heights. Now the Golan was in Israeli hands. The Runner himself was exhausted from the nonstop days and nights of those years. His clandestine back-up team in Syria and Beirut had worked to the limit, moving the Runner's material on secret routes from Damascus to the Mossad.

Tajar congratulated them all and arranged a schedule of lengthy vacations for them, keeping in place a network for minimum communications. The Runner was told to draw back from military affairs and concern himself with his civilian enterprises. In effect, he was to put intelligence aside for a time and act like a legitimate Syrian businessman.

Tajar had no difficulty persuading General Dror, the director of the Mossad, to accept this new tactic. The Runner and the back-up team were obviously in need of rest. Emotionally as well as physically, they were worn out. War hysteria had been rampant in Syria for months before June 1967, and defeat had brought rank instability in many Arab capitals. It was a dangerous moment for a deep-cover penetration. Complete inactivity was the only safe course for the operation, Tajar felt.

There's going to be a lot of bloodletting in Damascus, Tajar told Dror, a regular night of the long knives. The army and the security services will be at each other's throats hunting out traitors to take the blame for what they all did wrong. Treachery is how the Arabs explain defeat. They don't really have another way to justify it to themselves. It's part of their method of self-delusion, their weakness for the abstract.

Dror smiled. Along with everyone else, he respected Tajar as the Mossad's senior expert on Arab countries. He also admired Tajar's phenomenal success with the Runner operation. But as a pragmatic military man, Dror often found Tajar himself strangely abstract and incomprehensible. No one in his experience had ever devised plots as intricate as Tajar's. The Runner operation was already a dozen years old, a dozen years in the making, and Dror still wasn't sure he really knew where it was heading, even though he was the director of the Mossad and Tajar always *seemed* to be candid with him. Of course Tajar was quick to tell him what the operation's objectives were at any given moment, and the results invariably came in. But Dror sometimes felt lost all the same, as if he were a young lieutenant out tramping in the desert and Tajar were his bedouin guide signaling from the next rise in the distance. The guide got him where he was supposed to go but the route remained a mystery to him. Moreover, he never drew any nearer to the guide. Like any good bedouin tracker, Tajar was always up ahead signaling back to him, surveying a stretch of desert that Dror, the young lieutenant, hadn't come to yet.

Why do you think the Arabs are so given to abstractions? Dror asked.

Tajar moved his crippled legs with his hands. Ah well, he said, it's a very human characteristic, isn't it? Something everyone has tucked away somewhere. Who wants to accept what's at hand, after all? The desert's a harsh place. Who wouldn't prefer to think about the oasis in the distance? Even if there isn't one, just more desert? Who knows? It may be that the Arabs originally picked up the habit from us. Mohammed was illiterate well into manhood and it seems to have made a profound impression on him that these odd people called Jews were always reading a book, their book, created for them, and gathering great sustenance from it. Furthermore, when faced with hardship and defeat these odd people called Jews were always saying, *Next year in Jerusalem,* when anyone could see there wasn't a hope under the sun of them being in Jerusalem next year. When in fact, like most people anytime, the Jews were exactly where they were going to be until they died. Lastly, to an illiterate but thoughtful man, what could be more abstract than this invincible, invisible world hidden in a book? Naturally Mohammed wanted to have his own, so he learned to read and in time God dictated the Koran to him. So that much of the matter may go all the way back to Mohammed. The difference then becomes, I suppose, whom you blame for not being where you'd like to be in life. We tend to blame ourselves when things go wrong, while the Arabs are more apt to blame the fellow who lives next door. Perhaps we do that because we've been aliens who haven't been living in our own country for several thousand years. But now that we're sitting in our own country and it's this year in Jerusalem and we're there, while the Palestinian Arabs are going into a diaspora, it may be that we're going to become more like them and they're going to become more like us. It's curious, isn't it, General, how human beings affect each other, even enemies. Or is it especially enemies?

Dror nodded and turned the conversation back to the Runner operation. Within the Mossad, Tajar was known as a friend of Arab culture who was severely disturbed by the extensive Arab territory that had come under Israeli control as a result of the Six-Day War. There was no arguing with Tajar on this subject and Dror preferred to keep away from it.

Then we agree, said Dror, that the Runner operation should be quiet for a time. What about the Runner himself?

I feel it's important that I sit with him, replied Tajar. I have to talk with him about his son, and then there's the whole question of the future. The last few years have been . . . a severe strain for the Runner.

When do you plan to see him?

Next month in Beirut, said Tajar.

Good. An in-depth assessment is important. I'd like him to go on, of course, but you'll have to be the judge of that.

Yes. We can talk about it when I get back, said Tajar, gathering his crippled legs together.

◆◆◆◆◆◆◆◆

More than two years had passed since Tajar had seen Yossi. With the back-up team handling communications and the fortifications of the Golan Heights as its objective, the Runner operation had been clearly defined. Roles were precise and everyone knew what he had to do. The Runner himself was superbly methodical. His information fitted together and the maps, piece by piece, had grown more complete. Queries had been sent to the Runner, but as often as not he had already anticipated the Mossad's questions.

Most of Tajar's time, in fact, had been spent solving problems having to do with the functioning of the back-up team, whose work had to be continually adjusted in small ways to mesh with circumstances. In the end, due to Tajar's careful planning, the team had performed its tasks without error. The operation was tight and safe, deeply buried. Security was as strict as ever and only Tajar and General Dror knew the real identity of the Runner. To the members of Tajar's operational team the Runner was still a highly placed Arab in Damascus, a non-Syrian diplomat or military attaché whose sensitive role was of inestimable worth to Israel, to be protected at all costs.

As was his custom, Tajar treated the members of the Runner team as family, as his own sons and daughters. It was an old-fashioned way of running an operation, but with Tajar as clan chief it worked. Tajar's commandos, as they were known in the Mossad, were an elite within an elite, a long-range desert patrol operating behind enemy lines. They took orders only from Tajar, who reported directly to the chief of the Mossad.

Competence and loyalty were fierce among the commandos. Even if the Golan Heights hadn't been conquered in the Six-Day War, the commandos would never have doubted Tajar.

Besides security, there was a more subtle reason why Tajar hadn't met with Yossi in the period before the Six-Day War. By then Yossi had been in Damascus for over half a dozen years, or since the end of 1959. Tajar knew it would be a crucial time in Yossi's life. Yossi would have been living his clandestine role long enough for the novelty of it to have become routine. The initial exhilaration and sense of secret power would falter, lapse, disappear. Yossi's son would come of age and leave home. And Yossi himself would turn forty, and age when a man was suddenly apt to realize he was where he was going in life.

Tajar knew Yossi well and sensed these were things Yossi would want to face in his own way. Long ago Tajar had come to call Yossi the Runner because of Yossi's experiences as a boy in Iraq, running alone across the desert to the town where he had worked as a bookkeeper. General Dror, and Little Aharon before him, had often found it uncanny how Tajar could always predict what the Runner would do in any given situation. How can you know that? Dror had once asked Tajar in disbelief. When we describe something accurately, replied Tajar, aren't we always describing ourselves?

So Tajar knew it would have been a time of profound change for Yossi in any case. And the suddenness of the 1967 war, and Assaf's wounds in the war and the dramatic outcome of the war for Israel and the Arab countries, were all factors in addition to that, making the changes for Yossi more acute, more complex.

Still, Tajar wasn't prepared for the Yossi who walked into the room at the safehouse in Beirut.

Yossi had aged ten years. His hair was almost completely white, making his skin look darker. He stood very erect and seemed taller than before, an illusion caused by his carriage and the sparse bony planes of his face, which was as lean as a bedouin's. His moustache was thick and black, suggesting a younger man who had once lived in this body, and a heavy line cut down each side of his face. But what was most remarkable about him was his eyes. They were deep-set and powerful, the eyes of a visionary. Tajar had never seen eyes that burned so deeply.

For a moment Tajar was stunned, so arresting was this face. It would have caused him to stop and stare, to wonder, no matter where he had met it. But then Yossi smiled and his teeth flashed and dozens of little lines danced around his eyes. It was an immensely appealing smile, even warmer and more inviting than Tajar remembered, and at once it transformed this formidable figure into the best friend a man could ever have. Here was tenderness and confidence and strength, above all understanding. The deep lines in this face, Tajar realized, came from smiling.

They embraced warmly. Yossi stepped back and they gazed at each other with their arms clasped, holding on tightly with their hands, then hugged again. Tajar suddenly felt much older than he had a minute before then. He felt weak and clumsy, an awkward cripple, while Yossi was hard and strong, all muscle and bone.

How are you? they both said at once, feeling the breath of the other.

Blessed is the Name, they both answered, using that most Hebrew of expressions.

Once more they were standing apart, smiling and laughing as they held on with their hands and gazed at each other.

I've aged, said Yossi, but you look just the same.

Oh yes, said Tajar, I did all my aging when I banged up my legs. Now I don't get any older. I just lie in my hammock and watch the sky.

Yossi laughed. I remember that hammock of yours, he said. I have one of my own strung at the back of my garden in Damascus. People are always asking about it, they think it's a wonderful invention. I tell them it was a lazy habit I picked up in Argentina.

They laughed at the word *lazy*. Spoken by Yossi, it seemed

a grandly exotic notion, for he had the wind-hardened look of a man who only rested while mounted on the back of his camel, an instant here and an instant there between the steps.

Tajar was abruptly serious. You *are* well? he asked, not referring to Yossi's physical state. Yossi thought for a moment. Still that utter sincerity, thought Tajar. Then Yossi's smile burst out and lit his face.

More than enough, replied Yossi. Like any desert traveler, naturally, I also seek the next oasis.

◆◆◆◆◆◆◆◆

Their time together was brief in days and nights but exquisitely long in moments. For both of them it was a feast of memory to be savored and shared, with whole worlds of unknown sights and sounds to experience, to explore. And beyond all that were the nuances of feeling, those shadowy inner landscapes of the heart which could only be sensed when they were face to face.

They talked of Assaf and what he had gone through in the war, of his wounds and his recovery, his life in the Arab village of el Azariya and his friend the young Arab schoolteacher. Of Anna and her painting and the old stone house on Ethiopia Street where Assaf had grown up. Of Tajar and his snug cottage hidden behind the cactus and the rosebushes, the bushes still wildly out of control, the cottage still slowly crumbling at the end of its tangled, secluded compound.

They spoke of Jerusalem undivided now after the war, one city again, no longer separated by barbed wire and bunkers cutting across its stately hills.

Of the Mossad and Dror and Tajar's commandos, of Israel and the Arab territories occupied in the war.

Of the tiny settlement in the Negev where Yossi had met Anna, an army outpost now. Of the other settlement on the south coast where Yossi and Anna had lived by the sea after independence, a small city now.

So much has changed, said Yossi.

Oh yes, it happens quickly, said Tajar. The country grows, everything changes.

And Assaf is really taller than I am?

From only a little fellow, just imagine, said Tajar. He's at least an inch taller than you when he stands straight, which he's learning to do. The leg wounds held him back for a while but now he's overcoming that. A handsome young man who sometimes reminds me of Anna's brother, David. His good looks come from Anna, in other words. I know you wouldn't have it any other way. But his smile is yours, unmistakably. I always see you when he smiles and Anna also feels that. No wonder he's so independent, she says. That's the same smile we used to get in the Negev when we faced impossible odds and Yossi waved as he went off into the desert in another of his disguises. Who can resist it? she says. A smile like that is the hope of the world.

They spoke of Bell.

It's been over a year since I last saw him, said Yossi. I used to enjoy those visits to Jericho immensely, but then life became too hectic and I couldn't get away. And now, unfortunately, Jericho is on the wrong side of the river for me.

Tajar nodded. At the time of their meeting Assaf had only recently made the first of his trips with Yousef down to Jericho. Tajar explained Yousef's connection to Abu Musa, and through him to Bell.

So Assaf is also going to get to know Bell? said Yossi. Well it's not such an odd coincidence, really. Jericho hovers down there as a midway point on all the caravan routes, and the one-eyed hermit of Jericho has acquired quite a reputation over the years. You even hear people in Damascus speak of him from time to time, although not particularly the people I do business with. Bell is too out of the way for them. But if Assaf comes to enjoy the company of Abu Musa because of Yousef, that's certainly all for the best. Abu Musa's a marvelously clever old rogue. Have you ever met him?

No, said Tajar, for some curious reason I haven't. Neither him nor his partner at the gaming board, the giant called Moses the Ethiopian. Inexplicably and more's the loss, I've missed the antics of their forty-year shesh-besh game. But of course it's been decades since I knew Bell, in Egypt during the Second World War.

They talked of Damascus and Yossi's life in Damascus, or, rather, Halim's life in Damascus.

With its gardens and orchards, said Yossi, the city has great beauty. Then too, it has a river flowing through it and you know how special that is in this part of the world. When you have a river along with the desert you feel you have everything God can give. Unlike the Egyptians, though, the Syrians have never had the luxury of living off by themselves in history, so they have none of the easygoing habits that can bring. Every army from east or west, forever it seems, has conquered Damascus on its road to empire and people remember that, even if the memory is less than conscious. Intrigues and enemies and warring factions are what they've always known, that and an ability to survive which gives pride and also makes them wary, suspicious, shrewd, clever. They work hard and keep an eye over their shoulder. Some of the men I deal with are jackals, but no more than anyplace where life is difficult and power is hard to seize and dangerous to hold. The Syrians are many different peoples because of all the conquering armies, but even when people differ so much you're never far from those two fundamental lures of human nature, the river and the desert, with their opposing creeds and unresolvable promises. That's finally the struggle, I suppose, beyond empire and race and even beyond religion. Surely it has nothing to do with national boundaries. Since it's waged in each man's heart, in fact, how can there be an end to it? But for all that Damascus is still el Fayha, *the fragrant*, blessed with gardens and a river at the foot of its mountain on the transdesert routes of history.

Your days? asked Tajar. Your evenings?

Mostly I listen to people, said Yossi. The last few years I've been rushing around, but generally I spend more time in my garden. I do much of my business there. Meetings and appointments, it's my main office really.

You're able to relax then?

Oh yes. You know how it works out. A man who's doing well is expected to relax. That's what succeeding means, having more time to consider. It's the traditional way, as opposed to the Western or American way. So it's become like that for me, and people telephone or just turn up and we sit under my fig tree.

Do you smoke? asked Tajar, meaning hashish.

Rarely, said Yossi. I don't feel the need for it as much as some do.

Women?

Only the ones you know about. Sociable affairs and fairly distant, but regular enough to keep my attention from wandering.

Does it cause any difficulty that you've never married?

None. Some do and some do not, as they say, and a man who's thoroughly dedicated to his work is considered the same as married anyway. When I first arrived friends used to bring along their unmarried sisters and nieces, but now I'm accepted as a man who lives alone and devotes his time to his work. The uncle who can help. Everyone feels easy with that and values it, too.

Finally, then, their conversations came around to Yossi's future and the future of the Runner operation.

In other words, said Tajar, what do you see for yourself now? What do you want? You know everyone at home has nothing but praise for you. The operation has been extraordinarily successful and your contribution is beyond all measure. If you want to come back and begin a new life, it can be done any way you wish. Something quiet inside, or a different field and a new identity, anything. Or just living, if that appeals. You don't have to work. Dror is ready to go along with anything we come up with. I know you've considered all this, and of course we don't have to decide anything now. In a way the war is a turning point, for all of us and everything, but that doesn't have to be the case for the Runner operation. From everything you say and everything we know, the operation is as secure as ever. So you can also just live quietly in Damascus for a time, if that's what you want, and we can have this conversation again in six months. There's no hurry. We can bring an end to the life of the man known as Halim, now or later, without jeopardizing anything. It all depends on the way you feel.

I realize that, said Yossi, and of course I have thought a great deal about it. There were some hard times in the last few years, but I've gotten beyond the rough spots and what seems to have happened is that I've become Halim. With you I'm still Yossi, but it's more the way a person recalls his childhood, the person he used to be. He's still there inside me and always will be, but I've lived through several other lifetimes since then and in a way Yossi is foreign to me. A while ago you mentioned Anna's brother, David. Anna recalls him and you do, and Assaf must imagine him sometimes, and in that sense David still exists as much as anyone we think about, who may be as near as the next room. But in fact David's also been dead for twenty-five years, safe from harm and suffering, it's true, but also safe from change. Well that's something of the way I feel about Yossi. I miss him sometimes. It makes me sad to think of him sometimes. When you speak of Assaf's smile, for example, and how it reminds Anna of a young man in the desert long ago, slipping away with a wave from a tiny settlement that's now an army outpost . . . that makes me sad. When you said that my heart stumbled. I had to catch myself. For a moment it all came back and I felt lost, afraid. I was in the Negev again and leaving Anna, not knowing whether I'd get back and not knowing whether she'd still be there or still be alive if I did get back. Oh yes, I smiled then because it was all I had to give her. I was on my way to Gaza at night, across the open desert, so I smiled when I left her and our friends, pathetically standing guard duty around those little huts we had. But did she really think I preferred a cold desert night to lying in her arms? It's so strange what we know and don't know. Memory is strange and living through different lifetimes is strange and Bell is probably right. We add new vows to the old and forsake nothing and the soul becomes like the Holy City, the myth which is Jerusalem, a dream of ourselves which is forever unachievable, to be seen only by others, its wonders recounted to us in imaginary tales of distant places.

I understand that, said Tajar. And so?

Yossi smiled. Faced with Tajar and the past, there was still a touch of shyness in his smile, despite the hard years.

And so I'd prefer to live on as Halim in Damascus, said Yossi. I have no desire to see Jerusalem and be disappointed. When I was a child there were two mythical cities in my imagination, Jerusalem and Damascus. Because of circumstances I've come to know one of them, and one imaginary city is enough. That's where my dream of myself is. As for the rest, I have my work and I'm good at it, it means something and I'm useful in it.

Tajar nodded. And someday? he asked.

Yossi smiled again. Well if someday ever comes around, he replied, then I may become a hermit like Bell.

Who isn't really a hermit, said Tajar.

That's right, added Yossi, and that's his secret. You and I know that, and the shesh-besh players know it, Moses the Arab and Moses the Ethiopian, but it's a well-kept secret all the same. Isn't it so, Tajar?

Yossi covered one eye with his hand and pushed the rest of his face out of shape, pretending to be Bell. Then he dropped his hands and looked deep into Tajar's eyes and laughed because of life and fate, and Tajar couldn't help but laugh with him, marveling all the while at Yossi's strength and determination and above all the immense distance he had traveled in the last two decades.

And so? asked Dror.

And so all together, said Tajar, it's an astonishing experience to sit with the Runner. He's confident and self-assured and knows what he's doing and why he's doing it. Despite the enormous strains of the last two years, he's become even more at ease with himself.

Problems?

I kept looking for them and at first it didn't make any sense to me, replied Tajar. Damascus? An environment as hostile as that for eight whole years? Then suddenly it did make sense to me. At that moment I accepted the fact that he's become a different person from the one I used to know.

Who has he become? asked Dror.

Halim. He has become Halim, said Tajar. It's not a fiction anymore, not a cover, not a role. Halim is real, Yossi has created him. It's uncanny. He's even become something of a mystic, which you'd expect from Halim.

Dror saw that Tajar was looking off into the distance, lost somewhere in thought. Certainly Tajar's comments weren't as startling to Dror as they seemed to be to Tajar, but then Dror often found Tajar himself to be something of a mystic.

You didn't expect this? asked Dror.

Tajar gave a roundabout reply, a little of this and a little of that. Since leaving Yossi in Beirut, he had been trying to answer that same question himself. He still wasn't sure how he felt, but probably he hadn't expected it. It was true that Tajar had never spent so many years in one cover role. Nor had he handled an agent, before Yossi, who had done so. It was a new experience for Tajar and perhaps that was why he felt a little uneasy, a little confused. What did it mean that Halim was *real?*

But there was no reason for Tajar to go into this with Dror. These were personal questions, part of the endless dialogue Tajar carried on between himself and himself. None of it affected Yossi's integrity as an agent or the Runner operation. If anything, Yossi's transformation improved the operation by making it more secure. The back-up team was something else, a separate matter. But if Halim was just Halim, how could he ever be caught? What was there to uncover?

So the Runner wants to stay on in Damascus, concluded Dror.

Exactly, said Tajar. It's agreed there will be little or no operational activity until the aftermath of the war settles down. In the meantime he'll carry on his legitimate businesses. We also agreed to meet again in six months' time, more or less, to see where we go from there. But I don't foresee any change in his basic decision. He'll want to stay. By then the members of the back-up team will be ready for work again and we can reassign as necessary, depending on what we decide for the Runner.

Good, said Dror. And now you ought to take a little time off yourself. Will you be doing that?

Definitely, replied Tajar. My Greek needs improving. Homer is becoming incomprehensible to me.

FIVE

Tajar was back at work sooner than he expected. In the spring of 1968, about the time Yousef went into exile in the Judean wilderness, one of the commandos came to call on Tajar in his cottage behind the cactus and the rosebushes. A priority message had come through from the Runner in Damascus, alerting Tajar that a delivery of special significance was on its way. The material was due that night. The Runner had used an emergency procedure to signal Tajar and forward the material.

Tajar was waiting in the commandos' operation room when the delivery arrived at the Mossad near midnight. He read through it and spent the rest of the night preparing a report for Dror. The Runner's material showed that the Soviet Union was taking on the PLO as a full-fledged client in terrorism. For the first time Israel had been made a primary target of the KGB, and the Syrians were to be the link.

Before the PLO was founded in 1964, Syrian intelligence had trained Palestinian saboteurs and directed their efforts against Israel. After the PLO was organized, Syrian intelligence was still the main source of arms and training for the PLO. But until the 1967 war, the PLO itself was a negligible factor in Arab policy against Israel. The Arab goal remained outright conquest, to overrun Israel on the battlefield with conventional armies, a continuation of the failed military campaigns of 1948.

The disastrous Arab defeat in the Six-Day War changed all this. Overt aggression was impossible, at least for a time, and the PLO became a more important instrument. Supporting the PLO cause was also the only policy uniting the various Arab countries, busy as they were uncovering treachery in their own ranks and more particularly among each other. Nasser, the former hero of the Arab world who had promised total victory over Israel and instead had delivered total defeat, was no longer everyone's leader. Syria went its own way and used the PLO less as a weapon against Israel than against its neighbor Jordan, where it saw a chance of overthrowing King Hussein and expanding Syria. The Syrian intelligence services, in any case, had always been more intricately involved than anyone else in manipulating the PLO for their own purposes.

The Runner's connection to the Palestinian cause preceded the founding of the PLO. Years earlier, at a time when there were no Palestinian organizations, Tajar had asked the Runner to make himself known in the Palestinian refugee camps. Little Aharon, then the director of the Mossad, had ridiculed the idea as another of Tajar's vague, impractical notions, part of Tajar's lifelong obsession with obscure Arab movements and causes. But Little Aharon had let Tajar have his way because the Runner was only newly arrived in Damascus and had the beginnings of some valuable contacts in the Syrian army.

Thus the Runner's Palestinian connections were profound. The young men he had befriended in the refugee camps were now in positions of importance in the PLO. The man from Damascus known as Halim had been one of their first supporters and advisers, a friend whose garden and money and influence had always been available to them during the empty years. Furthermore, Halim's support was pure. He wasn't an officer of Syrian intelligence who paid them to do work useful only to Syria. Halim had a conscience and was incorruptible. He was a Syrian patriot whose true goal was the Arab revolution.

Early in 1968 rumors began to reach the Mossad that the KGB was taking a closer look at the PLO, through the KGB sections that worked with Syrian intelligence in Damascus. The KGB obviously had a new interest in the PLO, but the Mossad didn't know what form this interest would take. In the material sent to Tajar, the Runner documented the KGB's preparations for a PLO terrorist campaign. A new KGB section was being set up in Damascus to recruit PLO agents for terrorist training in the Soviet Union. Terrorist cells would then be grouped, armed, financed, and directed by the KGB. The Runner provided detailed information on the new KGB section in Damascus, including the names of KGB case officers and PLO recruits. From other sources the Mossad was able to determine that these terrorist cells would operate mostly in Western Europe, an area of far more interest to the Russians than Jordan or Israel or the Arab villages on the west bank of the river, between Jordan and Israel.

For the Mossad, it was a momentous discovery. Dror called the prime minister and there was a meeting in the prime minister's office. When Dror returned to the Mossad late that evening, Tajar was waiting for him.

A somber affair, said Dror. No one underestimates the power of the KGB. We'll be talking to the Americans, but the feeling is we'll have to go it alone for a time.

A time? said Tajar.

Years, probably. We have the proof the KGB is behind it but we can't divulge it, not even to the Americans. I spoke to the prime minister privately and he's adamant that the Runner's material is too sensitive to be shared with anyone. We can't take a chance on compromising the Runner, and if we control his material we can be sure that doesn't happen. The KGB operation is to be run from Damascus and we'll never have anyone so deeply buried there as the Runner. Security has to be tighter than ever. Having the Syrian security agencies as your enemy is one thing. Working against the KGB, in a place as hostile as Damascus, is quite another. So the Americans aren't going to be told how we get our information, and that means they won't trust it one hundred percent. They'll think we're trying to push them into helping us fight our war against the PLO. Of course they'll help, but not all the way, and what's worse, the intelligence services in Europe will be far less helpful. What do they care about the PLO's squabble with us? Nasty, yes, but also Arab-Jewish business, sandy Middle Eastern business, so why not let the Arabs and Israelis kill each other and work it out? That's the way the European services will see it. They won't want to get involved, even though most of the terrorism will be taking place in Europe. It's clear the KGB is going to work very hard to make this look like strictly the PLO against Jewish targets. So the Europeans will protect themselves and their oil supplies by staying out of it. And if there is a particularly vicious incident involving non-Jews, the PLO will simply say it was the work of some dissident group. The KGB's good at that, and the Europeans will want to believe it anyway.

Tajar agreed. The KGB would keep its role hidden by working through the Syrians, and the Runner's position in Damascus was too sensitive, now, to be shared with anyone. Eventually there would be other sources of information on the terrorist campaign, in the Mossad and elsewhere, and eventually some of them might become as important as the Runner. But for the time being Israel would have to face the terrorism alone, and the Mossad would have to counter it alone. The KGB knew all this, everything except the fact that the Runner existed. In Damascus, especially, the center of their operation, they would be watching everyone who could conceivably be harmful to them. Certainly they wouldn't just rely on the Syrians to safeguard a major KGB operation aimed at Europe.

The new problems for Tajar were vast, intricate, complex. For the Runner the danger was great. As Dror had said, no one underestimated the KGB and its immense resources. With careful planning the KGB would be able to use the PLO for years. The Third World, oil, anti-Semitism—the KGB had many factors to play upon with an instrument such as the PLO.

Tajar had another meeting scheduled with the Runner in Beirut, the follow-up to their first meeting after the Six-Day War. Now he cancelled this second meeting so he could work out a new procedure, taking even greater precautions. Not surprisingly, the Runner had already suggested this in the message that came in with his special material.

Tajar had to rework the commandos' functions to reflect the new involvement of the KGB. Above all, he was thankful that Halim and not Yossi was in Damascus, a man who was not only strong and self-assured, but real.

Real?

Tajar still hadn't come to terms with that idea, that fact. The commandos sometimes noticed a distant look in his eyes and assumed it was his preoccupation with the details of their new assignments. But in fact Tajar was still disturbed by Yossi's transformation into Halim. Having planned it, he understood it. Yet even he wasn't quite sure, now, where it would lead.

How far, he wondered, could a man really go in creating himself? How far, in other words, could the Runner run?

SIX

It was Abu Musa, especially, who urged Assaf to continue to visit Jericho after Yousef disappeared. He had developed a great fondness for Assaf, whose presence relieved the pain he felt for the lost company of Ali and Yousef.

Come bring us tales of mythical Jerusalem, he said to Assaf. The boys used to do that and we need it down here. Otherwise, Bell and Moses and I tend to succumb to the orange blossoms and flowers and live in a jasmine blur of eternal summer . . . unmindful that the world is not a dream, forgetful that the passage of days is not merely the rhythmic click of a shesh-besh game. Up there on the mountain of Jerusalem you have sharp winds and turbulence and raucous blustery noise. Won't you bring us news of this so I can shine as a knowledgeable patriarch when taking my morning coffee in Jericho's marketplace? Of course Jerusalem is a new place when compared to our serene ancient sun down here, but I for one like to keep in touch with the current fashions of men. By which I mean the latest religions and empires and so forth, whose followers are undoubtedly holding forth with fervent self-regard up there in the Holy City.

Or put another way, whose empire is it that now sways the world? asked Moses the Ethiopian, quoting the question asked nearly two millennia ago by St. Paul of Thebes, at the age of one hundred and thirteen, when speaking to a younger anchorite who had arrived more recently in the desert, St. Anthony, aged ninety.

Bell smiled at his friends and walked with Assaf from the porch to the gate.

Would it be all right if I did come to call now and then? asked Assaf.

We would be hurt if you didn't, said Bell. We miss Ali and Yousef and it makes a difference when you're here.

By the gate Bell pointed at Assaf's sandaled feet.

I know these now, said Bell. After years of sitting on my front porch and gazing out under the orange trees, I'm apt to recognize people by their feet. Abu Musa senses their hearts and Moses, well, he plucks their beings straight from the sunlight. So do come to see us whenever you can.

Assaf thanked Bell and agreed to come. With Yousef gone, he felt a growing kinship with the trio of wise men on Bell's front porch.

◆◆◆◆◆◆◆◆

That summer Assaf gave up his small house on the edge of the Judean desert. It saddened him to be in el Azariya without Yousef, so he left the village and moved back to Anna's old stone house on Ethiopia Street. His interest now was history, a passion he had picked up from Yousef. In the autumn he would begin studies at Hebrew University on Mt. Scopus, which he could see from the balcony in Anna's house where he spent all his time reading about the past.

Between Assaf's balcony and Mt. Scopus lay the valley where he had fought on a June night just over a year ago, the low ground of the Wadi Joz and the area known as Sheik Jarrah, which ran east to Damascus Gate in the Old City. Sheik Jarrah was said to have been chief surgeon to the armies of Salah al-din, the great Kurdish warrior who defeated the Crusaders in the Middle Ages and drove them from the Holy Land. The call of the muezzin from the mosque of Sheik Jarrah reached Assaf clearly, sometimes mixed with another inside Damascus Gate, depending on the wind.

At regular hours the Moslem calls to prayer, beginning with *Allah'hu akbar, God is great,* echoed up to Assaf's balcony across the former no-man's-land and caused him to lose his place in his book, to raise his eyes and daydream as he read of Crusader or Roman or Babylonian armies advancing to conquer Jerusalem on that track of low ground a thousand and two thousand and twenty-five hundred years ago.

The Israeli paratroopers in the Six-Day War had followed exactly the same route as all those other armies whose conquests of Jerusalem had been equally momentous events in other ages, in the make-believe of once upon a time, in all those distant eras now long since lost in the swirl of history. So for Assaf on his balcony above Ethiopia Street, such were the humbling lessons of Jerusalem and conquest, Jerusalem and time, as he studied and read and gazed out at the Old City, musing on the mirage of the present which was forever being born of the mythology of the past. And yet it *was* his history nonetheless, and his city's history—still the indelible mystery of place and man in it.

From his balcony he also listened to the grave ancient chants of his neighbors, the dignified Ethiopian monks across the street, whose solemn sing-song prayers soared above their lemon and cypress trees in the golden light of summer afternoons. Twice a day at four in the morning and again at four in the afternoon a bell drew the monks from their cells to the incense-shadowed vastness of their round stone church with its great purple-black dome, where they stood leaning on staffs and swaying like stately ghosts to the rhythms of their chants, so exotic and primitive and soothing, a timeless interlude for the hidden courtyards on Ethiopia Street. At other hours an elderly lone monk might circle the church reciting devotional poems in liturgical language, the low hum of his archaic dialects as persistent as a bee busily at work in the shade.

An order of young French nuns also lived on Ethiopia

Street, and in the reverent moments when the light of day faded over Jerusalem their angelic songs of prayer would suddenly pierce the air with breathtaking clarity. The young nuns sang with an exquisite beauty, with the very grace of nature itself and a promise of holiness like no other. To Assaf, indeed, it seemed the purest human sound God had ever made.

◆◆◆◆◆◆◆◆

Underlying the allure of the past for Assaf was an irresistible fascination with the life of his dead uncle, Anna's brother David, who had been killed in Cairo during the Second World War. Unlike his father, whom Assaf remembered with great clarity, his uncle remained a mystery to him. Anna had often spoken of her brother when Assaf was growing up, giving the impression that he wasn't dead so much as distant, gone to live in another country. This was particularly true after Yossi was killed. But to Assaf the life of his father had a meaning and a finality that his uncle's never could have, because he hadn't known him.

From the mixture of admiration and love and small detail with which a sister remembers her older brother, her companion in childhood, Assaf knew a great deal about his uncle. He also knew that he resembled his uncle in appearance and that his manner often reminded Anna of her brother. Yet somehow Anna's recollections of her brother were so deeply personal, so given to intimate memories of their childhood together, that Assaf never quite felt he understood his uncle as a man. The house and the street and the neighborhood in Cairo which Anna sensed so strongly—all of this was foreign to Assaf. Now that he himself was a young man he couldn't picture his uncle as he wanted to: not as his mother's older brother, the boy his mother grew up with, but as a separate person one might meet or see anywhere.

What kind of man had his uncle been? In seeking an answer to that, Assaf turned to Tajar.

Ah well, said Tajar, I only wish I could tell you more. I didn't know David well and what I recall I've already mentioned at one time or another. He was serious and dedicated but he obviously wasn't meant for undercover work. I always had that impression of him. The demands of a double life made him uneasy. If he'd been able to stick with smuggling Jews out of Egypt it might have gone all right, but when he got involved with deeper things he was over his head. He didn't have the outlook or training for that sort of business. But then he got caught up, drawn in, and it was too much.

Did you know what the deeper things were? asked Assaf.

Not in any specific way, replied Tajar, but later in the war I came to have a vague notion of what had been involved. It was what we'd call espionage, no question about it, and that's how David got into trouble. You have to remember that Rommel and the Germans seemed very close to overrunning Egypt and seizing the canal, and the British were desperate. Many Egyptians favored the Germans from a nationalist point of view, to get the British out, and Cairo was crowded with refugees from Europe. So there were innumerable cells and obscure organizations all carrying on their own secret causes. Men moved back and forth in disguises and there were British and German penetrations everywhere and informers up and down the line. And the tank battles were very close, only hours away in the desert. The lines changed constantly and units were destroyed or disappeared. There was also traffic to and from Europe, especially Greece, fast boats and clandestine air drops. So what it amounted to in Cairo was chaos, a very dangerous kind of chaos for anyone involved in espionage. And of course it was easy to become involved without knowing it, which is what happened to David. He was on the edge of something. He wasn't really a participant himself, but through others he was connected to a maze, and somewhere in that maze there was extremely vital information. Or an extremely important agent, either to the British or the Germans, and as a result David was killed.

It seems hopelessly blurred and indistinct, said Assaf. I can't get ahold of it. Or of him.

True enough, replied Tajar. History is often that way. We only pretend it's clear in retrospect. There are always conflicting truths and especially that immense confusion, that chaos. Add to it the cross purposes of war where there are never two sides or a dozen sides but a hundred and a thousand sides from which people pursue their bewildering variety of causes, each one vital to them, each one worth enormous sacrifices, and then beneath those outward causes consider the conscious outwitting of others through pretense—what we today know as espionage—and you have the constantly shifting images of a tapestry we call history. Each of us, in fact, creates history. Each of us decides what was, what used to be. Anna knew David in a certain way and she clings to that and insists upon it and of course she's right, *it's* right, from her point of view. He was her brother and she grew up with him and David was this and that and such and so. For her, it's as simple as that. But it can't be that way for you or me or for anyone else. I have an impression of David which I recall from having seen him a few times in certain circumstances. But perhaps he was in a particular mood when I happened to see him. Or perhaps he was thinking about something I didn't know about. Perhaps his words and his manner had nothing to do with what I thought I heard and saw. Who can say? We know, well, so very few people in our lives.

Assaf frowned. Then he smiled.

You make it sound nearly impossible, he said.

Looking back, it is, said Tajar. Which of course is why the past, history, is so intriguing. We know how much it could explain to us if only we could unravel its secrets. Tell me, why is it that your uncle interests you so much?

Because Anna says I remind her of him, replied Assaf. And because if I knew more about him, then I'd know how I resemble him and how I'm different.

How you're unique? suggested Tajar.

Yes, I suppose that's really it, isn't it? It's another way to find out who I am.

So David seems to be the key to that precisely because he is such a mystery, said Tajar. And also, perhaps, because he was killed a quarter of a century ago in Cairo, a place and a time which are also a mystery to you. But what about your father? What of Yossi? Is he less a mystery to you?

It seems so, replied Assaf.

Why?

Because I feel I know him much better. Because everything about him is so familiar to me. Am I wrong, though? I was only eight when he died and you were his best friend. Do I see him clearly? Was he as I remember him?

Oh yes, certainly he was, said Tajar. I only wanted to point out that the apparent mysteries of the past are not always as enlightening as we like to think. My own feeling is that David, now, can't tell you what you want to know about yourself. Despite Anna's recollections of him, or my own.

Assaf laughed.

You're contradicting yourself again, he said. If the past is intriguing because it's important, why shouldn't I pursue it?

Tajar also laughed.

Exactly, he said. But can its mysteries ever compare to what goes on around us today? As for contradicting yourself, welcome it always as putting you closer to the truth. The tapestry shifts from moment to moment, just as the unchanging desert never stops changing.

SEVEN

I find it strange all the same, Tajar said to Anna later. Why should a vigorous young man with his whole life ahead of him be more obsessed by the past than a creaky, battered old camel like me? It's upside down, backwards. I urge Assaf to seize today and he nods sagely and goes on to ponder what was and what might have been. Does that make sense to you?

Anna smiled. I guess it has to, she said. He doesn't have a past or much of one, so naturally he peers in that direction to help him find his whereabouts. If you and I don't look back it's because we know what we'll see. And also because we've already done that enough.

Tajar moved his crippled legs with his hands to a more comfortable position. As so often, they were sitting on Anna's balcony and gazing down on the courtyard crowded with flowers.

I suppose you're right, he said. Anyway, I've never been cut out to be a mother. I don't have the patience.

Anna laughed. I don't think God or the state ever intended you to be a mother, she said. But you do have patience, much more than most people. To me, the important thing about Assaf is that he's become so outgoing. He takes far more pleasure in people than he ever did, even before he was wounded. When friends of mine are here he wanders in and laughs and tells stories and is actually charming. People remark upon it.

They notice how he has changed. Deep down he's as serious as ever, but he gets along with people now and that's just wonderful. It's because of Yousef, mostly. Knowing Yousef set him to thinking in so many ways. He's come alive since then.

Anna paused and looked down at her hands. Her voice was soft, uneasy.

Our poor Yousef. Has anything? . . .

No, sadly, replied Tajar. There's been no news at all, I'm afraid.

Yousef's self-imposed exile was a painful subject for Anna. She became silent and withdrawn when she thought of it, for it was all too easy for her to imagine Assaf having done something like that if the circumstances had been different. All these years later, as Tajar knew, Anna still recalled how her brother had retreated into himself when faced with a world that was too much for him, and the memory hurt her even now. She couldn't bear to think of her son closing himself off that way, which was exactly what she had feared might happen after Assaf was wounded. His deliverance from that, by way of Yousef, caused her heart to ache all the more for the lost one —Yousef—since it brought a measure of shame to the joy she felt. To Anna, Assaf's new success with people seemed inextricably linked to the suffering of another, and that she found intolerable.

Tajar understood this.

Look, he said, it's just not so that what Yousef has done is connected to Assaf. Yousef would have done it anyway, whether he'd met Assaf or not. His exile has to do with the Six-Day War and the PLO and Jews and Arabs not living together in Palestine, and the grand city of Jerusalem and its poor neighbor on the other side of the Mount of Olives, his own tattered little village of el Azariya, and with his brother's senseless death and his need to do something after it that would count with himself. Those are the things, the facts, that influenced Yousef to do what he did. Assaf's friendship only added to Yousef. It gave to Yousef. It didn't take anything from him.

And yet their destinies are linked now, Anna said softly. They have to be . . . how can it be otherwise? I feel it because I know Assaf feels it, so what do facts matter? Assaf visits Jericho more than ever, and what are those visits but a pilgrimage to his common ground with Yousef? To a place they shared and do share, Assaf now and Yousef in memory, down there near the river on the other side of the Judean desert. Isn't that what Jericho and the house in the orange grove have become for Assaf . . . a place of pilgrimage?

◆◆◆◆◆◆◆◆

After leaving Anna that evening Tajar shuffled back to his cottage at the end of the wildly overgrown compound and stretched out in his hammock beside the rosebushes. Wrapped in blankets against the summer chill, he gazed up at the starry night over Jerusalem and tried to put his feelings in order. He was thinking mostly of Yousef and Anna and Assaf, but his thoughts kept drifting away to Jericho and the house in the orange grove . . . Bell's house.

Soon after Yousef disappeared, Tajar had put a permanent tracer on him because of his friendship with Assaf. When the Shin Bet or the border police acquired information on Yousef, it was forwarded at once to Tajar. The security services had no idea why someone in the Mossad could be interested in a man as low-level and inconsequential as Yousef, a former village schoolteacher in hiding, a nominal member of the PLO who wouldn't take up arms. Yousef's name was buried in a long list of PLO supporters whose routine activities were reported to the Mossad, when there was anything to report. Of course the security services would have been far more interested in Yousef's quixotic behavior if they had known their information on him was going to someone as important as Tajar. But that was the last thing Tajar wanted. Even the commandos, who logged most of Tajar's communications within the Mossad, didn't know about the tracer on Yousef. Those reports, meager as they were, reached Tajar by a different route.

> Subject said to be living in caves east of Hebron.
>
> Subject said to have friends among the bedouin, or among the village boys, who cache small amounts of food for him when grazing their flocks.
>
> Subject said to have been living in the southern Judean desert during the middle of the month.

Always vague and fragmentary accounts. Never an actual sighting or an actual contact, only hearsay and rumors from the villages on the edge of the desert. But for Tajar that in itself was remarkable, for it meant Yousef was adapting quickly to his fugitive life. He was learning to survive in the desert as an unseen presence and Tajar respected that. Inevitably, perhaps, it also reminded Tajar of the special talents of the Runner.

Tajar understood well enough the attraction of Jericho for Assaf now that Yousef was gone. Indeed, Tajar himself was strongly attracted to the house in the orange grove, although for different reasons. Soon after the Six-Day War Tajar had planned to pay a visit to Bell, hoping to renew their acquaintance, but then Assaf's friendship with Yousef had intervened and Assaf had met Abu Musa and Bell, which complicated everything. The Runner was now on the other side of the border from Jericho and could no longer go there, but professional judgment told Tajar the only safe course was caution. Reluctantly, he put aside for a time his desire to appear at Bell's front gate.

Then came the astonishing revelation that Anna also knew Bell.

Tajar had never suspected that Anna might connect the one-eyed hermit of Jericho with the former British intelligence officer who had helped her in Cairo after David was killed, who had also provided her with papers to come to Palestine. Bell had gone by a different name in Egypt and had lived in Jerusalem for only a short time after the world war, obscurely and quietly, before moving down to Jericho. For nineteen years Jericho had been part of Jordan and there was no reason why Anna should know who Bell was. Before 1967 the one-eyed hermit's reputation had existed on the other side of the border, on the other side of no-man's-land, and it wasn't something Anna could have heard about in west Jerusalem. Tajar knew about Bell because of intelligence files, because he had always been interested in Bell and had made a point of keeping track of the former head of the notorious Monastery in Egypt. But no ordinary Israeli could know anything about Bell.

Bell, after all, had buried his past life, his clandestine life in espionage, with great care. Not even Abu Musa knew anything about it.

◆◆◆◆◆◆◆◆

The story came out when Anna told Tajar of Assaf's first visit to the house in the orange grove in Jericho. Anna had paused then to smile at Tajar.

The hermit Assaf speaks of, she said, is the man who did everything for me in Cairo. But since it's your business to know things, you've probably known that all along. Have you?

Tajar was astounded. Well . . . yes, he replied. As a matter of fact, I did know it. But it amazes me that you do, because his past is a very well-kept secret. Once he left Egypt, Bell, as he has called himself since then, went out of his way to put his old life behind him. And I'd say he has had great success in doing just that.

You knew him in Cairo, didn't you? asked Anna. Through your work then?

That's right.

And he was important, wasn't he?

Oh yes. Very.

I've always thought he must have been, said Anna. And I've always imagined you must have known him, even though I've never said anything about it. I asked him once, later, why he had done so much for me in Cairo. I knew it was connected to David but not how, exactly. He wouldn't talk much about it, or he couldn't, but he said there had been a terrible mistake with David and that was why he did what he did for me. It touched me so deeply, looking back, his caring that way and taking the time to do something about it. Cairo was such absolute chaos then, and for a man as important as he seemed to be to come on his own to find me . . . well, he could have sent someone but he didn't. He came himself. He was the first person to come, you know. I was alone in the house with all the doors and shutters locked when he turned up to help me. I was lying in the corridor downstairs near the back door, the door to the courtyard. The floor was stone. It was hard and cold and dark and I was terrified, half out of my mind. There was nothing left, just nothing. Somehow he got into the house and lit a candle and all at once there was his face above me in the darkness . . . *life,* and what a face. He brought me back from the dead and I've never forgotten any of it. . . .

Even now, all these years later, Anna shuddered at the memory of that darkness and terror when she had thought she was slipping into madness. Her hands came up in front of her in a pathetic involuntary motion. Protection against the darkness? A plea to the angel of death to be merciful? She gripped her arms and tightened her fists, forcing down the fear and memory from long ago. After a moment the shudder passed. Quietly, she resumed her account.

So with his help I came to Palestine, she said. Then one winter after the world war ended I was walking down a street in Jerusalem, not far from here. The street was narrow and it was raining hard and blowing and I was struggling along with my head down against the wind, all wrapped up so I couldn't see much of anything. A car came along and I had to get out of the street because it was so narrow, so I pushed into a doorway and there was a man doing the same thing beside me. He was coming from the other direction and if it hadn't been for the car right at that moment we wouldn't have seen each other's face, just each other's feet slogging by in the rain. But we both looked up to find a place to push into and there he was. It was him, with most of his face hidden by a scarf and a hat and his coat collar. You can imagine my shock. I hadn't seen him since Cairo and I had no idea who he really was. I didn't even know his name and of course I didn't know what had become of him. We just stood there staring at each other.

Anna fell silent. Suddenly she smiled.

That face, she said. How could anyone ever pretend to act in a normal way with a face like that just there all at once in front of you? No one in the world has a face like that.

Anna went on smiling, a gentle smile.

It's like a mask, she said. Some inhuman kind of mask that's so extreme and unlikely you can't believe it at first. That great bulging staring single eye, and the bulging black eye patch, and the scars and all the rest of it. It's a face you have to be warned about, to prepare yourself for, otherwise you just stare and stare because it's like nothing you've ever seen. Now I can smile about it because I came to know what was beneath that mask, but I couldn't then. His face paralyzed me then. And meeting him like that, both of us drenched with the water streaming off us, huddling in a doorway . . . it was absurd and ludicrous and wonderful, and fearful and joyous and ridiculously awkward all at the same moment, just everything. I was paralyzed and my heart leapt, both at once. But I'm afraid I'm making no sense at all, trying to describe it all these years later. . . .

They stood in the doorway until finally one of them suggested they get out of the rain. Bell, for that was his name now, lived nearby and offered coffee and a fire. They went to his small apartment where the rooms were half underground with walls of stone several feet thick, the broad windowsills on a level with the garden outside, a snug and cozy retreat on such a blustery winter afternoon. Bell poured brandy and built a fire in the stove and soon they were warm in front of it.

The rooms were heaped with books. Bell was studying Arabic, he said. He read and did little else. He had some disability pay from the war and intended to live on it, to begin a new life in some remote corner.

Anna told him of her own years since Cairo, of her wanderings in Palestine. Bell was reticent, polite, sometimes shy. He wanted to be cordial but it was apparent he hadn't put his old life behind him and didn't know how to behave with Anna, who in a way was from that old life. Yet she wasn't really a part of it and Bell had nothing to fear from her. To reassure him, she promised at once never to say anything about having known him in Cairo.

But no, then she realized it was his own face that was making him reticent and fearful. He didn't seem to know how to behave with a young woman. From what he said she gathered he had no friends in Jerusalem and saw almost no one other than the Arab scholar who came to tutor him. In Cairo she had thought he was important, but now she realized he had probably been much more important than she had imagined. Without an official position and the status that went with it, and the automatic relationships that went with it, he didn't know how to act, especially with a young woman. He was unsure of himself, even lost. Alone now with his face, with his freedom, he hadn't yet learned how to make his way.

The rain splashed on the windows and they drank more brandy and became lovers that afternoon. Far more than him, it was Anna's doing. She had much to thank him for, more than she ever could, but there was also something beyond even that. So seldom could one make a profound difference in the life of another, and Anna sensed she had that gift then, for in his way he was as alone and fearful as she had once been in Cairo. As they lay in front of the little stove and the rain beat down in the half-light turning to darkness, Bell told her as much. Since the shattering of his face, he said, it was the first time he had been with a woman in a regular way, as if he were just a man who could meet someone and. . . .

They saw each other for several weeks. Anna came to him every afternoon and stayed through the night and it never seemed to stop raining the whole time they were together. Love was the delicious smell of olive wood smoke and rain softly beating down outside on the garden above them, and brandy and an early darkness and a warm cheery stove hidden away from the world for long tender evenings. Then she was busy for a few days, and when she came again Bell said he had decided to move to Jericho. He had found his remote corner of the world, he said. They held each other and Bell smiled. A warm smile. Anna knew his face by then. . . .

So that's what he did, she told Tajar. Then not long after that I left Jerusalem too, and found my way down to the Negev. And the British were leaving Palestine and the Arab countries invaded, and a new life began for me as well. I've never told anyone about it, not even Yossi. There seemed no reason to. It was a long time ago, twenty years ago, and it was a few weeks that belonged to two people. Since then I've never heard from Bell, or of him, not until Assaf came back from Jericho with his story of the three wise men and the house in the orange grove, with its forty-year shesh-besh game and a one-eyed holy man who oversees it with a glass of arak in his claw.

I don't doubt Bell knows Assaf is my son, said Anna. One of them down there must have asked Assaf about his background, or Yousef could have talked about me or whatever, and Bell would have realized who Assaf is, I'm sure. Not that he'd say anything about it. But it's strange looking back, isn't it? It seems we all have these rare and beautiful moments hidden away within us, turnings we could have taken in life but somehow . . . didn't. Once or twice during those few weeks with Bell, you see, we both considered . . . well what? A life together? We didn't come out and say it in so many words, but it was there in front of us, seriously so. And if we had decided to try that, given his nature and mine, it probably would have gone on for a lifetime. As it happened the time wasn't right then, or so we thought. He needed to be sure of himself and to know he could manage on his own with his face, although I never had any doubts about that. And I thought I still needed to be able to wander, to be free to move around and find myself, although it couldn't have been so very important to me because soon after that I ended my wandering, with Yossi.

What's strange about it to me now, said Anna, is that I know it could have worked with Bell. Oh yes, it could have worked and all the years would have been very different. Not better, but different. And how true it is that the turnings on the path are often so subtle, so unsuspected at the time, that we pass them by with a wave and a smile and a near arrogant ease. Yet when we look back in life the reasons for our choices seem unbearably flimsy and silly, which is confusing and even frightening. A *totally* different life which could have worked just as well as the one we have? That's something none of us likes to think about. Instead, we try mightily to forget our other worlds that might have been, and with good reason. But all the same those rare and beautiful moments from the past live on within us, no farther away than the smell of an olive wood fire or the sound of rain beating softly on a garden, time's unquiet ghosts, haunting our memories with secret whispers of *what if?* . . .

◆◆◆◆◆◆◆◆

Tajar lay in his hammock that summer night, gazing up at the stars above his cottage. Once long ago Anna had told him there were three men who counted in her life, himself and Yossi and one other. Now he knew who that third man was and it didn't surprise him. Bell's was a powerful life, lived deeply. That Anna had felt it so long ago only showed how deeply her own feelings ran.

Her memories of Bell and the fondness of her recollections set Tajar to thinking in many ways. There was no question he had always loved Anna. He knew that. And everything she now said about Bell also applied to him and was meant for him. He and Anna had shared those rare and beautiful moments of which she spoke. They both were aware of that, and what if? . . .

Years ago when they met, Anna was wandering and Tajar was energetic and ambitious in his work. They knew each other and parted, with a wave and a smile. Then later they met again after she had married Yossi, and all that was to be came about.

Of course they were still together in other ways and shared many of the things a man and a woman could have. Not the same roof, it was true, and not sexual love . . . an automobile accident had seen to that. But they were much closer than many people who were married. And yet, what if he'd had the sense and the wisdom to try to make it permanent with Anna the first time they'd met? Wouldn't their life together be even richer now?

As she said, it was confusing to think about such things and more than a little frightening. With Bell, if she'd made that decision, her life would have turned out very differently. But not so with him. With him it probably would have become much as it was now, the two of them living in Jerusalem with Tajar having his work and Anna her painting, perhaps a hammock strung on one of the balconies of the old stone house on Ethiopia Street, or in the courtyard below with the flowers. . . .

Tajar's eyes flew open. He was looking up at a vast sky of stars. He had been drifting off to sleep in his hammock when suddenly he had thought of Assaf. All of this had started with Assaf's passion for the past and its secrets, with Assaf's interest in his uncle in Cairo during the world war and his trips to Jericho after another war a quarter of a century later, where he had met Bell who was linked to everyone, past and present.

But would there even have been an Assaf if Anna, if Tajar, if Bell, if Yossi? . . .

Tajar laughed, gazing up at the Jerusalem night. How wonderful were the young with their limitless belief in what might be. So grandly did they believe they could even go beyond it and make-believe, truly conjuring up the might-have-been in all its splendid glory.

What a magnificent gift, thought Tajar. What joyous folly. Just by being, Assaf has told me extraordinary things about myself, and about Anna and me and the past, and especially and above all about right now.

And Bell?

Yes, more than ever Tajar wanted to see Bell. He still thought some time should pass before he made his journey to Jericho, but inevitably he would do it. They were connected in too many ways for it not to come to pass.

EIGHT

After Little Aharon's reign of more than a dozen years as director of the Mossad, it had been decided that five years was an appropriate term for the chief of intelligence. As General Dror's term came to an end, many in the Mossad hoped one of their own senior executives would be chosen to succeed him.

Tajar never considered this a possibility, nor did he think it was in the Mossad's best interests. The army's influence had greatly increased since the Six-Day War, and Tajar felt a civilian director would be at a disadvantage dealing with the prestigious generals and former generals who were now so powerful in government. Dror stayed on longer than expected as the generals and former generals maneuvered against each other, promoting their various candidates as his replacement. In the end a general was chosen, but the choice surprised them all.

General Ben-Zvi, on the verge of retirement, was as astonished as anyone by his appointment. He had no experience in intelligence and was not the sort of fighting general for which the army was famous. By any standard, in fact, Ben-Zvi was the least glamorous of Israeli generals. Most of his career had been spent in staff positions, particularly in training, then during the Six-Day War he was on assignment in Europe as a military attaché. As the other generals joked, for a professional officer not to have fought in the Six-Day War was akin to a man not consummating his marriage.

The prime minister had outmaneuvered his powerful generals, yet the army couldn't complain because Ben-Zvi was one of their own. There was disappointment within the Mossad but none of the enormous internal turmoil that had accompanied Dror's appointment the last time around. Tajar, in any case, saw wisdom in the selection. Quoting Ben-Gurion, he said it was a tragedy that Israel's generals had begun to think of themselves as generals. Ben-Zvi's lack of swagger would serve the Mossad well, he felt. He even admired the fact that Ben-Zvi wasn't a military hero.

On the other hand, Ben-Zvi was a conscientious officer who believed in professionalism. He worked night and day at the Mossad to master his job and combat the new kind of secret warfare faced by Israel: the international terrorism of the PLO, backed by the KGB. He wanted to draw the best he could from his staff and delegate authority when possible, but only after he knew what was involved. Having been a trainer, he valued instruction and was quick to recognize Tajar's immense experience and unique skills.

By then a mystique had grown up around Tajar in the Mossad. He was a legend even to those who had only the vaguest notions of the Runner operation. To the few senior executives who did know something about the operation, the legend was firmly based in fact. And to the director of the Mossad, the only man beside Tajar who knew the true identity of the Runner, the fact that the Runner was an Israeli seemed a near superhuman accomplishment.

But for most of Tajar's admirers the mystique was more general than that. Tajar, after all, was a man from Little Aharon's generation whose preeminence went back even further than Little Aharon's. As time went on Tajar's importance during the pre-independence years continued to be revealed in memoirs and histories. In 1945, for example, when Ben-Gurion went to New York to ask a handful of influential American Jews to begin raising money for the coming struggle in Palestine, he took only two men with him to help him explain his case at that historic August meeting in Manhattan: his treasurer at the Jewish Agency and Tajar, his expert on Arab countries. And when Ben-Gurion needed a man to negotiate in trust and secrecy with Emir Abdullah of Transjordan in 1948, it was Tajar who drove alone at night through Jericho to the villa of the emir, King Hussein's grandfather.

Further, many of the senior men in the Mossad were former Tajar commandos of another era, selected and trained by Tajar decades ago when he was all the country-to-be had in the way of a foreign intelligence service. Yet Tajar still wasn't so very old, only in his early fifties, which showed what awesome responsibilities men had taken upon themselves, at an early age, in order to create the state.

Thus it was only natural that General Ben-Zvi, even more than Dror before him, needed what Tajar had to offer. So Tajar in his quiet way became Ben-Zvi's unofficial instructor and adviser, the trainer's trainer, working behind the scenes to make the studious general a master in Israel's lonely new secret war. Ben-Zvi was in the habit of working late at night in his office, reading reports, and that was when Tajar dropped in to talk with him. Ben-Zvi knew Tajar made his visits at night in order to be inconspicuous, so that his appearances would attract as little notice as possible within the Mossad. Tajar was always the modest tutor, and he didn't want to embarrass Ben-Zvi by drawing attention to himself.

Besides, said Tajar, smiling, you have decisions to make in daylight. Only at night is there a moment to reflect and ponder.

Sometimes they talked for an hour or more, sometimes less. If some specific problem was troubling Ben-Zvi, Tajar might recall a case from the past that seemed similar. Or he might suggest someone Ben-Zvi could discuss the matter with, or simply ruminate on the alternatives as he saw them. Tajar was careful to stay away from solutions and always stopped short of suggesting courses of action, for as he said, it was Ben-Zvi who had to be the director. At the same time he often consoled Ben-Zvi, since the general was apt to take his failures deeply to heart.

Ours is a profession of failure, Tajar told him. Unlike paratroopers, we don't drop out of the sky and storm positions and then raise our flag in triumph. It's not land we deal with, it's just people. So if you think of it as a sad profession, you won't be so disappointed. Orwell said that any life when seen from the inside is simply a series of defeats. Well that's the only way we *do* see life: from the inside. Appearances are for others, our work is to get at the truth. But recall that in order to get at the truth, we have to deal far more deeply in subterfuge than society's criminals. That's the sadness and it takes a strong man to rise above it and not be dead inside. Others peddle cynicism and hatred but we can't afford to. *You* can't afford to. So when you come across a man without feelings, pack him off to retirement on a kibbutz where he can raise vegetables, because that's what he understands. . . .

Along with death and hatred, there were many failures for the Mossad during those years when the PLO's terrorist campaign was at its height. Or at least the terrorists were able to continue with their terror, especially in Europe. The only real way to combat it was by building up files on the terrorist cells with the aim of penetrating them, and that kind of work took immense time and effort.

For years there was no cooperation from the West European countries in combating the terror. As long as the campaign appeared to be merely the PLO against Israel, Arabs killing Jews, the Europeans refused to help. Oil above all, but also Third World opinion and the propaganda and manipulations of the KGB—there were many reasons why the Europeans wanted to stay out of the conflict, as Dror had predicted.

Eventually the European attitude changed, as the Mossad was able to document the KGB's role in the terror and the PLO's connection to European terrorist cells. This was especially true after an Israeli commando raid on PLO offices in Beirut in the spring of 1973, when files were captured linking the KGB through the PLO to an international terrorist network, with detailed descriptions of money and arms, contact men and future plans.

Ironically, these files captured by the Israelis helped a number of moderate Arab governments and leaders to survive, when information on terrorist networks in their countries was passed along to them by the CIA, the information having been given to the CIA by the Mossad for that purpose.

◆◆◆◆◆◆◆◆

The Runner operation, overall, turned out to be less vital against the terrorists than Tajar had expected. In the beginning the Runner provided crucial information on the KGB's involvement with the PLO, but before long the KGB moved its control of the terrorist campaign from Damascus to the island of Cyprus. The Russians found there were too many security leaks within the PLO in Damascus, where the Syrians had long been accustomed to running PLO factions for their own ends. But Cyprus had a weak government and its Greek and Turkish populations were always close to civil war, backed by agents from mainland Greece and Turkey, so for the KGB it was a convenient transit point from which to direct terrorist traffic between Europe and the main PLO training camps in Lebanon.

An ideal gathering ground for jackals, as Tajar told Ben-Zvi. No bomb thrower could possibly look out of place in Cyprus, no matter what his cause or nationality.

The Runner himself seemed to slip into a kind of malaise during those years. Or so Tajar secretly felt, without confiding his concern to anyone.

The Runner was still a steady source of high-level information on the Syrian government and Syrian intentions, and Ben-Zvi had nothing but admiration for the Runner and for Tajar's handling of the case. To him the operation was the very essence of successful espionage, a model of careful planning over a long period of time, its accomplishments the standard by which any penetration was to be measured.

But the working objectives of the Mossad had gradually

changed since the Six-Day War. On the tactical level there was the constant preoccupation with the details of the terrorist cells, their potential targets and routes of supply and command, a quest which led from Beirut and the PLO camps in Lebanon to Cyprus, and from there to Europe. And on the strategic level the emphasis had shifted to nuclear power and the build-up of the Arab air forces by the Soviet Union, highly technical intelligence that was beyond the scope of the Runner operation. In those subjects as well, the quest for information was often outside the Middle East, in both East and West Europe and in the CIA satellites circling the earth.

Or perhaps Tajar only imagined that the Runner was undergoing a period of malaise when he met with Yossi at safehouses in Beirut. It might have been that the frustrations everyone felt at home in dealing with the terrorists, or even his own sense of lessened responsibility, were causing him to see an uneasiness in Yossi which in fact wasn't there. Expectations had been great after the total victory of the Six-Day War, and now nothing seemed to be coming from them. Or rather, the security and hope for a better future weren't coming about. Yossi had never been as dazzled as most Israelis by the outcome of the war, although perhaps more so than Tajar because of his own enormous contribution to it. But now, little by little, it seemed that Yossi was becoming as deeply troubled as Tajar over the future.

Yossi's mood disturbed Tajar but he was careful not to show it at their infrequent meetings in Beirut. His task was to encourage Yossi and that was what he did, subtly, in many little ways. From long experience Tajar knew even better than Yossi that a feeling of futility was the most dangerous enemy of all to the operation. In his own mind at least Yossi could never simply stand still, never just remain in place, because that wasn't part of the life the two of them had created for the Runner. It was the nature of the operation that the Runner had to keep on running.

So the bombings and murders and hijackings went on and on with a few terrorists sometimes able to seize the attention of much of the world, as they did when they killed Israel's Olympic athletes at Munich in 1972, with only a minor and bumbling show of resistance on the part of the Germans. That terrorist group was known as Black September, named after the month when Jordan's Arab Legion had expelled the PLO from Jordan in a particularly bloody campaign of Arab against Arab.

But to Tajar the most gruesome episode of all was the massacre at Lod airport in May of that year, when three young Japanese men flew into Israel on an Air France plane from Rome, opened their suitcases and threw grenades and fired automatic weapons at random around the arrival hall of the airport, killing and wounding over a hundred passengers.

The Japanese belonged to a tiny terrorist group grandly called the Red Army, of no consequence at all in Japan, which had come halfway around the world to carry out a suicide mission for Black September. The majority of those killed at the airport were Puerto Rican pilgrims, Roman Catholics on a visit to the Christian sites in the Holy Land. The one Japanese who survived, in explaining himself, said he had wanted to become a star in the heavens, visible in the night sky throughout eternity.

Japanese idealists massacring Puerto Rican pilgrims in Israel? In the name of revenge by Palestinian Arabs against Jordanian Arabs? In the hope of becoming a star in the heavens?

Another demented, grotesque act using the cause of human dignity as a mask for madness. Even given man's sad weakness for self-delusion and the clever manipulations of the KGB, the evidence of darkness and insanity in human affairs sometimes seemed overpowering to Tajar.

NINE

Bell's morning walks began at first light. He could no longer go all the way down to the river now that it was the border between Jordan and Israel, but he still set out east each morning to cross the parched empty plains of Jericho, the Dead Sea shimmering off to his right and the dark mass of the hills of Moab looming high in front of him on the far side of the valley. Just before the wire fence of the military zone, he turned north on the second leg of his circle and walked up the valley parallel with the river. The first rays of the new sun were breaking over the Moabite hills when he turned again, west this time. The sun bathed his back with a gentle warmth as he made his way home toward Jericho's lush greenery, the jagged heights of the Judean desert softly pink and glowing beyond the oasis. Bell walked at a brisk pace, savoring the ancient beauty and moods of that wild, haunting landscape.

His walks lasted about two hours. When he got home he showered and ate and washed out his laundry from the previous day, then settled into his chair on the front porch with a large glass of Turkish coffee. The orange grove was already buzzing with its characteristic morning hum at that early hour, the insects busily at work before the sun drew high.

Bell always passed one or two Israeli patrols on his morning walks, open command cars with mounted machine guns driving near the border where the soldiers checked the swept sand beside the wire fence, looking for footprints or other signs of a clandestine crossing during the night. The soldiers waved to Bell and he waved back, for they were as familiar with his routine as he was with theirs. Every few weeks a command car veered off its course to approach him and Bell had a short talk with the soldiers. They were reservists, none too young, serving on their yearly call-up. A visit from a command car only meant that a new sergeant had arrived for duty on the sector and was checking things out for himself.

The new soldiers who hadn't seen Bell close-up tended to stare, unable to hide their morbid fascination with his face. Those who had seen him before made a point of studying the surrounding desert. One of the soldiers always spoke Arabic, so that was the language Bell used. But if a sergeant addressed him in English, Bell answered in English. The interviews were brief and polite. Anyone who did duty near Jericho soon came to know Bell and was able to recognize him from a distance.

The border had been dangerous once, but not seriously so since the Jordanian army had fought and expelled the PLO from Jordan in 1970. When there were infiltrators now they were generally men who were trying to avoid the Jordanians as much as the Israelis. The bridges near Jericho carried a great amount of legal traffic back and forth across the river between the east and west banks, all Arab, but there were always men who didn't want to face policemen of any kind, as at most borders.

Most mornings after coffee Bell read straight through to noon, but there were days when some curious memory came to him on his walk and he found the hours slipping away as he sat with an open book in his lap, pondering a distant episode in his life.

It had been like that this morning. He was out in the desert and had just turned north on his circle route when a command car passed to the east, near the border. A wave from a soldier, Bell waved back. The dust in the wake of the command car disappeared over a rise and Bell suddenly thought of Stern, a man who had been dead nearly thirty years. For the rest of the walk Bell had noticed almost nothing of the hills and the valley and the light, so intense were his memories of Stern all at once. He thought about that now as he relaxed on his porch, listening to the hum of his orange grove.

During the Second World War in Egypt when Bell had been in command of the Monastery, Stern had been his most valuable agent. Stern was a gifted man of many disguises, able to go anywhere, and it was because of him that Anna's brother had been killed. Stern had been a friend of their family in Cairo, of David and Anna and more particularly of their father before them. There was never any professional connection between David and Stern, but a mistake had been made in the Monastery and someone had assumed there was a professional connection, so David had been run down by a lorry in Cairo at the time when Stern was also killed.

Bell had greatly respected and admired Stern. He had never met David nor even known who David was until after his death. But because of his feelings for Stern, Bell had gone out of his way to help David's sister after Stern and David were killed. And after the war that had led to his few weeks with Anna in Jerusalem, which in turn had brought him to Jericho.

During his brief time with Anna in Jerusalem, Bell hadn't dared to let himself think there might be something more for the two of them. He was too afraid then of his face and his freedom to imagine her love could be anything but the paying of a debt, a young woman's way of escaping the ugly memories of her past, perhaps by embracing ugliness itself for a moment. Thus Bell, lacking the courage to hope, had turned his back on Anna and left Jerusalem, running away out of fear to seclusion and Jericho and a life of obscurity on the edge of the desert.

Well, it was simple enough, he thought now. Anna was often on his mind these days because of Assaf. And so in the desert that morning his memory had abruptly tumbled back through the years to Stern, all the way back to Egypt and the

Monastery where it had actually begun for Anna and him, although neither of them had known then that it was a beginning, so long ago in Cairo.

Stern . . . Anna . . . secret histories.

I suppose we all have them tucked away inside somewhere, thought Bell, these precious and secret events with their secret beginnings. Understanding as little as we do, we always seem to be connected to others in ways we never suspect, in a sweep of time we can't fathom, in moments we're only able to recognize years later. As if for each of us the important things in life become but one single story in the end, one beautiful secret dream we grasp too late.

Bell smiled at his abstractions, at the way he was trying to make sense out of the secret histories he carried within him. Or is it just that I grow old? he wondered. Is it just that all these years later I still can't forgive myself for leaving Anna and Jerusalem?

Regret? thought Bell. The utterly useless pain of recalling lost chance and lost opportunity? Surely I should know better than that by now.

And yet the folly of losing Anna and going off to live alone sometimes seemed so incalculable to Bell, such a monstrous insult to life, that the sacrilege of it overwhelmed him and drove him to a bleak despair which no amount of atonement could lessen. For years he had lived as a recluse and yet his turning away from the woman he loved had been entirely his own doing, and the humiliation it had caused him ever since then had come only from his own self-loathing.

Yes, and what was the use in the end of blaming it on his face? On fate? On the chance catastrophe of a spyglass once held to his eye and struck by a bullet, shattering his face and his faith in life, in himself? What excuse was that for turning away from love?

It was infinitely sad to Bell, for sometimes it did seem to him that all the moments in life were one and that a man had but one chance to make the world within himself as he wanted it to be, as it should be, as it was right for it to be. And in that, he knew, he had failed completely.

Anna, he thought. If only I'd had the courage years ago. . . .

◆◆◆◆◆◆◆◆

Assaf took a degree in history at Hebrew University and went on to graduate studies. He still visited Jericho once or twice a month and spent even more time there in the winter, when the seductive ways of the sunny oasis were especially appealing. He had his own room now at Abu Musa's where he kept books and clothes, coming and going as he pleased, reading and walking down Jericho's dusty lanes and working in Abu Musa's orange groves, where he repaired the waterways of sun-baked mud.

Abu Musa was overjoyed with the arrangement. He was careful not to interfere with Assaf's freedom, but there was always time in the course of the day for the two of them to be together. In the late afternoon Assaf accompanied the old Arab to the daily shesh-besh sessions on Bell's front porch, where Assaf sat and talked with Bell or listened with Bell to the rambling monologues carried on by the two players. Ever serious and now scholarly as well, Assaf took great pleasure in the far-ranging subjects conjured up with such ease by his three friends.

But it was Abu Musa, in particular, who devoted himself to Assaf. All the knowledge of his long life now seemed dedicated to Assaf, who filled the need in Abu Musa's affections for the innumerable young people of his family from whom he had been separated over the years.

The boy is a blessing in my old age, Abu Musa confided to Bell. Not until Ali was killed and Yousef went away did I realize how seldom we speak in life and how little we say. Why, my friend? Why is age so reticent? When I was young I yearned to hear and know of life and yet so little was said to me, I realized later. My wife's father was a great friend and we were close and he told me many things, but how much more he could have told me. He was a man who had done everything a man can do, yet he never really let flow the depths of his being to me. And why? Because he felt it would have been unseemly? Because of his position and mine? Because he was a great desert chieftain and had to take care that I could always respect him? No sign of weakness, therefore? No hint that he was anything less than wise and strong? A terrible mistake, I tell you, the same mistake I made with Ali and Yousef and won't make again with Assaf. I ask you, what do I have to hide? The fact that I'm not half the man I wanted to be? The fact that these little pieces of wisdom I string together add up to not much at all? The fact that the respected village patriarch solemnly pondering his coffee in the marketplace can't help but recognize an unmistakable kinship with every passing fool of his era? They've *endured.* That's what the fool and the patriarch have in common and that's what they represent, and all else is incidental.

Abu Musa's great body shook with laughter.

And so I've put an end to mystery and silent cunning in my old age, he said to Bell. Every pathetic feeling of mine I will lay bare to the young traveler Assaf and he can make of them what he will, knowing that at least one desert wayfarer has told him all there is to tell about one oasis.

◆◆◆◆◆◆◆◆

Of Yousef, however, Bell said little. Abu Musa knew Yousef wanted it that way so his life as a fugitive would cause no harm and as little suffering as possible to others. And to Assaf, Bell said nothing at all about Yousef. In their own ways they all understood the burden of knowledge Bell carried because Bell had always been special in Yousef's life, and because Bell was a foreigner, neither an Arab nor a Jew, and also simply because Bell was Bell.

On moonless nights Yousef still came to the ruins of Herod's winter palace on the outskirts of Jericho, sneaking down the wadi to the banana plantation and crossing into the ruins to see Bell, although he came less frequently as the years went by. Yousef's appearance had changed so much the others probably wouldn't have recognized him. Now he was very thin and worn, as slight a figure as Ali had been in his youth. He moved lightly, like a desert animal, and every sound in the darkness had a meaning to him. A stirring as soft as a breeze in the night and suddenly a presence would be crouching behind a rock near the spot where Bell sat looking out over the plains from a corner of the ruins. The presence waited for whole minutes and drifted closer, still invisible in the darkness to anyone but Bell. When finally the desert creature spoke his voice was so quiet Bell had to strain to hear him.

So it went season after season and year after year. Yousef liked to hear of the doings of his friends, what Abu Musa and Moses the Ethiopian were discussing during their shesh-besh games and what Assaf was studying and what Bell was reading on his front porch in the mornings. Yousef spoke readily enough of himself when Bell asked him questions, but it was Bell who did most of the talking because Yousef was unused to it. His life in the desert had accustomed him to listening, as Bell understood.

Bell often thought what a strange life it must be. The region where Yousef spent much of the year was in the vicinity of the Wadi Kidron, one of the deepest of the ravines that wound down through the Judean wilderness to the Dead Sea. The wadi began as the Kidron Valley just below the eastern walls of Jerusalem, the valley that separated the Old City from the Mount of Olives. From there it curved south and east, cutting ever more sharply down through the hills and the desert, a ravine of high precipices and many inaccessible caves, so fiercely hot in the summer months it was known to the bedouin as the Wadi el Nar, *the wadi of fire.* Centuries ago it had served as a route for travelers journeying up to Jerusalem from the Jordan Valley: an east-west traverse between the Way of the Kings up the valley floor and the Way of the Patriarchs stretching up the central ridge of the land from Hebron through Jerusalem to Samaria. The crumbling remnants of ruined monasteries overlooked its deep barren gorges and the hovels of forgotten anchorites were hidden away in its ancient cliffs.

Living in such a place, it was no wonder Yousef seldom talked when he met Bell. With that vastness of solitude around him day after day and night after night, with the intense cold of the desert winters and the awesome heat of the summers and the spirits of other eras as his only companions in the wadi of fire, it was no wonder that Yousef had grown accustomed to listening.

How many interminable hours of sunlight are there in such a place? wondered Bell. How much darkness in even one night? It must be a kind of eternity he lives in, a realm of dreams and visions that the rest of us sense for only the briefest of moments in the course of our weeks and months. Wholly another world and existence, conceived in a multitude of time as infinite as the stars.

Do you see an end to your life in the wilderness? Bell once asked him, in the spring of 1973 after Yousef had been living as a fugitive for a full five years.

Yousef was silent for a time. I don't really know about that, he finally replied. But I have decided there's a man I'd like to meet to talk about it. He has a great reputation among some of our people and I believe you used to know him. A Syrian. Halim is his name. He lives in Damascus.

Yes, I did know him, said Bell. Not well, but what I saw of him was impressive. Does that mean, then, you'll be leaving the desert and crossing the river?

Not right away, replied Yousef. I don't even know yet whether he'll agree to meet me. But if he would, then we'll see. There's no hurry about it, there's no hurry about anything I do. But you'll know first if I decide to cross the border.

It would be a great relief to Abu Musa, said Bell.

I know, whispered Yousef, and went on to ask about Assaf and the shesh-besh games and the books Bell had been reading since their last meeting in the ruins of Herod's winter palace.

◆◆◆◆◆◆◆◆

Bell was excited that Yousef was at least considering an end to his exile in the desert, the first sign in five years that he was having a change of heart. Bell realized the news was meager and tentative and perhaps more of a hope on his part than anything else, but he still wanted to share it with Abu Musa and Moses. This he did the next afternoon when the three of them were alone on his front porch.

Moses looked up at once from the shesh-besh board and smiled and nodded in encouragement at Bell. Abu Musa, however, turned away from the board and busied himself for a time with his waterpipe, which had gone out. A somber mood seemed to have come over him, which surprised Bell.

Of course it's still too soon to know what will come of it, ventured Bell.

Abu Musa fumbled a while longer with his waterpipe and finally gave it up. He sighed and gripped his hands together in his lap.

It may be too soon to know, said Abu Musa, or it may be that the affair has gone on too long already. You don't hear as many tales from the local coffeeshops as I do, my friend. Do you know what the villagers in the hills are saying of our Yousef? They call him a man who casts a long shadow in the moonlight. You see Yousef on nights when there is no moon, on nights when it's dark, or so I imagine. And if you do you miss that aspect of him. You don't see his shadow in the moonlight.

Bell wasn't sure what Abu Musa meant by his allusion to Yousef's shadow in the moonlight, which of course he never did see. As well as he knew Abu Musa, the old Arab's elliptical desert imagery could still elude him sometimes. He said as much now.

Abu Musa sighed again and gripped his hands more tightly together. Oh well, he said, it's just that for most of us life is such an *ordinary* matter. Day in and day out that's what we know, a persistent *ordinariness* which is sometimes tedious but which is also reassuring in the end. For some, though, it's not that way and so it may be with our Yousef. I would rather that he still be flesh and blood and not a shadowy promise of redemption that lives in the moonlight of people's dreams. Oh yes, I would dearly prefer it but I am but one man with my own hopes, and you are, and Yousef I fear has gone beyond all this and become something else to many people. Become what? A myth in the hills? A myth of the desert up there? Perhaps, and perhaps even a holy man of sorts. . . . To my mind a holy man who drinks is fine. The drinking merely means he is still a man while pursuing his holiness, a sensible approach to an admirable vocation. And I don't mean to say Yousef sought what he has become. He was always a modest and well-balanced young man and I don't believe for a moment he had this in mind when he went into the desert. But this is five years later, and don't you realize what it has cost him to live alone up there in eternity?

Abu Musa sadly shook his head.

Everything, he said. Quite simply it has cost him his whole life. And I don't mean he has gone mad, although it must be like that in a way, existing as he does in another time and dimension, on a different planet circling a different sun, lost somewhere in the stars. . . .

Abruptly Abu Musa reached out and clutched Bell's good hand in both of his own. He held on tightly, tears in his eyes.

Don't wish too hard for what cannot be, he said. It's good and right for a holy man to believe more than the rest of us, that's what makes him what he is. And you believe in Yousef because you love him and have always loved him, ever since he was a child wrapping his arms around your knees to hold himself up. But you must accept the fact that Yousef is gone and will never come back. *Never.* He couldn't even if he wanted to. He's elsewhere now and the villagers in the hills have their beautiful dream of him, a dream of hope and freedom and redemption. *Their* Yousef now. Not ours. . . .

Abu Musa still gripped Bell's hand, overcome with sadness. In the silence that followed, Moses the Ethiopian slowly lumbered to his feet and rearranged his bright yellow robes with great ceremony. Just as slowly he seated himself again on his bench and fell to studying the shesh-besh board.

A dream such as that, he murmured to himself, must also have been known in those villages two thousand years ago, when Jesus stood on the Mount of Temptation and turned his back on Jericho. But perhaps that's always so in a place as ancient as this, where memories and oranges ripen inseparably in the sun.

TEN

Nineteen seventy-three was a disastrous year for the Israelis. With a fearful sense of inevitability, Tajar watched fortune scatter the seasons with an abandon that allowed nothing to go right. To him it was as if some elemental force in the cause of nations had shifted momentum and was driving silent winds across the land, reworking fate and creating new designs for the secret structures of time. After all the years of struggle he sometimes thought he could sense invisible danger as an animal does, and now his very fingers seemed to feel it whispering to him in the glancing touch of a doorknob, in the heavy grip of his crutches, in the worn smooth stones of Jerusalem when he stopped and rested his fingertips on an ancient wall and closed his eyes and listened.

Tajar had a curious experience that spring.

One still Sabbath morning he was lying in his hammock in the clearing beside his low stone house, far back in the overgrown compound where he lived hidden from the world behind a tangle of wild rosebushes and the giant cactus which reared across the entrance of his tumble-down gate. He had a book in his hand but he wasn't reading. He was gazing up at the fresh spring sunshine spilling through the cypress and olive trees, feeling strangely distant from even the slumbering quiet of Jerusalem, when all at once his eye caught the movement of a butterfly shooting past overhead. Another butterfly fluttered quickly by and another, both identical to the first. They were neither large nor small and of commonplace coloring, orange or yellow with black markings.

Again a single butterfly shot past, again followed by a cluster of three or four. He looked more closely and decided the color was definitely orange. Idly he watched the procession of butterflies repeat itself, then suddenly realized it *was* a procession and wasn't ending.

He sat up in the hammock and stared. Still the butterflies kept coming, dozens of them jerkily fluttering past him on the same course, seemingly caught in a narrow stream of swift-flowing wind. But there was no wind. The air was utterly still. And the butterflies all came in a line from the same direction, from the far end of the compound where the gate was, skimming along above the rosebushes and shooting over his hammock and flittering away out of sight beyond his house, a steady flow of them on and on, now one or two and now a cluster, not a single butterfly deviating from the mysterious tunnel devised for them through the sunshine.

Tajar was astonished. He had never seen anything like it. For whole minutes the butterflies went shooting by like a flock of migrating birds, hundreds of them bending their erratic flight to a course, then the stunningly beautiful procession ended as abruptly as it had begun. The stream of butterflies vanished and there was not even one stray orange fantasy in the air overhead, fluttering with black markings across the clearing above his hammock, inscrutably pursuing the route from south to north up the length of his compound.

Tajar found it disturbing, unfathomable. Butterflies were notorious for directionless, patternless flight. Where had they come from and why? Where were they going?

The butterflies made Tajar uneasy that spring day. Later he told Anna about it and she too was astonished, though less mystified than he was. To her it seemed only a wondrous and beautiful event, inexplicable certainly, remarkable because it was so far from the ordinary.

But for Tajar this chance glimpse at the incomprehensible counterorder of the universe was truly startling, far more so than any random clash of chaos could have been behind the tangle of wild rosebushes in his walled compound, where a huge ancient cactus guarded the gate with a thousand sharp swords.

◆◆◆◆◆◆◆◆

The major ambition of the Egyptian leader Sadat, as he always said, was to make up for the humiliation suffered by Egypt and the Arabs in the Six-Day War. The war fought in October 1973 did that.

It wasn't a military victory for the Egyptians and the Syrians. After some initial advances on the battlefield the two Arab armies lost. Egypt conquered six miles of desert along part of the Suez Canal and Syria gave ground. Success swung away from the Arabs long before the end of the fighting, when Israeli tanks were twenty-five miles from Damascus and forty-five miles from Cairo. But wars are measured in more than ground, and the Arabs felt triumphant because they proved they could fight. In Israel, there was a brutal end to the euphoria that had followed the Six Days of victory and creation the last time around.

The new war began on the Day of Atonement, the holiest day of the Jewish year. By tradition Yom Kippur marks the day when the ancient Israelites received the second Tablets of the Law and thereby knew they were forgiven for the sin of worshiping the golden calf. It is a day of repentence, of fasting and prayer and meditation, with the intent of receiving the forgiveness of one's fellow man, which in turn will allow the forgiveness of God. It addresses man's weakness and ability to envision the ideal, and celebrates God's help to the penitent.

Israel has a small standing army and can only fight a war after calling up its reserves, in which all men serve until the age of fifty. In such a small country mobilization is enormously disruptive. In May 1973, after the Israeli commando raid on the

PLO in Beirut, the PLO attacked the Lebanese army and for a time it looked as if the Syrians might invade Lebanon to assist the PLO. Military intelligence in Israel was against mobilization but the army issued a call-up, which turned out to be unnecessary.

In July 1973 the Mossad was overtaken by a terrible blunder. A Mossad team, on the trail of the PLO terrorist responsible for the Olympic massacre in Munich, was led to the small Norwegian town of Lillehammer where it killed a Moroccan waiter, the wrong man. Norwegian police arrested those involved, the first incontrovertible evidence that Israeli assassination teams were operating against terrorist leaders of the PLO. The affair was given publicity and the Mossad was in trouble at home.

In September 1973 a train carrying Russian Jews emigrating to Israel was hijacked by PLO terrorists in Czechoslovakia, creating great turmoil in Israel. The PLO unit was one of those run by Syrian intelligence.

The Egyptian army always held its annual training maneuvers in the autumn. In September the Egyptian army was on the move beyond the Suez Canal, which had been the border with Israel since the Six-Day War. In the north on the Syrian front there was also activity, but Israeli military intelligence did not foresee war. In its opinion the Egyptians were on their annual autumn maneuvers and the Syrians were engaged in defensive arrangements.

In October 1973 the Egyptians and Syrians had surprise on their side for the first time. Their lines of supply were short, both along the canal and on the Golan Heights. They had the initiative and their motivation was to recapture their own territory lost in 1967. This time Israeli forces had to cross the Sinai to reach the southern front, but Israel's military leaders were contemptuous of the Arabs' ability to wage war. Israeli military intelligence was convinced the Arabs wouldn't go to war unless they were first able to strike at Israel's airfields, as the Israelis had done against Egyptian airfields in 1967, since tank warfare in open country depends on control of the air. Israeli intelligence was aware the Russians had supplied the Egyptians and Syrians with new kinds of antiaircraft missiles, but they didn't rate these weapons very highly.

All together, it was a massive failure of Israeli military intelligence, combined with overconfidence on one side and clever planning on the other. Despite the many signs of war, Israel didn't call up its reserves in October as it had in May.

War began on the afternoon of the Day of Atonement, October 6 that year, when there was complete quiet in Israel. A thousand Egyptian artillery pieces opened up a bombardment along the Suez Canal and 8,000 Egyptian infantrymen crossed the canal in rubber dinghies. Opposing them in the fortifications of the Bar-Lev line were 600 reservists of the Jerusalem Brigade, who were not even on alert. The Egyptians overran the line and that night moved five divisions of troops and 500 tanks and a forward missile defense system over to the east bank of the canal. That same afternoon in the north, on the narrow front of the Golan Heights, the Syrians attacked with more tanks than the Germans had used in Operation Barbarossa, the German invasion of Russia in 1941.

Tajar always felt useless when war came. He could find ways to keep busy by helping others at the Mossad, but his own work was entirely in preparation for war, and when war broke out he could only sit and be anxious and wait for rumors and messages from the battlefields like everyone else.

The news that October was horrible. The Sinai provided protection in the south, at least to those who weren't near the canal, but the Israelis couldn't afford to give up land in the north or the Syrians would be in Israel itself, the plains of Galilee open to them. So the Israelis stood their ground on the Golan and whole units disappeared in the first hours of battle, swallowed up by the massive assault of Syrian tanks.

For Tajar, war was also the time when he recalled his earliest years growing up in Jerusalem with his brothers and sisters. He thought of them at other times but never in the same obsessive, intense way. Again and again whole incidents would suddenly flash before his eyes with startling clarity. Why did those images recur at these moments? What trick of the brain abruptly resurrected such long forgotten sensations? The process obeyed some primitive surge from deep in his being. He tried to concentrate on the work at hand but the recesses of memory compulsively thrust him back in time, as if to remind him how vast was the sweep of life and to reaffirm it, instantly and forever, in the hours of death.

They had been a large family, six children in all, Tajar the youngest. Perhaps there had sometimes been strife and acrimony but he didn't remember that, or at least it wasn't the sense of his memories. What he recalled was warmth and well-being and the protection of his brothers and sisters, who would never let any harm come to him. He was small in these scenes, only four or five. His brothers and sisters seemed twice as tall as he was and were therefore powerful guardians against the dangers of the world. Sometimes the whole family was on a picnic outside the walls of the Old City, sitting together in the evening on the slope of a hill, escaping the summer heat of the narrow alleys of Jerusalem. There were always ruins for him and his brothers to play in and perhaps some British officers might come prancing by on their horses, saluting the boys. Or it was winter and everyone was sitting around in the kitchen and the living room, reading and doing lessons, the only sounds the shuffle of pages and the rhythmic click of his mother's knitting needles. Darkness came early in the winter and everyone read, warmed by the tea his sisters made, all of them bending over their books and dreaming of the Holy City, of the land of Israel and Jerusalem and someday.

There had been little money but he had never gone to bed hungry. Their house was small, with one room for the boys to sleep in and one for the girls. Later a tiny storeroom was turned into a private room for his eldest brother, a great event the children all took pride in because it showed how much there was to look forward to when you grew up.

All of this had been a few years after the First World War when Tajar was four or five, when Turkish rule had just ended in Palestine and a new era of progress and hope had begun with the British. Now Israel was fighting its fourth war and Tajar's mother and father and all his brothers and sisters were long since dead. When you grew up the youngest in a family, it was strange to find yourself always the oldest person in the room, as Tajar did at the Mossad. Like warfare, espionage was for young men. It consumed your ideals and burned you out. But for an automobile accident that had made him a cripple, Tajar would have been burned out by now. As it was he sat uselessly at his desk and felt sick at heart as the young men of his country hurried off to the fronts in the north and the south.

Hurrying . . . to what?

At night in Jerusalem, driving through deserted streets a few hours before dawn, Tajar had seen a young soldier hurrying along in the darkness. He was a reservist in uniform with his rifle and dufflebag slung over his shoulders, one hand gripping each strap as he rushed along with his head down, on his way to meet some bus or car that would take him to his unit at the front. Was the boy old enough to have fought as well in the last war, Assaf's war? Chance ruled the world. If the boy was twenty-four he had fought in the last war. If he was twenty-three, this was his first war. In any case he was young and intent, hurrying. Tears rose in Tajar's throat and he found himself choking at the sight of the boy hurrying alone in the darkness and silence of the deserted streets . . . *O God have mercy, to what?*

On the first afternoon of the war the Israelis lost forty planes to the new Russian missiles, mostly over the Golan Heights. Overall the odds on the ground, initially, were ten or twelve to one in favor of the Syrians, far more in the case of the Egyptians. The Syrians reached their maximum penetration in less than forty-eight hours and after that were driven back. But the situation on the Golan was so desperate in the beginning that Israeli tanks were sent up singly to fight on the plateau, without forming units, as soon as crews of reservists arrived to man them. Two Iraqi armored divisions and a Jordanian armored brigade joined the Syrians, but on the fourth day of the war the Syrians had been driven out of the Golan. On the sixth day Israeli counterattacks were launched into Syria itself.

The Israeli counteroffensive against the Egyptians took longer because of the intervening mass of the Sinai. On the ninth day of the war more tanks were engaged along the Suez Canal than the 1,600 British and German and Italian tanks that had fought at El Alamein, two hundred miles to the west during that same month in 1942. On the eleventh day of the war the first Israeli paratroopers crossed the canal into Egypt. By then the Egyptian Third Army was cut off and trapped in the Sinai.

◆◆◆◆◆◆◆◆

As was customary, the United States and the Soviet Union eventually brought an end to the war.

In terms of land, given the inferiority of Egyptian and Syrian air power and their reliance on defensive antiaircraft missiles, it was unlikely the Arabs ever thought they would carry the war into Israel. At most they could have hoped to recapture some of the territory they lost in 1967, on the Golan Heights and in the Sinai. In this the Syrians failed completely. The Egyptians managed to hold two shallow bridgeheads east of the canal, while losing a pocket west of the canal.

But in other ways the Arabs knew success. They fought hard and inflicted heavy casualties, proving to themselves that Israel on the battlefield was not the invincible force it had appeared to be in 1967. In Egypt the war was celebrated as a great victory.

The destruction on the battlefield in less than three weeks was immense. The dead were over seven times greater on the Arab side, but for Israel with its small population the cost was enormous. In eighteen days of fighting the Israeli dead, relative to population, were nearly half of what the United States suffered in all of the Second World War.

And for the United States and the Soviet Union, thought Tajar, it was also an opportunity to test their new weapons on the battlefield. To see how well their new weapons killed, much as outside powers had done during the Spanish civil war. For the big and the powerful, it was always easy enough to find new killing grounds where others would do the dying for them.

And so another war, thought Tajar. Disaster for Israel, new pride for the Arabs, a chance for the superpowers to play with destruction—and an intolerable slaughter for everyone, an appalling squandering of ingenuity and promise for all mankind.

Where is the *last* war? Assaf had once asked when he lay ripped and mangled in a hospital, recalling the terrified words of a little girl who had huddled in a corner beside her family as the shells shrieked overhead: *I'm so frightened. This is my first war.*

What's the *matter* with people? Assaf had asked. What's wrong with their hearts and their minds? This isn't survival or life or anything at all a man can speak about. It's just horror. *War. . . .*

Alone in Jerusalem, alone at the back of the compound of wild rosebushes guarded by a giant ancient cactus, Tajar sat in his small stone house, his spirit crushed. When the new war finally ended he had come back here and hidden himself away so no one would witness his despair and his longing, his indescribable agony. But now, alone at last after the shattering days of horror and waiting and hoping, of praying for his brothers and sons and nephews, he let his heart go and wept for all his friends through the years who were no more, for all the brave young men who had gone to war after war decade after decade, who had gone and gone and gone and would never come back.

Inconsolable, alone, Tajar wept and wept, hidden away by himself because it was strength people needed from him, now and always. The strength of belief and courage and hope, the strength to dream of what could be.

Oh yes, *the dream.*

Because people counted on Tajar and he knew that. The living counted on him, but no more so than the fallen. After all, if the survivors didn't believe, who was there? What was there? And what then would become of the dream?

Part 3

ONE

For many years until he was brutally killed in the sordid tribal warfare of Lebanon, the little journalist Ziad was Halim's closest friend in Damascus. A Syrian by profession as much as by act of God, as he was fond of joking in the coffeehouses, nervous and smiling and ever brash as he sank more deeply into failure, Ziad was never able to achieve his lifelong dream of escaping his homeland. The great capitals of Europe were always his secret goal, above all the glittering wonders of Paris. But circumstances trapped him early in life and chance receded, and like any man with too weak a grip on hope he sank back into what he already knew and made a routine of it.

Europe was his eternal *over there*, an unreachable land of freedom far from the stifling clutter which was his real lot in the world. Halim—who was still Yossi undercover in the beginning—would have loved him as a friend no matter where they had met and under whatever conditions. For despite all his faults Ziad was a peculiarly lovable man, although perhaps an outsider like Yossi was better able to see that.

Yet circumstances counted in any friendship and particularly for someone as isolated as Yossi had been when he first arrived in Damascus, struggling to make a place for himself in a dangerous enemy capital. There was no way he could ever forget all the help Ziad had been to him then, nor could Ziad himself ever realize the extent of his gifts to Halim, for the simple reason that Halim could never speak of them. It was what Tajar would one day refer to, in consoling Yossi after Ziad's terrible death, as the *lost* factor of friendships in the world of intelligence. Or what Abu Musa in Jericho, going beyond espionage to more fundamental failings of human nature as he saw them, had once referred to in Halim's presence as the pitiful silence of the human heart.

The hard facts of the matter were that Ziad made very real contributions to the early achievements of the Runner operation, without ever knowing it. Through Ziad's ridiculous posturing in the coffeehouses, Halim first made the acquaintance of the vain young lieutenant who was the nephew of the Syrian army's chief-of-staff. Through Ziad's desperate attempts at womanizing, Halim became a close friend of the colonel in command of Syria's paratroop brigade on the Golan Heights. And eventually through Ziad he also came to know the Syrian minister of information, a rigorous intellectual who could open almost any door in those days. But for Halim there would always be another dimension to the closeness he felt for his great friend: the small, strictly personal things Ziad had done for him when Yossi was newly arrived in Damascus and groping inside himself, truly alone and truly frightened.

Halim met Ziad on his first exploratory trip to Syria from Argentina, the visit that was supposed to decide whether he would move to Damascus to go into business. The editor of an Arab weekly in Buenos Aires had given Halim the name of a nephew who worked as a journalist in Damascus. The nephew took Halim to a coffeehouse where journalists gathered and there, among other acquaintances who greeted them, a small and noisy man sat down at their table.

This was Ziad. When he heard Halim was from Argentina he immediately began calling him *gaucho.* Several days later he found Halim sitting alone in the same coffeehouse and joined him without being asked. He was loud and boastful and seemed to have a small man's need for making his presence felt. He dismissed Argentina as backward . . . the place where the devil lost his poncho. Isn't that the expression you use down there for a totally useless corner of the earth?

Ziad had a superficial knowledge of many things. He lectured Halim on the politics of South America and then launched into a detailed account of the sexual practices of an Indian tribe in Brazil, his voice rising. He was vulgar and crass and so busy spewing out opinions that saliva collected at the corners of his mouth, yet no one at the other tables took any notice of him. Only once did he interrupt his noisy recital of his own prejudices and that was to ask Halim what he thought of a certain French painter. Halim had never heard of the man. So this was Ziad in his coffeehouse role—a pathetic buffoon, a shabby clown promoting himself.

Or at least that was the way he acted when confronted by a stranger like Halim, a man who had actually been somewhere in the world and done something. But when he was alone with Halim he was very different. Then he dropped his public pose and became quiet and thoughtful and morose. In only a short time Halim came to know Ziad well on their walks along the river, and he wasn't surprised to learn that the little journalist was a sad and vulnerable man.

Ziad was a few years younger than Yossi, therefore a few years older than Halim, according to the biography put together by Tajar. His background was as poor as Yossi's, although for a time it looked as if he too might rise above it as Yossi had done. Like Yossi, he was the only surviving child in his family. Disease had carried off the others. His father and mother had run a fruit and vegetable stand in the Hamdia souk, the traditional Oriental bazaar in the old section of Damascus. They had gone out before dawn to acquire their produce from peasant dealers, then haggled at their stand all day and into the evening with customers who demanded a discount and threatened to go next door.

A few piastres gained here, a few lost there. It was numbing and brutal work that always required a smile, a deferential politeness. Ziad said he never remembered seeing his father and mother when they weren't exhausted. The drooping eyes, the permanent slump to the shoulders, the old rough hands which were always busy stripping decaying layers off green vegetables to get at a core that could be sold. It just never ended for them, he told Halim.

For their son they naturally hoped for a better life. Ziad was clever and was able to get into a French school run by Catholic fathers, though he was a Sunni Moslem. From the French school he was able to enter the University of Damascus to study law. It was a time of political turmoil and young Ziad became involved with the radical activities of the emerging Baath Party, which advocated social reform and made a special appeal to the new educated classes. The army revolted and one coup followed another. Ziad was suspended from the university, then expelled. He drifted into journalism, which he had been doing part time for the party. His father died, embittered and unreconciled to his son's failures. Overnight his mother became ancient and half-senile, fearful of crowds and afraid to leave the semidarkness of their tiny cavelike apartment above the souk, which was unbearably hot in the summer and icily cold in the winter.

For years his mother lived on alone in her dismal room, supported by Ziad, who came by several times a week to cook her hot meals in the late afternoon before he went out drinking. She was too frugal to use the new lamp he had bought her. He would find her huddled in a corner like some terrified noctural animal, buried away in the shadows under a heap of tattered shawls, his gifts of blankets and a fan and a heater and warm clothes carefully packed away in a cupboard, an old woman with only half a mind who muttered to herself about vegetables.

Once, much later, Ziad took Halim to see these rooms in the souk where he had grown up. They left the alleys of busy shops and made their way back through filthy stone tunnels worn down by centuries of squalid poverty, crept up a narrow stone stairway that was so steep it was more like a ladder twisting and turning between old walls in darkness, the crevices stinking of urine and rotting animal flesh. Finally they came to a low door and Ziad knocked, announced himself, fitted a key. The door opened and they stepped forward. Halim could make out nothing in the shadows. And then all at once a ghastly light lit the cave where they stood, dead white and flat, remorseless. Ziad had turned on the switch by the door as they entered.

The light was neon because neon was cheaper, the original light put in by Ziad's father. The single neon bar hung from the center of the low ceiling and lit the dreary room without depth or contours, a horrible macabre moment. Halim was stunned. In the corner two eyes and a creature cowering under a pile of rags—his friend's mother. Only a short distance away, the seething noisy alleys of the souk where crowds pushed and shouted and every manner of thing was for sale. And here above the alleys this cave of silence, impenetrable in its waste and sorrow. Nothing seemed alive in such a light. It was the illumination of nightmares and death.

Welcome to my secret past, said Ziad. This is my mother and this is where I learned to dream of the world.

◆◆◆◆◆◆◆◆

Because he spoke French and read French newspapers, Ziad liked to think of himself as much better informed than the average journalist in Damascus. He fancied himself a theorist of international politics and was always working his ideas into conversations by drawing grand designs in the air with his busy fingers, here a great power, there a plot. He bought his French newspapers secondhand from clerks who worked in hotels where French travelers stayed. He always had a French newspaper under his arm when making his rounds of the coffeehouses, but since the front-page news was old by then he had the newspaper folded to an inside page of commentary. Interesting piece on the Congo, he would say as he slipped into a chair, adding cryptically: I'm making some notes. Later he resold the newspapers to students at his old school.

Ziad was at his strongest when lecturing bored acquaintances in a coffeehouse. The folly of human affairs was obvious to him then and his face had the worldly grin of an ancient Greek mask of comedy. But if asked a question on the Congo, the mirthless laughter in his eyes betrayed him. His expression turned brittle and he covered his fear by getting his hand up in front of his face and sucking deeply on his cigarette. He needed time to think. What should he say? He threw back his head and blew a long stream of smoke toward the ceiling. Despite the maneuver, Halim had the indelible impression of his friend's face abruptly cast in the other extreme of classical drama, a rigid mask of tragedy. But in only an instant Ziad had recovered, and whether his answer was inadequate or ridiculous didn't matter. Once again he was rushing on in a headlong tumble of words, grinning and talking and talking, desperate to fill the silence inside himself.

When Halim first met him Ziad was prospering in a minor way as a journalist. Or at least he seemed as close to it as he would ever come in the corrupt crosscurrents of bribery and scandal that passed for journalism in Damascus, where every newspaper was the tool of a political party and some loose amalgam of commercial interests, whose enemies it viciously attacked day after day while negotiating with those same enemies, through intermediaries, for a sweeping reversal of editorial policy in exchange for money.

In case things turn out differently tomorrow, Ziad said to Halim. It's just the traditional Levantine sense of contingency. Why be caught publishing yesterday's truths about today's national heroes and saviors, when we all know they're going to turn out to be tomorrow's unscrupulous villains and national traitors? It's no secret you can't run a newspaper that way. In a way it's even fair. Everyone on the outside gets a chance to buy success, and everyone on the inside gets a chance to sell out his friends and principles. And the public, or at least those who remember yesterday, get a chance to read about it and be entertained.

They were out on one of their walks by the river, crossing the Nabek Bridge in the middle of Damascus. The bridge was packed with ancient overflowing buses and old French taxicabs and donkeys pulling carts, with men carrying huge loads on their backs and women selling flowers. People hurried through the dust and the noise and the clatter, their eyes intent on the far shore. Ziad pulled Halim over to the railing and gestured at the muddy river, then at the city.

But you, gaucho, how are you going to know the way things work? asked Ziad. You left Syria at the age of three and you made your way well enough in Argentina, but this isn't a place where laborers eat steaks twice a day. Oh they warned you in Argentina, I know. No pampas and no beef over there, they said, just politics and people. Too much of the one and too many of the other, they said, laughing, and you laughed with them. Because at the same time they were also telling you other stories, weren't they, gaucho? The old men became sentimental and never tired of recalling their beautiful memories. Nostalgic in their faraway land, faces glowing, they described the summer nights of their childhoods when all of Damascus seemed to drift down here to picnic on the banks of the Barada, to lounge on the shores of the river and forget the heat of the day, children playing under the trees in the shadows and lights twinkling on the water and cool breezes whispering up where family and friends were gathered around for long pleasant evenings. Oh just lovely memories when they recalled their homeland. But they don't come back, gaucho, do they? Idle memories are enough for them over there, where pampas and beef mean a man can make a life with only hard work and honest labor.

Of course they admired your idealism and wished you every success, said Ziad. Why shouldn't they? So all your life you've heard these lovely stories about your homeland and wondered about it, and what did it matter that it might be more difficult over here, where there's just politics and people. Worthwhile things *are* difficult. You're young and you've already achieved success in the New World, so why not the Old? Why not Syria? But what do you know about it, gaucho? Do you have any idea what an Alawite or an Ismaili or a Shiite is saying this month beneath what he appears to be saying? Do you know the way the Kurds or the Druse or the Armenians or the Orthodox or the Assyrians are getting along with any of these others this week, and why? Or who's with the Egyptians at the moment and who's against them among the older nationalist groups or the civilian and military wings of the Baath, or the various factions of the army, and why? Because it doesn't really matter so much *what* they're up to, as *why* they're up to it. It's the why that's going to affect what happens next week. And all these rivalries and jealousies and alliances are going somewhere, just as the people and buses and carts on this bridge are going somewhere, intent and hurrying. But *where?*

And even a coffeehouse is never just a coffeehouse, said Ziad. It's a secret society where alert and suspicious members meet to exchange information and get a sense of shifting fortune. You're a Syrian and a Sunni by birth, gaucho, and no doubt that seemed a long-lost identity to you over there in Buenos Aires, a birthright that would provide you with a place in Damascus. But it's just not so. You'll need to be much more, to know much more, in order to go into business here. Syria is a land of ancient fragments, chaos remembered, a primeval place of fanatical discord. Our great gifts to early Christianity were those strange men like St. Simeon Stylites who erected pillars off in the desert and stood on top of them for fifty years, day and night and winter and summer. What possessed them? Is there anything men won't do? It's the Syrian disease and people are like that in this part of the world. They hold onto things. If a prejudice was good enough for the fifth century, it's good enough for us. The more heretical the belief, the more we embrace it. Schismatic Moslem sects have always thrived here. We still have Nestorians and Chaldeans, Christian sects that are so obscure no one else in the world has heard of them for fifteen hundred years. There are even people whose common tongue is still Aramaic, the language of Jesus.

So perhaps back there in Argentina you thought you had an identity as a Sunni and a Syrian, said Ziad. And no doubt you thought you could come over here and rediscover it. But identities change when we cross oceans. Don't you know that, gaucho? Here, you're not what you were back there. Here, there's not enough to go around and never will be. It's a poor country with too many tribes and too many religions in too many variations, without oil, without pampas, with a few fruit and olive trees and too much desert . . . just people and politics, as they told you in Argentina.

Ziad laughed. He took Halim's arm and they left the railing overlooking the river, falling in with the busy crowds swarming across the bridge. Still holding Halim's arm and steering him between the carts and people, Ziad went up on tiptoe and stretched his neck to whisper in Halim's ear.

Of course I could begin to tell you about it, whispered Ziad. That's my business, my profession: how it all works. So if you still want to leave Argentina and move to Damascus, I can show you how to get started.

◆◆◆◆◆◆◆◆

Halim was wary of Ziad in the beginning. It was Tajar who overcame his reluctance at their subsequent meeting in Geneva, when Yossi was returning to Buenos Aires to conclude his affairs there. Yossi was simply being overcautious, Tajar thought, now that the time had finally come for the Runner to move to Damascus.

I'm sure there's nothing to fear, Tajar said in Geneva. Let our little journalist friend help. Open up to him. You're apprehensive and that's natural, but you don't have to underestimate yourself. Ziad obviously respects you, Yossi, and my own feeling is that he's fascinated by what Halim intends to do, wants to do, imagines he can do. In you he sees things he misses in himself, and there's no question he can help you in a very practical way right now. He dramatizes matters to emphasize his own importance, his value to you, but that's all right. You can always distance yourself from him later. By helping you he'll be boosting his self-esteem, which is the point of it for him, I imagine. You'll be doing him a favor by letting him help you. A man like that must suspect even now that he's never going to go very far in the world, but he feels you may.

Anyway, it's not material things that concern him with you, said Tajar. Your eventual success in Damascus as a businessman, as a man who knows people who count and moves among them, all that is too far away for him to think about, inconceivably far away. Life for him is week to week. A month from now the army may have revolted again and there may be another government. That's the way it is in his world. He doesn't know long-term. How can he?

So his interest in you is personal, said Tajar. If he were thinking about bettering himself and promoting his career, he'd be spending his extra time in Baath politics. But the fact is he doesn't. The fact is he would rather spend his extra time with you. Why? Because he's intrigued by the whole idea of the mad gaucho from Argentina. Because he knows himself and knows he'll never be mad or a gaucho, an adventurer from some distant foreign place, some exotic faraway culture, *taking a chance.* Because he knows he's sane and reasonable and a little timid, which is to say ordinary. The way you've described him tells me we see him in the same way. He's a little man with good perceptions and talent, trapped in a place where that's not enough. Likable, harmless, useful. I've known men like him before, in Damascus and elsewhere.

I'm sure, replied Yossi, thoughtfully.

What is it? asked Tajar.

Oh, I was thinking of Argentina, said Yossi. When my Syrian acquaintances there used to speak of life being hard in Syria, because it's a poor country, there was often a hint of something more in their voices. A suggestion meant for me perhaps, an unspoken word, a perception they shared, looking back. Not something they wanted to say out loud because that would have meant demeaning their homeland and their memories. I felt it on this trip, especially when I was with Ziad. *Ruthless* was that unspoken word. You have to be that way to succeed in such a place, when you're born there and grow up there, and Ziad doesn't have it. He lacks it entirely.

Oh well, ordinary for his time and place, like most people, said Tajar. Of course I wouldn't imagine he'll go very far. But then most people don't . . . anywhere, do they?

TWO

The first years of the Runner operation in Damascus were devoted to Halim establishing his export business. With his introductions from Syrian businessmen in Buenos Aires and his Swiss letters of credit, he had no difficulty putting together shipments of leather goods and obtaining export licenses. The shipments went off to Belgium and more orders came in.

Halim worked alone in his business, using the small hotel where he lived as his office. The hotel occupied the top floor of a large building off Martyrs' Square in the center of downtown Damascus. It was not yet a big city but it was growing rapidly, in confusion, and private flats and commercial and government offices tended to be all crowded together in the same buildings. Construction was haphazard after the Second World War and new Damascus was as much a hodgepodge as the old. Halim's building was typical with shops and coffeehouses on the ground floor, the offices of dentists and lawyers and small businesses and municipal departments on the two floors above that, then three floors of apartments where families lived, with the hotel on the top floor.

The same two creaking cage-lifts serviced all the floors, so every manner of person could be found coming in and out of the building. The lifts were at the end of a cavernous entrance hall, poorly lit, and people tended to slink through this near-darkness like fugitives, no matter how confidently they entered from the bright sunlight. Far back in the gloom an elderly guard reigned from his perch on a high stool. The guard wore a vague khaki uniform and was armed with a Mauser, a huge antique rifle from the time of the Ottoman Turks. The rifle was merely ceremonial: a shiny brass plug with a red tassel was fitted into the end of the barrel. But this was the guard's undisputed domain and here he ruled with the ill-humor of a stranded Tatar horseman, gruffly directing a band of ragged urchins who fetched coffee and ran errands for the offices upstairs.

Only Syrians stayed at the hotel. The bedrooms were comfortable, even spacious, and a few were occupied by old women who lived there permanently and spoke French more often than Arabic. But most of the guests were men from the provinces with business to do in the capital, or people visiting relatives. The polite deskmen were careful with messages, and the younger bartenders were ready to provide discreet information on women and gold and hashish.

Halim often worked on one of the balconies outside the public rooms of the hotel, where he could do his correspondence and bookkeeping while looking down on courtyards with palm trees and banks of flowers, a low red-tiled roof somewhere among them. The streets near Martyrs' Square were always noisy and crowded but there were also grand old houses with overgrown gardens hidden away between the newer buildings, and the balconies of Halim's hotel offered a glimpse of these graceful memories of an older Damascus.

Ziad pretended to find Halim's living arrangements insufferably bourgeois. Secretly, though, he liked the peaceful comfort of the hotel, exotically named the Brittany, which was far removed from the hectic coffeehouse scheming he lived in so much of the time. Halim would still be at work when Ziad arrived at the end of the afternoon. Ziad would poke his head through the beaded curtain separating the barroom from the balcony and announce himself, then settle into a leather armchair and order Scotch. Ziad loved Scotch but he could never afford to buy it. Here it went on Halim's bill. The bar was a sedate room with wood paneling and potted plants and a ceiling fan. There were also free bowls of peanuts. Ziad sat in splendor with his French newspaper open on his lap, watching the sinking sun through the windows and feeling himself a man of the world.

A second bowl of peanuts arrived with Ziad's second Scotch. By then Halim was gathering up his paperwork and soon it was time for them to go out and roam the city, to visit coffeehouses and meet people and take long walks, ending up at some restaurant Ziad knew.

On other evenings Halim generally ate in the hotel dining room. It was astonishing how many friends he made there in a short time, men of different backgrounds from different parts of Syria. In many ways, Tajar had told Yossi, your first year in Damascus will decide everything. People get an idea of someone and it lasts.

Halim was aware how Ziad's company enhanced his own position with other people. Ziad's futile self-display in public, so desperate and awkward and shrill, could only emphasize Halim's more thoughtful manner. Ziad had to pretend to understand every subject and would make any claim, while Halim never talked about something he didn't know. So the contrast between the two of them was striking, and Halim seemed all the more inviting and worthy of confidence because of Ziad's boisterous antics.

In the beginning Yossi deeply felt the dangers of Damascus. Keeping watch and informing on others, after all, was the traditional free entertainment of the city. In a casual or venomous manner, people idly repeated scurrilous news as a way of passing the time while they waited for something more interesting to happen, much as they also split sunflower seeds with their teeth and spit out the shells around them as they walked or tarried . . . *By the by, have you heard? . . . did you know? . . . his mother . . . her grandfather . . . that one . . . yesterday . . . the last time. . . .*

This commonplace pastime was a way to enact a private revenge on life, to defend against personal inadequacy and unkind fortune, a neverending litany on the weaknesses and misfortunes of others which hovered between simple gossip and outright slander. Imagined petty intrigues were slipped into any conversation, if for no other reason than to show that the speaker was clever and suspicious. Spite and jealousy and politics were pervasive and demanded constant attention. Rumors had to be tested and insinuations passed along, for how else could they be verified? It was part of the social fabric for everyone to inform on everyone else, and beyond these routine habits lurked the professionals, the plainclothes policemen and the innumerable agents who were employed by the various security services.

Yossi was only fifty miles from Beirut, where he could meet Tajar. He was only a hundred and thirty-five miles from Jerusalem itself. Yet he often felt farther away from Tajar than he had in Argentina. After the vast expanses of South America, he found it strange to readjust to these tiny distances separating people and enemies in the Middle East.

So Yossi was intensely aware how alone he was, cut off with no one to turn to. Every confidence he made in the hotel dining room or in the offices where he did business, every step he took on the path to becoming Halim, only made his isolation clearer to him. His life was profoundly remote and there was no relief from solitude. At first this aloneness was hard to bear and he often confided in Ziad, revealing his fears and loneliness as a stranger—not as Yossi of course but as Halim, an immigrant from faraway Argentina, absent from Syria since the age of three. As for Ziad, he was more than sympathetic. In fact he loved this intimacy and was eager to understand Halim's feelings, which were exactly what he had always yearned to experience in life and knew he never would, an aspect of his own secret dreams of adventure, of breaking away from the confines he had been born to and going to live in a foreign land.

A concern, an understanding which was always generous and genuine—this was Ziad's gift to Halim in the beginning, and certainly for Yossi the gift was far from small. Yossi was aware someone else might have done as much for him when he first arrived in Damascus, some other friend he might have made during that early, crucial period. But the fact remained it was his little friend Ziad who listened to him and shared his feelings when he was vulnerable, before he began to acquire confidence in his status as Halim.

◆◆◆◆◆◆◆◆

Shesh-besh caused the first great change in Halim's life in Damascus. The game was newly popular in Europe when he began exporting tables, and they became an enormous success. Other companies soon entered the market, but by then Yossi had already made enough money to recompense the Mossad for all the costs of the Runner operation to date.

Tajar was astounded when he read the Runner's financial reports. He smiled and hummed to himself. Intelligence operations never made money. They either spent it or lost it. The Runner was unique in many ways but of course no one would ever know it except Tajar and the director of the Mossad.

In Damascus, Halim's manufacturers were ecstatic with their share of the profits. The tale of Halim's shesh-besh triumph in Europe crept into the coffeehouses, and Halim's reputation as a shrewd businessman was assured. Halim rented offices on a lower floor of his hotel building and hired a clerk and a bookkeeper. He began to look for a permanent place to live. The government fell and the influence of the Baath Party increased, particularly in the army. Through Ziad, Halim became friendly with the arrogant nephew of the new army chief-of-staff.

They're Druse and therefore the uncle can never be president, confided Ziad. That makes it a safe appointment, unthreatening to the older political parties. But the uncle is known to lean toward the Baath, and this shows how our strength is growing. Another year or two and we'll have it all. . . .

Ziad's *we* was the Baath. His interest in the party had suddenly revived now that it was moving closer to power.

Halim's shesh-besh success gave him a reputation as a marketing genius with the right contacts in Europe. Businessmen approached him with proposals and he studied the projects carefully before investing his time and money. He was thorough and hardworking and honest. He favored partnerships and was exactly the kind of man anyone would want for a partner. He liked the idea of developing import schemes to balance his export trade. He also showed a flair for practical engineering projects. Once he had even thought of becoming an engineer, he admitted.

And then with a shy smile: If we could choose whatever we wanted in the world I suppose I would have been an inventor in the early nineteenth century, in Europe or America, one of those cranks who tinkered around in his workshop and found a practical solution to something real, on his own.

Halim had this conversation with a businessman he had befriended a few years previously at the hotel. The man owned a well-established machinery company which had begun to slip. Together they worked out an ambitious partnership. Halim would invest capital for new imports and be responsible for marketing and development. His partner would continue to run the firm and be in charge of its service and repair operations. Halim redirected the company into air-conditioning, which was soon making money. He also developed a special capability in exhaust systems, first for plants and then for trucks. They repaired army trucks and went on to the more complicated systems of armored personnel carriers. The basic equipment was Russian and not the best, nor had it been designed for Syrian conditions. Sand got into everything.

With his machinists, Halim worked out modifications for the intake and exhaust systems. The new parts were tooled in the company's shops and worked well when installed. They made still more improvements when army transport officers took Halim and a master machinist into the field to check performance on the spot.

But that was only one of Halim's many projects during those years. He was always busy and worked long hours. He now had a manager running his central enterprise, his export-import office, and was generally involved in two or three other business ventures as a partner, in addition to the machinery company. His work took him back and forth through Syria, frequently to Beirut and sometimes to Europe. He also went to Jordan to visit the Palestinian refugee camps there, a humanitarian problem that had begun to concern him.

Still, he was careful to stay out of politics in Damascus, which he could do as a businessman who had come from Argentina and was unencumbered by the usual intricate networks of past favors and loyalties and allegiances. Of course there was no question he was a patriot. He had returned to Syria for that very reason. And everyone knew his sympathies were with the progressive policies of the Baath, the party of social reform and nationalism. His friends suspected he might take a more public role when enough time had passed for him to feel firmly established. He might not, but that was the usual way with businessmen who owed their success to hard work and caution.

Although he had little time to enjoy it, Halim was obviously very fond of the house he had found for himself. It was one of those old Damascus villas he had always admired, with rustling palm trees and an overgrown garden tucked away between newer buildings, a relic from a more leisurely era. The house itself wasn't so large and much of it was given over to wholly useless verandahs with broad stone steps to nowhere, which must have once commanded a view. The villa had been on the outskirts of Damascus when it was built and now it was well within the city, but the grounds and the trees and walls still gave the house a great sense of privacy. Halim could walk to his office and did so every day, strolling briskly along tree-lined streets and greeting dozens of people on the different routes he followed to vary his walks. Because Damascus was growing so rapidly, squalor stood next to luxury and Halim passed through many kinds of neighborhoods.

Ziad wasn't surprised at the sort of house his friend had chosen. Since their days on the hotel balcony he had expected Halim would eventually live in one of these crumbling old villas, hidden away behind high walls and crowded in among ancient fruit trees. Ziad knew his friend would take no notice of the primitive electrical wiring and water pipes which ran along the walls inside the rooms. Naturally it was the tangled garden that would enchant Halim, with its disused fountains and broken, discolored statues. The statues were half as old as Damascus itself, relics of the Greek and Roman and Byzantine periods, worn both white and black by two millennia of rain and sun. How many gardens have they stood in? mused Halim. How many eras have they calmly watched come and go?

Of course, *tradition*, Ziad said, laughing. It takes a man from the wide open spaces of the New World to appreciate such a romantic ruin of a house. What does it matter that it has leaky roofs and bad plumbing and huge drafty rooms which are impossible to heat in the winter? The garden alone justifies all. Here Aristotle can contemplate the bust of Homer and marvel at the poet's blind stone eyes and wonder whither time marches . . . yes?

There was another government coup. Tanks rumbled through downtown Damascus and this time the Baath seized power outright. The more outrageous land speculators were arrested, allowing this sure means of instant wealth to slip into other hands, perhaps those closer to the new educated classes and the army. The general who had been the Syrian military attaché in Buenos Aires became the new president. Halim sent flowers to his former shesh-besh partner, congratulating him, and became a guest at presidential receptions. Ziad was able to find a job for himself in the ministry of information, the most substantial position he had ever held.

Halim began entertaining in his home and Ziad turned up with his new friends, mostly Baath army officers. Ziad also brought along women to these evenings. With the ways of regular journalism now behind him and no longer a source of income, with his success now dependent upon army officers, he had come up with a new service for those in power—pandering. Always pathetically unsuccessful himself with women, he now found he could enjoy their company on the strength of the important men he would introduce them to. Slightly hysterical and already a little drunk, he appeared at Halim's door early in the evening with a woman on each arm, and rushed off to try to gather up a few more who might or might not be waiting for him. Then he gulped Scotch and spent the rest of the evening flitting around Halim's living room, refilling glasses and telling raucous anecdotes.

Halim himself acted as a quiet host at these gatherings, in keeping with his more reserved manner. While Ziad chattered noisily from group to group, Halim was apt to be in conversation with someone off to the side.

Most of the women brought along by Ziad were secretaries from government ministries, but occasionally he captured a more glamorous prize. One evening he turned up with a popular singer, a vivacious and ambitious young woman. Halim introduced her to a colonel and took the two of them for a stroll in his garden, applying all his charm to making the encounter a success. For the colonel, who was the new commander of the paratroop brigade on the Golan Heights, that evening in the shadows of Halim's garden was the beginning of a passionate love affair with the singer, and he always felt warmly toward Halim for bringing her into his life.

There were also other kinds of friendships for Halim. The austere minister of information, educated in Paris and the leading intellectual of the Baathist regime, was a man of a different sort. Halim met him through Ziad but thereafter they got together without Ziad, the better to discuss Latin American politics and pursue the minister's scheme, first suggested by Halim, of securing financial support for the Baath from the Syrian community in Buenos Aires. Halim wrote letters to Argentina and collected some funds for the minister. But as the minister said, the amount of money wasn't as important as the principle of Syrians overseas taking part in the rejuvenation of their ancient homeland.

◆◆◆◆◆◆◆◆

Halim was busy, always busy. The machinery company in which he was a partner had been given a contract to improve the ventilation systems of bunkers on the Golan Heights, which accommodated armored vehicles as well as artillery and tank crews, a whole complicated series of connecting underground fortresses. Each bunker was different and presented a slightly different set of ventilation problems. Halim worked on the diagrams with his master machinists, making modifications and finding practical solutions.

For his central office Halim still used the suite of rooms he had acquired originally in the large building off Martyrs' Square, the building with the hotel on the top floor. Now he had to find space in the suite to work on these ventilation schemes. The only free area was the seating arrangement at the end of his own room, where a company director normally sat with his guests over coffee. Halim moved the overstuffed chairs to his manager's office and put in draftsman's tables and lighting fixtures and banks of deep flat cupboards with dozens of drawers to hold the blueprints and diagrams. When his partner came by and found Halim and the master machinists pouring over their papers, he joked that Halim's room looked more like a crowded architect's den than a successful businessman's office.

It was crowded and there were papers everywhere, but nothing was done by chance in the Runner's life. The entrance to Halim's offices lay at the end of one of the two corridors that ran the length of the building on each floor. The elevators opened between the first and the second corridors. In the second corridor was the room with toilets and sinks for the smaller offices on the floor which were without toilets of their own. The entrance to Halim's offices was in the first corridor, but his rooms extended to the blank wall of the second corridor. And the far end of his own room, now crowded with draftsman's cupboards and tables, backed exactly against the wall where the toilet stalls were.

In redesigning the room the Runner had done some special work of his own. If he set the screws in the back of one of his cupboards in a certain way, a man in the second corridor could enter the toilets and lock himself in the last stall, unfasten a panel in the back wall and another panel in Halim's wall, and reach through into Halim's cupboard—to remove the cardboard cylinder that had been placed there for him. The panel in the toilet stall could conceivably have been opened by chance, but if that happened it would have revealed nothing. The next panel through Halim's wall, giving access to Halim's cupboard, couldn't be discerned. Nor could that second panel be opened accidently, since only a correct combination of screw turns on Halim's side allowed it to open.

There was risk involved. No dead drop was ideal when bulk material had to be transferred frequently. Either the Runner repeatedly carried compromising material on his person to some neutral location in Damascus, or the dead drop had to be adjacent to his office. Tajar felt the lesser risk was for the Runner never to have the compromising maps and diagrams on his person. Better for the couriers to bear that danger and make it their main concern. The arrangement also freed the Runner to be only Halim when he moved around Damascus, a subtle and important consideration to Tajar's mind. Thus setting the screws at the back of the office cupboard was Yossi's task. And later when Halim walked out of the office he could simply be himself, a man who carried nothing he need fear.

Risk was inherent for the Runner, but Tajar knew the risk was lessened the more Halim could be Halim. In any case, Tajar expected the dead drop to be in use for only a limited period of time. The underground fortresses on the Golan were extensive, but not infinite.

So there were intricate risks and dangers in the Runner's progress, and precise precautions and continual readjustments. To Ziad as to anyone else who knew him in Damascus, Halim's early steps in the Syrian capital had always seemed to follow naturally and easily one upon the other: where he lived and where he worked, the hotel on the top floor and then the offices on a lower floor of the same building, the villa out of the center of town, the way his life and business came to be what they were. But behind it all were the careful decisions of a master planner.

◆◆◆◆◆◆◆◆

Hectic, busy years for the Runner then, and soon there were to be many changes around him because the Middle East was slipping toward the Six-Day War, that utterly disastrous defeat for the Arabs. God was said to have created the world in six days and rested on the seventh, and certainly the 1967 war completely reworked the destiny of the Middle East in only six days. But it did so with a secret promise of years of brutal struggle instead of a seventh day of peace. Ziad lost his job and added espionage to his list of failures. After the war, the young nephew of the former army chief-of-staff lapsed back into the obscurity of his Druse village. The minister of information, more fortunate than many, went into exile as the Syrian ambassador in Paris. And the paratroop colonel took part in a failed coup attempt and then escaped to Baghdad, only to reenter Damascus clandestinely with the help of Iraqi agents, disguised as an old peasant woman, to be immediately arrested and tried and shot, all within twenty-four hours.

Yet for Halim looking back, those times before the Six-Day

War were the good years, the years of building and moving forward, before chance and skill changed the maps of fate so drastically. Tajar used to tell Yossi that the identity of Halim would come over him very gradually in Damascus. Before the Six-Day War this seemed to be so to Yossi, and the two aspects of his life never met. Yossi and Halim remained separate people. They had different tasks and different lives, different emotions and different sensibilities, in keeping with the controlled schizophrenia of a deep-cover agent. Halim's life was decided by circumstances outside himself, by the background Tajar had constructed for him, and by the ways business and society worked in Damascus. Halim's life was subtly aggressive. Exploiting opportunity was the purpose of it. And Halim could do this without second thoughts because the justification for it lay elsewhere. The Runner operation justified what Halim did.

Yossi's life, on the other hand, was minutely prescribed. There were exact instructions for everything Yossi did, particularly after the fortifications on the Golan Heights became the goal of the Runner operation. Tajar's back-up team was responsible for moving the Runner's material, and Yossi didn't know these men for security reasons. Halim crossed paths with hundreds of people each day, all kinds of people in all kinds of places. His life was arranged that way on purpose. The disguised and coded messages between Tajar and the Runner might be embedded between the outer and inner cardboard layers of what looked like a common cigarette box, discarded and crushed and empty, its bottom torn open so that it would be of no use even to a child or a tramp. The crushed cigarette box was put in a certain place, and elsewhere a commonplace mark was made at a certain place on a wall or a tree, by Halim or by a member of the back-up team, explaining exactly what had been done. The cupboard transfer for bulk material remained the same at Halim's office, but coded messages back and forth were always kept separate from that.

Tajar continually revised these procedures, always striving for naturalness and simplicity. When he met Yossi in Beirut, an important part of their time together was devoted to reviewing Halim's movements and contacts, so Tajar would have the knowledge to work out safe new methods connecting the Runner and his back-up team.

Thus Yossi's work was rigid and inflexible. It was mechanical, outwardly complex but demanding nothing of his inner self. Yossi was neither aggressive nor opportunistic. He didn't exploit people or situations. That kind of activity belonged to Halim's sphere. Yossi as a person, a former paratrooper who had gone on to more specialized training, had no need to question anything. His objective was clear: the high ground of the Golan. The Runner operation as a whole—Halim, Yossi, the communication and transport systems maintained by the back-up team—worked as a machine run by Tajar. In fact Tajar did more than run the machine. In effect, he was the machine.

All that changed with the Six-Day War. It took some time for Yossi to realize it, but the comfortable schizophrenia of his several lives irrevocably came to an end with that war, which had seemed to be his and Israel's greatest triumph. Thereafter he had no choice but to become Halim, a man who was as much a Syrian in his complex way as Ziad.

THREE

Damascus was appalled by the magnitude of the Six Day defeat. Overnight the Runner operation became completely inactive. Halim retreated into the quietest of his business enterprises and saw as few people as possible, like everyone else. The danger grew as shock gave way to recrimination and bloodletting in the government, in the Baath and the army. Yossi, hidden away inside of Halim, suddenly had a great deal of time to roam through his house and garden. He was joined by Ziad, who was out of work and in need of drink. Ziad came to spend long summer evenings alone with him in the old villa. Together they sat for hours in heavy thronelike chairs on Halim's broad empty verandahs, above the wide stone stairs leading down to nowhere, their thoughts drifting in the shadows as they imagined the open fields and caravan processions which were no longer there in the distance.

Defeat—brutal, overwhelming, ignominious—caused Ziad to look back over his life that summer. He became obsessed with the past and often recalled the stirring visions and noble causes of his student days, all sadly come to nothing.

Yossi also looked back over his life that summer, though in a much different way. The news of Assaf's wounds from the war troubled him far more than he was able to admit to himself at first. The fact that Assaf had come so close to death destroyed the exhilaration Yossi might have felt over Israel's victory and his own contribution to it. To be suddenly inactive after years of hectic effort might have brought a letdown in any case, but added to this depression was a profound sense of remorse.

There was nothing he could do for Assaf. There was no way he could ease Assaf's pain or comfort him, no way he could even see him. This caused a terrible sense of inadequacy in Yossi, and the fact that he understood his situation so clearly did nothing to lessen his bleak mood of uselessness. He felt he had betrayed Assaf and the betrayal brought him intense pain. Even the house he was trapped in was all at once painful.

Yossi's house in Damascus was very much like Anna's house in Jerusalem, at least in its interiors. Tajar had described the Jerusalem house to him and of course the similarity wasn't surprising. The stone houses on Ethiopia Street had been built by the Nashashibi family, one of the important Arab clans of Jerusalem under the Turks and the British. When various branches of the family had gotten together and erected an enclave of connecting homes and courtyards early in the century, they had followed accepted custom and built their houses in the Damascus style: a large central room with high ceilings of painted wood arranged in geometric designs, tall recessed windows and wrought-iron doors opening onto courtyards or balconies, the smaller rooms for sleeping all giving off this central gathering place for the family, with the kitchen and pantries and storerooms tucked away out of sight at the end of a long corridor. As an arrangement of space it was the typical old-fashioned design for a large Arab family of means. The spaciousness of the central room and its painted wooden ceilings, in particular, were what signified the Damascus style during the Ottoman era.

Thus the apartment where Assaf had grown up in Jerusalem was almost a replica of Yossi's house in Damascus. The grounds were different and Yossi's house was single-storied. But when Yossi wandered through the great central room of his old villa, he sometimes had a haunting premonition that

Assaf was there somewhere, lying wounded in a bed behind one of the doors, waiting for Yossi to find him. The sensation came to Yossi without warning, a sharp rush of excitement as fleeting as it was irrational. Restless and pacing, his thoughts on some practical matter, he would chance to glance up at the orderly patterns of the ceiling and all at once feel a presence near him, a special significance to one of the doors. . . . Was Assaf in there?

The feeling was so strong he might turn toward the door or even take a step in that direction. But then the truth would strike him like a blow and crush his heart in a moment of unspeakable anguish, a pain far worse than any he had ever known. He realized it was his own guilt that was torturing him in this cruel way, but he could do nothing to evade the torment. Yet it was also true that he only had this experience when he was alone and could think of himself as Yossi. It never happened in the company of someone else, not even Ziad. Tajar's training of Yossi had been so profound that even these powerful bursts of emotion were overruled by Halim's unshakable discipline.

So Halim's safety and solitude remained intact, but there was an inevitable price to be paid for it. In a matter of months Yossi's hair turned mostly white. It was also during this period that his face came to have the lean carved look of a permanent desert traveler, and his eyes acquired that startling penetrating quality which Tajar found so mesmerizing when they met again in Beirut after a separation of several years. By then the Runner's transformation was so complete that Halim's radiant smile was the only outward sign to remind Tajar of the eager young man he had sat with on the shores of the Mediterranean near the Negev a decade and a half ago, and there revealed his dream of an extraordinary clandestine operation they would build together, and an adventurous new life for Yossi which would be uniquely devoted to the purest of ideals.

As for the Runner, he was simply trying to survive in his innermost being, and what surprised him most was how remote his old self now seemed. He found himself recalling Yossi as he might recall a childhood friend. He knew every detail about the life of this other person, but it was all a memory from another world. Yossi's hopes, Yossi's fears . . . they were simply no longer his. Halim understood disguises, and the lean new face he saw in the mirror, with its deep-set eyes and white hair, meant little to him. It was the inner changes that astonished him as Yossi slipped away into the past.

The steps of survival were always so small, it seemed to the Runner. Yet how vast was the sad finality of these changes he was witnessing.

◆◆◆◆◆◆◆◆

Through the long quiet evenings they shared on Halim's dark verandahs that summer, Ziad mistook his friend's distant mood for the gloom of defeat pervading Damascus. Ziad had lost his job at the ministry even before the war broke out, a casual victim of one of those periodic shuffles that accompanied minor weekend intrigues in the army. Some pro-Egyptian officers had been arrested, some people fired. Ziad was caught having coffee on the wrong side of the corridor one morning.

He was disappointed, but he knew after the war he would have lost his job anyway. Important men were being arrested and jailed, and Ziad wasn't even important. People used him. He ran errands. Now he was doing part-time work for several newspapers. The only real friend he had was Halim, who treated him as an equal. With Halim there was never any need for him to hide and to play the buffoon. He could always reveal his fears and be himself, because of the bond between them. He wasn't used to such good fortune in life and never ceased to be amazed by it, and grateful for this place he had in Halim's heart.

But then Halim wasn't like other people. Halim had grown up in Argentina and chose to live in a crumbling villa from another era. He recalled grand tales of a mythical Damascus and dreamed of being a Syrian and an Arab, which meant he actually believed there were such things. To Ziad these were abstract concepts, unconnected to reality and meaningless in the end. Reality to Ziad was the nexus of family and tribe and chance, and money and skill and religious sect, which determined a man's place in the souk. There were many little souks and the one great souk that included them all—Damascus—which for thousands of years had been the chief place of a satrapy or province or border state often called Syria, sometimes Greek or Roman or Persian or Turkish or Mongolian, sometimes Moslem or Christian or pagan, a meeting place for caravans, a way-station for conquering armies from Europe or Asia or the vast hinterlands of the deserts. This abstraction was what Halim liked to think of as his homeland, Syria. And to Ziad, *Arab* had even less meaning than that. To him it was a term as vague as *Latin American.*

You know it means nothing, he said to Halim. What does an Amazon Indian hunting in the jungle with a blowgun have in common with a stiff Chilean of German descent tending vineyards on the slopes of the Andes? You had no trouble understanding that over there. Why pretend it's any different here?

Halim only smiled in answer to Ziad's arguments. Of course it was true Halim had visionary aspects to him, undeniable touches of the mystic. Halim even believed in the cause of the Palestinians, who were merely a tool to everyone else, a convenient source of manpower to be drawn on for private wars. So astute and practical in business affairs, Halim had this strange other side to him when it came to viewing the politics of men, an ability to disregard the everyday facts of life and find an ultimate faith in human destiny. Ziad couldn't fathom the paradox. He knew the world didn't work the way his friend envisioned it, but he was still fascinated by Halim's faith. Halim was a dreamer and Ziad couldn't help but love him for that.

But above all, it was Halim's acceptance *of him* that affected

Ziad most deeply. Life for Ziad was a hard, perpetual performance of skill and trickery and dissembling, a desperate and neverending attempt at false bravado. He utterly lacked Halim's charm and easy way with people. It wasn't that he meant to harm himself with his awkward behavior. He wasn't perverse. He simply had a clumsy touch with others and couldn't avoid the feeling that he was sinking in life, without ever having had a chance to rise. He felt out of place in almost any situation. Inevitably his feelings betrayed him and then he was out of place.

Only with Halim was it different. Halim's presence reassured him. When they were alone together he truly felt calm inside himself, as if blessed, because Halim accepted him as he was. This seemed nothing less than a miracle to Ziad, a gift from heaven.

In fact he often thought of his friend in exactly those words. For me, he said to himself, Halim *is* a gift from heaven.

◆◆◆◆◆◆◆◆

As the months passed Halim began to devote more of his time and money to helping his Palestinian friends. Again the Runner was busy, reporting on Palestinian activities.

In Damascus it was a time of instability and uncertainty. Halim's former friend, the minister of information, was brought back from Paris and sent to jail for life. A younger cousin of the ex-minister, who had become the head of a Baathist intelligence agency while still in his early thirties, committed suicide by jumping out an office window in the defense ministry, or was murdered. A fierce struggle developed between the civilian and military wings of the Baath, with Iraqi agents and pro-Egyptian elements active against each other. Protection money from Saudi Arabia and the Gulf oil states, beyond the regular subsidies, was available to those who knew how to extort it. In this turmoil Syria practically closed its borders to Westerners. Even influential Syrians rarely traveled beyond Beirut. King Hussein of Jordan, in danger of losing control of his country to the PLO, went to war against the PLO militias and drove them out of Jordan into Lebanon. Syrian tanks invaded Jordan but drew back when Israel warned of war and Saudi Arabia warned of a cut in money.

It was a serious failure for the Syrian army, which had been acting under the influence of the civilian cadres of the Baath. The Syrian defense minister, a career army man, seized power and made himself president, which was a victory for the military wing of the Baath. But more important, the new man was the son of peasants and from the minority Alawites, a poorer Moslem sect which was traditionally scorned and oppressed by the majority Sunnis. Further, it turned out that the new president was not merely the head of another coalition of officers. He ruled alone, something no Syrian had done in centuries. His first act was to arrest his mentor in the Baath, the former president, and have him sentenced to life imprisonment in a notorious desert dungeon.

Ziad was cynical and excited.

An Alawite as president? he said to Halim. An inconceivable thing, it's never happened before. People will see him as representing all those who have always been wronged, which is naturally most of the country. So now we have a real *presidente*, our very own Perón to be the father of the shirtless ones, but far cleverer in the ways of the souk and not a banana dictator. Oh no, a genuine Levantine leader who knows how to scheme and cut throats. A despised Alawite? An ex-peasant whose first act is to turn on the man who made him? Despised minorities produce patient, angry men, and people will love him for that kind of treachery. Secretly, it's what they all dream of. And this ex-peasant even had the foresight to change his name to *Lion* as a young man. The king of the beasts as our dictator? It's apt. It fits. Maybe he'll even be strong enough to get back our land from the Israelis. Dominate or be dominated? Anyone who is different is inferior? This Alawite knows how it is. He has to. He *is* an Alawite, after all.

Ziad was also enthusiastic because once again he sensed a new future for himself. A new government meant new loyalties. A dictator meant new kinds of opportunities. And a dictator from a minority sect which was despised by most Moslems meant there was suddenly a chance for little men, failed men, to rise in society.

◆◆◆◆◆◆◆◆

Ziad found his new life—in espionage. He was hired by one of the new men, a captain in Syrian intelligence whose agency ran a Palestinian militia which was establishing itself in southern Lebanon, after having been expelled from Jordan. The new Syrian government was continuing the old government's policy of not mounting operations against Israel from Syria itself, to avoid reprisals. With Jordan now closed to the PLO militias, the Syrian secret services were redirecting their money and arms into Lebanon.

The intelligence agency Ziad worked for was one of a dozen secret services maintained by the Syrians. These secret services were independent of each other in their budgets and tasks and authority. All of them kept their own files, controlled their own agents, and pursued the goals set for them by the man at the top of their organization, who might be a major or a colonel, a minister or the president. Some of the intelligence agencies were much larger than others, with those run by the army and the defense ministry being the largest of all. But size didn't necessarily signify importance. An agency employing many thousands might not be as influential, at a given time, as a much more secret organization with only a few dozen key agents. These intelligence agencies operated out of the defense ministry, the foreign ministry, the interior ministry, the army, the Baath, the president's office—all the centers of power in Syria.

The agencies were seldom separated into the usual spheres of intelligence: foreign or domestic, espionage or counterespionage. Most of them worked both sides of any question, since friends and enemies abroad were as crucial to the power center in Syria as friends and enemies at home. Nor were the military and political functions separate, since there was no strength in one without the other. The military agencies also had political targets, and the civilian agencies also worked in the army.

Some of the Syrian intelligence agencies had more specialized interests. The Baath Party in Syria had long run an intelligence agency devoted solely to Iraq, where a Baathist party was also in power. This civilian service concentrated on manipulating and subverting Baathists of consequence in Baghdad, under the guise of fraternal relations with like-minded comrades, while countering the constant subversion by Iraqi Baathists in Damascus.

Egypt, as the largest Arab country, was another special case. In the past Syria had been briefly controlled by Egypt in a political union, and there were still pro-Egyptian officers in the intelligence agencies run by the army and the defense ministry. But the intelligence agencies run by the interior ministry were fervently anti-Egyptian. Jordan, as a neighbor, was the province of the secret services run by the army and the foreign ministry. Liaison with the KGB was ostensibly handled by a secret service in the foreign ministry and another in the defense ministry, but in fact a second defense ministry agency was deeply involved.

As a matter of course most Syrian intelligence agencies tried to penetrate each other, or at least have a source in the others with access to some of the files. This was done most aggressively by the secret services run by the Baath—its civilian wing, its military wing—which planted men wherever it could in addition to its regular counterintelligence service, which it ran as a counterweight to the counterintelligence service run by the interior ministry.

Secret money from Saudi Arabia and the Gulf oil states, an important source of funds for covert operations, was another special case and was channeled through the secret services of the defense ministry. But other agencies could acquire it for selected targets, or if they had the right connections. In one way or another all the Syrian secret services operated in Lebanon and all of them used Palestinians. In the Middle East, Beirut was the meeting place for the agents of every secret service, not just those of Syria, and the Palestinians were the foot soldiers and mercenaries who ran the errands.

A gigantic Mafia-style operation was the way Tajar described Beirut. Lebanon, he said, is gangsterism on a scale the world has never even imagined before.

Lastly in Damascus, there were the small secret services run directly by the president's office, the most special case of all. In the past these highly clandestine services had never been involved in field operations. Their job was to keep the president informed on the other agencies, even though in order to get where he was the president would already have been in control of some combination of the army and defense ministry intelligence agencies, and more recently those of the Baath as well.

These competing secret services in Damascus were always in the process of splitting apart and swallowing each other as fortune changed and a new group or new individuals gained power at the expense of others. The agencies sprang up, disappeared, completely altered their targets and size and influence. Sub-departments drifted away over a weekend to find a new home in another agency, or were liquidated, or suddenly became independent in another ministry on the other side of town. Even the most stable among them—the military intelligence agencies—radically shifted in importance as power accrued in some army field command or was pulled back into the central offices of the defense ministry. What was astonishing was that the total number of secret services in Syria—twelve—remained constant and had done so since the end of the Second World War, when the French left.

This devious confusion bewildered the Syrians as much as anyone, but fortunately for the Runner there was an expert who understood the Syrian intelligence services far better than most Syrians did, certainly far better than any other non-Syrian. That man of course was Tajar, for decades the Mossad's wizard on arcane Arab lore of any kind.

It's the magic number twelve that has always puzzled me, Tajar once said to Yossi. No other country in the world has half that many intelligence agencies, but the Syrians *always* do. Why? It's curious. Why have all these fellows tripping over each other? The Russians get along with just one or two. The Americans, who like free enterprise and competition, allow for three or four. And all other countries, even the most untrusting and paranoid, make do with no more than that. But not the Syrians. The Syrians insist on a dozen of the monsters. What a headache. How can they keep track of anything? The cost, the duplication, the inefficiency—it's simply staggering. From time to time one of the Syrian agencies gets greedy and gobbles up three or four of the others, and you think some sense is in the air, some logic, the powerful are doing what you expect the powerful to do. But what happens? A few months go by and three or four new agencies have suddenly oozed their way into being, mysteriously squeezing in from the sidelines somewhere. It's extraordinary and I've never been able to explain it adequately. It's some kind of natural law of Syrian secret services, an archetypal infatuation with chaos, a passionate embrace of ultimate *suspicion.* Perhaps it's a state of mind that comes with centuries of having your destiny in the hands of foreigners. Of course the Italians and Greeks have these tendencies in a minor way, so some of it may be simply Mediterranean anarchy: the sun beats down, the skies are always fair, one can't help but imagine real things must be going on around the corner and undercover and out of sight. . . . But no matter. When it comes to sheer *distrust,* no one in the world compares to the Syrians. It's their unique contribution, on the order of the pyramids of Egypt. Like the pyramids, their distrust is monumental. As for the natural law and the magic number, that practice may have gotten started eight hundred years ago when Salah al-din was riding out of Damascus, leading the

Moslem forces against the Crusaders and throwing the foreign devils out of the Middle East bit by bit. We all know he was a great general who managed for a time to get all the Moslems behind him, but as a Kurd he must have had his doubts.

About? Yossi had asked, and Tajar had nodded, laughing.

My point exactly, Tajar had replied. About everything and everyone, I suspect. That's why he was such a great and glorious general and such a successful leader, because he *did* have so many doubts. So many, in fact, that he knew one intelligence agency wouldn't do the job. Not even three or four would do the job. He had too many elements to contend with in his own forces, so he conceived the idea of a dozen secret services to keep a balance to things. And perhaps that memory became deeply embedded in the Syrian psyche eight hundred years ago and has been there ever since: for success, no less than twelve will do, like a country with its tribes. . . . Why not, Yossi? It's as reasonable an explanation as any other. Because it just makes no sense that a country should *always* have a dozen intelligence agencies when the powerful ones are continually gobbling up the less powerful ones. Surely from any rational point of view, it's incomprehensible. . . .

Oddly, as if to substantiate Tajar's quaint theory, the new man Ziad called *el presidente,* Syria's first dictator in centuries, didn't change the system. What he did do was have all of Syria's twelve intelligence agencies report directly to him—something that had never happened before, or at least not since the time of Salah al-din, as mythically described by Tajar.

FOUR

After a lifetime in the poverty and Moslem austerity of Damascus, Beirut was a new world for Ziad. The bars and nightclubs where rich Arabs from the oil countries came to escape the puritanism at home, the luxurious shops and hotels and the blond women from northern Europe, the hashish and money and sex and alcohol which were everywhere, the cheerful avarice and blatant intrigue, the ever-changing parade of Europeans and other foreigners seeking quick profit from the sheiks and oil millionaires on holiday—it was all a lurid fantasy of material and erotic plenty, ripe with decadence.

And Ziad loved to think of himself as a spy. He found it immensely exhilarating to have a clandestine purpose and to be passing himself off as a foreign correspondent in Beirut. Now that he was a secret agent embarked on mysterious international missions, who could say what might follow? Perhaps these trips to Lebanon, he mused with Halim, were only the beginning of much greater opportunities. Perhaps they might even lead to a career in Europe, in Paris?

In fact Ziad was merely a low-level courier. Using his newspaper work as cover for his forays, he carried money and directives to the Palestinian militia in southern Lebanon controlled by his captain's agency. He left Damascus early in the morning, sharing an oversized taxi with six other passengers, strangers, Syrians and Palestinians with business to do in Beirut. The passengers were all nonchalantly puffing cigarettes and pretending not to look at each other, Ziad smoking as many cigarettes as anyone. In appearance the group was as ordinary as any band of messengers and thugs setting out for a day's work in Lebanon. The elongated Mercedes became an impenetrable cocoon of smoke as Ziad huddled in one of the jump seats, safe in the middle of the car with a noncommittal smile on his face. They raced across the valleys and down the mountains, scattering goats and peasants and donkeys, horn blaring without letup, hurtling toward the glittering skyline of Beirut rising high above the Mediterranean.

From Beirut Ziad slipped off south by buses and taxis to the refugee camps in the south, returning by the same route with sealed envelopes for his captain in Damascus. Often he slept in the camps. When he was lucky he managed a night or two in Beirut, staying at some cheap hotel which doubled as a brothel.

His captain had given him a briefcase with a false bottom, which he was very proud of. In this false bottom he carried the money and directives in sealed envelopes. He had been told never to let the briefcase out of his sight and therefore took it with him when he went out in the evening to prowl Beirut's bars and nightclubs. In order to stretch his meager pocket money, he did his serious drinking at the open-air stands for laborers which were to be found in any alley. There he would throw off tumblers of cheap arak, then chew mints to mask the smell of arak on his breath as he wandered deeper into the night, examining the photographs on display by red-leather doors and savoring the florid promises of extravagant floor shows, the special acts of obscenity direct from Sweden and Holland and Germany, listening in evil-smelling alleys to the whispered offers of smooth-faced boys and giant glistening black women from the Sudan, knowing that somewhere behind one of these grimy doorways the ritual of a French *circus* was taking place—a small amphitheater heavy with peculiar animal odors and the smoke of hashish, the narrow wooden benches in utter darkness above a sawdust-covered pit lit by bright lights, deafening music pounding the fetid air, two sweaty handlers in the pit, a male donkey between them with a rag tied over its face, the beast in a frenzy and bucking wildly because the mask over its eyes and nostrils gave off the pungent scent of a mare in heat, and beneath the donkey a slovenly fat woman insensate from drugs, heaving in the harness that held her.

And then finding his own place at last behind a red-leather door, his private little corner in some nightclub for the evening, a stool in a dim crowded room where he could lean on the bar when he felt dizzy and sniff his single Scotch and have a clear view of the floor show, of the blond women moaning with their snakes and cucumbers in the harsh white glare of the spotlight, then squatting on the fringes of darkness to suck up thick phallic rolls of money from outstretched, straddled hands, the wandering pink and blue searchlights of the room playing over his face and catching his eager smile in garish half-tones . . . an adventurer ready for the world, ready for anything.

To Ziad these private evenings of isolation in the alleys of Beirut were a baroque fugue of sin, a dream of wickedness far removed from the pathetic sexuality he had known his whole life: alone in his barren, wretched room at night, furtively pouring over magazines of naked women as his right hand churned and his mind danced through a phantasmagoria of human parts. Yet it wasn't that he couldn't have wanted more than pornography from sex. Sometimes he did imagine more when he saw a romantic French film in Beirut. It was just that sexual reality for him was always reduced to pornography by the harsh ways of his society, by the strict separation of men and women and the primal fears of his religion.

He did a minor trade in Swiss watches, smuggling one or two at a time into Syria in the false bottom of his briefcase, along with the sealed envelopes. One night in Beirut, drunker than he realized and made forgetful by the enchanting pink and blue lights, he left his briefcase in a bar. The moment he awoke the next morning with a shattering headache, he knew what had happened. He vomited in the sink of his sordid hotel room and rushed through town to the bar, where a cleaning man knew nothing. Miserable and sick, Ziad sat in the foyer until a man in a suit finally showed up at noon and retrieved the briefcase from a cupboard, which also revealed a shoe and a cane and a soiled address book, the lost-and-found remnants from the previous evening of glory. Ziad tipped the man outrageously and rushed back to his hotel room to examine the false bottom of the briefcase. It hadn't been opened. One of his hairs was still pasted across the secret opening inside—a trick he had learned from a spy movie. He was ecstatic and celebrated by getting drunk in an alley behind the hotel.

Ziad was absurdly enthusiastic over his new role and had to tell Halim all about it. He told Halim far more than he should have and Halim was seriously concerned for his friend's safety, both with his employer and in Lebanon itself. Ziad didn't seem to realize that along with its freedom and glitter, Beirut was a city of real danger. The bars of Beirut were not the same as the coffeehouses of Damascus, which Ziad had grown up with and understood intuitively. Life could be dangerous in Damascus, but Syria was also ruled. Only those in authority could kill people. The dangers of Beirut, with its gangsterism, were totally different.

Halim was worried by his friend's reckless behavior. He felt he had to caution Ziad. Halim knew Beirut well from the export-import business he had done there over the years, and he knew a briefcase carried into bars and alleys at night could be mistaken for something worth stealing, a delivery of drugs or foreign currency. There were safe places to store baggage —lockers with keys in public places. Thus under the guise of warning his friend in a practical way, the Runner now found himself in the odd position of training Ziad in some of the fundamentals of his new job in Syrian espionage.

Fortunately for Halim, there was never any question of the Runner having to use what he learned from Ziad. Ziad's kind of low-level information was readily available to the Mossad in Lebanon. The Runner operated at a much higher level, using as sources the well-placed Palestinians whom he had befriended years ago in the refugee camps of Jordan.

⧫⧫⧫⧫⧫⧫⧫⧫

The KGB began to find Damascus a hazardous place from which to direct the PLO agents of its terrorist campaign in Europe. The Syrians ran so many Palestinian groups of their own, for so many different purposes, that the Russians were finding it impossible to maintain security among *their* Palestinians. The Syrian intelligence agencies routinely penetrated each other, and although the KGB's use of the PLO wasn't a target for them, information on the KGB's operations invariably slipped out. To regain security, the KGB moved the headquarters for its European terrorist campaign to the island of Cyprus. There, the internal conflict was between Greeks and Turks and the KGB could exert greater control over its Palestinian agents flying in and out of Europe.

Unhappily, it means the Runner is going to have much less to tell us about airplane hijackings and other things, Tajar said to General Ben-Zvi, the director of the Mossad. But I suppose it was inevitable that the Russians should learn their lesson like everyone else. Having the Syrians as allies is one thing, but working out of Damascus is another. As the Egyptians used to say, quoting their brothers the Iraqis, who had it from their brothers the Jordanians, who borrowed the saying from their brothers the Palestinians, who were repeating an old proverb of their brothers the Lebanese: With brothers like the Syrians, who needs? . . .

Led by Sadat of Egypt, the October war of 1973 was launched against Israel. Syria's tank brigades fought well on the Golan Heights and briefly it looked as if they might win back the territory taken by Israel in the Six-Day War. But Israeli air power was too sophisticated for the Syrians and their army was beaten with dreadful losses. Once more Ziad came to sit through long evenings with Halim on his friend's broad empty verandahs, above the overgrown gardens where the villa's solitary broken statues could be glimpsed among the trees and hanging vines, elegaic guardians of lost memories.

Ziad was especially gloomy. It's hopeless, he said. I was sure we were at least going to break even this time. But no matter how well we fight, we lose anyway. The Russians give us last year's weapons in abundance, but the Americans give the Israelis next year's weapons and there's no comparison. Courage has nothing to do with it. Technology decides the outcome and we can never fight them as equals. If we did we might win, and who knows, maybe even the Russians don't want that. What's the point of it all? We're simply used as murderous toys. . . .

As after the previous war, the Russians rearmed the Syrians with improved weaponry and the Americans rearmed the Israelis accordingly. In matters of electronic guidance for shells and missiles and bombs, and counterelectronic systems to overrule them, nothing could compare to tests under actual battlefield conditions.

More then ever Beirut flourished as the Middle Eastern entrepôt for pleasure and money and arms and drugs, the convenient meeting place for everyone with something or someone to buy or to rent or to sell. The oil embargoes had arrived with the October war and oil became the great black weapon of the world as the price shot up. The industrial nations of Europe scrambled to strike covert deals with the sheiks of the desert. Enormous sums were to be made by entrepreneurs at every level. Western banks and corporations came to Beirut to help the oil princes dispose of their stupendous new wealth. And everyone in Beirut had to be serviced: the bankers and sheiks and corporations, the myriad business representatives from every country with oil or in need of oil, the arms dealers and smugglers, the drug merchants from Africa and the West, the intelligence agencies from all the countries of the Middle East, the intelligence agencies from the major countries of Eastern and Western Europe, and the biggest players of all with their spy satellites roaming the heavens—the KGB and the CIA.

Plots and schemes and *trade.* This for that in Beirut, with a cut for the smiling industrious people who provided the sun and the waterskiing, the seaside hotels and the dark back alleys, the appropriate setting for any transaction.

Trade in every guise had been the vocation of the Lebanese coast since the time of the Phoenicians, five thousand years ago. The temples of true believers had always been elsewhere, beside the Nile and the Tigris and the Euphrates and in Jerusalem and Damascus.

◆◆◆◆◆◆◆◆

It was almost a surprise for Halim to realize how great a distance the Runner had traveled in the last years. A pattern had settled over his business enterprises and he no longer had to concern himself much about them, now that he wasn't trying to start up in new fields. The same earnest manager still ran his office in the building that had the Hotel Brittany on the top floor. The man had been with him more than a decade and they were old friends. Halim seldom had to interfere with his decisions.

In addition to his export-import business, Halim was generally involved in two or three partnerships which turned some profit. He wasn't wealthy but he was successful for a Syrian. He gave part of his income to charity as would any worthy Moslem in his position. The Runner's back-up team was Tajar's expense, but the Runner himself cost the Mossad nothing. In any case the back-up team was smaller than it had been before the Six-Day War, when the Runner was concentrating on tactical intelligence and moving a great deal of material, quickly. The cupboard-toilet dead drop was almost never used anymore.

Halim still rose early and walked to work for the exercise,

taking different routes to vary the scenery. By now he knew hundreds of people along the way, familiar faces from over the years who greeted him and passed along the neighborhood news, sold him his cigarettes and newspaper, inveigled him to pause for a Turkish coffee. When he entered the lobby of his office building, the Tatar horseman on guard there solemnly raised his antique Mauser rifle with the red tassel at its end, in the morning ritual of salute. Halim conferred with his manager and dropped in on his bookkeepers, always a pleasantly nostalgic pastime for the boy hidden away in him who had once done bookkeeping.

At least once a week he rode the creaky cage-lift up to the top floor to have coffee in the hotel lounge and visit with his old friends who still worked there. He went out and walked to appointments in downtown Damascus, then met a business acquaintance for lunch near Martyrs' Square or by the river. He took a taxi home after lunch and observed the siesta hours, unplugging his phone and resting or reading until late afternoon, when he was known to be at home to visitors. He carried the phone out to the gathering of chairs beneath his fig tree, and there people came and went.

Halim welcomed them all, his Syrian friends, his Palestinian friends. He listened and advised and helped when he could. His friends knew where to find him and came around the house through the garden, after first calling and setting a time. Halim boiled Turkish coffee for every guest and later set up a table with drinks beneath the fig tree. It was a comfortable setting, relaxed and private. Occasionally he went on to dinner with some of his visitors but returned home early to read and listen to music. Several times a week he met one of his women friends for dinner at a restaurant beside the Barada, but even then he was home early the next morning to change clothes and walk to the office. It was a single man's regular life of work and routine, friends and commonplace pleasures.

Life was also a nexus in the usual Arab fashion. His office manager was a cousin of the machinery company owner who had been his first business partner in Damascus, the man he had met over dinner in the Hotel Brittany. The owner had now retired from his company and been replaced by his son, whom Halim served as a senior business adviser. Halim had been given a place of honor in the son's wedding and was an unofficial uncle to his firstborn, a boy. Halim had also helped his manager by guaranteeing a loan for a new apartment. Halim's cleaning woman, who arrived in the morning and worked until he returned home in the early afternoon, was a poor relation of the manager's wife from a village in the north. And so it went, with obligation and loyalty tightly connected in the usual manner of a traditional society.

The pain Yossi used to feel over Assaf was hardly there anymore. Very slowly the torment had dimmed, the anguish receded. Halim still experienced it sometimes when he was alone in the garden, not in the house. But even then the feeling was remote, a memory rather than a physical sensation that suddenly gripped his chest and threatened to strangle his heart, as it once had done. Only the sadness afterward was the same, the immense longing he was left with when the spasm passed, an emptiness for what was gone.

As if in compensation for his loss, a small compensation but nonetheless real, he had come to love his old house again. Here he had suffered and survived his terrible anguish and now it was truly his home, his place in the world. He loved its crumbling grandeur and tangled gardens, its noble old-fashioned rooms with their great window-doors opening onto the verandahs. He felt safe and comfortable sitting beside the fire on rainy winter nights, listening to music, and never tired of wandering along the verandahs on warm evenings and gazing up at the stars. Israel seemed very far away to him now and more than ever a dream, an imagined place. It was *over there*, like Ziad's dream of Europe and Paris: a distant place and beautiful, a rare and certain treasure to be loved, to be cherished, pure as only an abstraction can be.

But there was never anything abstract about Tajar in his

thoughts. Tajar was also far away but Tajar was his dearest friend and more, his father and brother and keeper, the conscience of his finer self. He felt so close to Tajar that he often spoke of him in conversations with friends in Damascus, under the pretext of recalling the widower-cousin in Argentina who had given him his start in life. Naturally, this was most true with Ziad. It was curious but in some ways Ziad was more familiar with Tajar—under a different name, in a different time and place—than he was with almost anyone else in the world, save for Halim himself.

Halim had always hoped Anna would remarry, and his memories of her had an idyllic charm to them. The memories dwelled on the intensity of their lives at the little settlement in the Negev that was soon to fall. . . . Those few huts in the vastness of the desert. The still nights and glorious sunrises. The two of them together at the dawn of the world when hope and love had sparkled in the very grains of sand sifting through their fingers.

The women he knew now were loving in their way, but it could never be the same again because he wasn't the same. Now, the unfathomable joys and sadness of life were no longer still ahead of him.

Yet he had achieved what he always wanted. He had been determined to create his own life and that was exactly what he had done, with Tajar's help. Choice after choice, decision after decision, he had pushed on to create Halim, the Runner, himself—a long and arduous journey. And he was here in this house, and the accomplishment was unique. He knew that.

But there were also strange moments of indefinable power when Halim saw something else. On evenings when there was a moon and his overgrown garden came alive with shadows and eerie moonglow, he sometimes found himself gazing down from the verandahs and glimpsing ghosts among the trees. These were the broken, discolored statues he had inherited with his old house. The clearings that had once surrounded the solitary statues, like the paths that led to them, had long since been lost to vines and bushes and hanging branches. He knew they were no more than statues, and yet they would suddenly rise up to haunt him as images of the important people in his life—Anna, Assaf, Tajar, Ziad. . . . Each statue solemnly off by itself. An enduring stately presence in its own secret grove. A mystery standing alone in the moonlight.

There were so few of them, so few people in his life. But were there more in any man's life?

He wondered about that. He also wondered about the conceits of solitude. Because lately, as if to mock these illusions, another ghost had abruptly begun to appear in his garden at night.

Yes, Bell. That crooked, shattered, fate-blasted face . . . smiling in broken discolored marble. Of all the ghosts only Bell seemed to smile, and Halim found this oddly appealing. The idea intrigued and amused him at the same time because to his mind, the hermit of Jericho was the ultimate spirit of disguise. Who but God, after all, could ever create a mask as unworldly as Bell's face?

♦♦♦♦♦♦♦♦

Ziad continued to make his regular trips to the squalid refugee camps in southern Lebanon. The practical training given him by Halim was to bring him to the notice of his superiors, with unexpected results.

The Runner operation, through no fault of the Runner himself, entered a period of torpor which was vaguely troubling to Tajar. Before the 1973 war the Mossad was almost totally occupied with the international terrorist campaign of the PLO, so effectively financed and directed by the KGB. The director of the Mossad, General Ben-Zvi, spent all his time on it. When the KGB transferred control of the campaign from Damascus to Cyprus, Tajar and the Runner operation slipped in importance for a time. But that was to change.

Looking back later, Halim was able to see it all clearly

enough. Wars marked the great changes in the life of the Runner: the Six-Day War in June 1967, the Yom Kippur War in October 1973. Up until the June war he had lived as two people, as Yossi and Halim, with part of himself still in Israel and another part in Syria. From then until the October war he had gone through the painful process of learning to be but one man in Damascus—Halim. And thereafter came the third great shift in his career, which was to involve him so intimately with Lebanon.

Of course both Halim and Tajar had always known this third stage would come. It was only to be expected that sooner or later, one of the important Syrian intelligence agencies would make Halim an offer he couldn't refuse.

FIVE

Halim had come to know Bell at Tajar's suggestion, in order to add a different dimension of time to the Runner's life, as Tajar had said then, when Jericho was still part of Jordan. Yet Tajar didn't renew his own acquaintance with Bell when the opportunity came after the Six-Day War. The reason Tajar gave himself for this was professional. It was a matter of security. Assaf had become closely connected to the house in the orange grove in Jericho, through his friendship with the fugitive Yousef.

The excuse was plausible and even real, but it wasn't in Tajar's nature to fool himself, and he also knew how easily the demands of security could be adapted to personal needs. The secrecy of espionage wasn't always a mask presented to others. It could also be a mask to oneself, a hiding place, and in fact there were deeply personal reasons why Tajar hadn't gone to see Bell.

The most important was that Bell had once lived Tajar's kind of life but had gone on to choose a different path. Tajar was a little afraid of that. And then there was the fact that Bell had once been the grand master of espionage and Tajar the novitiate, long ago in the Monastery in Egypt. And finally, there were Anna's feelings for Bell.

So it was complicated and there were many subtle reasons why Tajar had put off his journey to Jericho. But the passage of the years changed that, especially the profound despair

Tajar felt after the Yom Kippur War. Suddenly delay and caution seemed futile. Why go on avoiding Bell? All at once it seemed a cowardly act of omission in facing himself. He decided to make his pilgrimage to Jericho and not surprisingly, the decision brought a kind of relief that lightened his heart.

◆◆◆◆◆◆◆◆

Everything having to do with Bell tended to be unique in Tajar's eyes, and he would never forget their first meeting after a lapse of thirty years. Tajar turned up at Bell's gate early one summer morning when it was likely Bell would be alone on his front porch. The iron gate creaked noisily under his hand. He took a deep breath and called out: *Anyone at home among God's oranges?*

The insects buzzed in the orange grove. Tajar imagined his feet being studied beneath the trees, from the porch. No, Bell wouldn't recognize these old shoes with the aluminum crutches planted beside them. A generous, welcoming voice came back: *But for the grace of God we are all strangers at a strange gate.*

And so it began. Tajar shuffled forward through the orange grove and there was Bell standing in front of his dilapidated chair, looking exactly as Tajar remembered him. With a face like that, a man didn't change. Tajar stopped in front of the porch, smiling broadly.

The last time we met was by the Nile, said Tajar. I learned a great deal from you then, but it's the student who remembers the teacher, isn't it? I had legs in those days and you took me for a walk in the desert to help me and calm me, because I was frightened. I was leaving on a mission that night which seemed very dangerous, and you said . . .

◆◆◆◆◆◆◆◆

Bell was pleased to see Tajar, who was surprised at how well Bell remembered him. When he had served under Bell during the Second World War, Tajar had been no one of any particular importance, merely another of those experts in disguise, the anonymous Monks, who were sent on long-range missions by Bell's secret organization hidden away in the desert near Cairo. Yet as soon as Bell placed him, which he did very quickly, the recollections came back at once.

Just as surprising, Bell seemed totally unconcerned that Tajar had turned up on his porch that morning. Without quite putting it in words, Tajar hinted that intelligence had become his career. Yet Bell seemed to accept his unexpected appearance as a commonplace event. For the hermit, apparently, all things were equally routine and fantastic. Bell was as relaxed as Tajar himself would have been at home in his hammock, contemplating his rosebushes.

They talked of many things, going back to the time when they had known each other three decades ago in Egypt.

And so you went on to do important work, said Bell. You must be very proud of that. It's a splendid way to spend one's life. If I'd had a cause such as yours ahead of me, the building of a homeland, my life would have been very different. But there was nothing so grand waiting for me at the end of the Second World War, in fact nothing grand at all. Quite the contrary. What lay ahead seemed petty and mean and narrow. The days of the British Empire were over and it was obvious they would be trying to withdraw with a measure of order, which meant fighting ugly little wars of retreat. I wanted no part of it. And because I'd been born in India and had never really lived in England, I suddenly found myself a man without a country. Permanent exile seemed to be all there was, so I ended up here.

Bell smiled in his strange twisted way.

Like all men I was born at the wrong time, he said. A mostly blind Argentine wrote that. It's miraculous to me what people see despite the darkness and anguish they live in. Mostly we hear the roar of the world but there are real tunes of glory and this land, more than most, has heard them. Perhaps that's why it has always been fought over. . . .

When he opened Bell's gate that morning Tajar still hadn't decided whether to mention Anna, which also meant speaking of Assaf. He had hoped the candor between Bell and himself would go that far, and now after only a few hours it seemed completely natural to speak of them. Bell was excited and pleased and showed it. How fortunate you are to have known her all these years, he said. Bell spoke of his fondness for Assaf, and then of the lost Yousef and the dead Ali. After that, he fell silent.

Better to say it? asked Tajar at last.

Oh yes, replied Bell. I was thinking of Anna. Of all my acts of cowardice and stupidity, none compares to that piece of folly. Once in Jerusalem I had the whole world within reach and I let it go, let her go, turned away. It was utterly inexcusable and I've never forgiven myself for it. Fools that we are, we learn everything too late. It seems unimaginable to me now. Why did I do it? How? But there are no answers to comfort a human heart, or to justify or explain it, and the tragedy is always the same. Love was there and *I* lost it, *I* turned away. Oh yes. . . .

The time came for Tajar to leave, the long morning of remembrance and renewal at an end. Bell walked with him to the gate.

My car is just down the way, said Tajar. I'll come again.

They embraced and Tajar began hobbling away. Bell leaned on the gate watching him go. The road was deserted in the midday heat and Tajar hadn't gone very far when a thought came to Bell.

That evening we walked in the desert, Bell called out. The time when you were leaving that night. Where were you going?

Tajar stopped and turned his head. To Syria, he called back. I was on my way to Damascus and it seemed very dangerous, but you pulled me through.

He waved a crutch in salute and hobbled on down the road, raising little puffs of dust with his crutches.

◆◆◆◆◆◆◆◆

Tajar drove slowly out of Jericho that day, working the special hand levers in his old car that made it possible for him to drive without legs. He went slowly because he was reluctant to leave the bright colors of the oasis, the splashes of purple bougainvillea and orange-red flamboyants, and to leave Bell and the house in the orange grove. He was thinking how aware Bell was of the advantages of his, Tajar's, life and what he had done with the years. Of course. Tajar had been busy in the world and his mark was deep on men's affairs. Yet it was human nature to miss what you lacked and Tajar couldn't help but think how appealing Bell's life seemed, with its solitude.

Tajar laughed at himself, at his own weakness for misgivings. If Bell had been in his place in life, Bell would have done exactly what he had done for the last thirty years. Tajar knew that for a fact. And if he had been Bell, well then naturally. . . .

All the same, it was fascinating how the dream could change.

He was thinking of his father and his father's father, those pious poor rabbis who had endured the squalor and oppression of Jerusalem under the Turks, men of profound longing for whom the Holy City on the mountain had always been an imaginary place, an unrealizable dream, much as it was for Bell, who had lost the great love of his life there. Yet for he who had been born in Jerusalem and lived there and had come to know it as the capital of his country—for Tajar—his imagination was now turning elsewhere, he found. Bell was the one who was in exile, seemingly in exile. He wasn't. And yet?

Tajar smiled at his musings that day. He shook his head and laughed as he busily pushed and pulled levers, driving his car without legs up the mountain. The road curved and he caught a last glimpse back at the plains of Jericho and the Dead Sea, and beyond them the hills of Moab where God had shown Moses the promised land which Moses could never enter.

Of course we learn everything too late, thought Tajar. Life, our Jericho crossing, our Jericho mosaic . . . there it is forever glimpsed from afar.

◆◆◆◆◆◆◆◆

After Tajar left, Bell stood lost in a reverie with the fierce sun beating down on him. What a splendid man he is, Bell kept thinking. What a grand life he has built for himself since we knew each other so long ago.

Bell, alone in retreat all these years, had only two or three friends for whom he counted, whereas Tajar, this hobbling and smiling cripple from the mountain, had tirelessly pursued his worthy cause and truly become a world to many people. Inevitably, thought Bell, a paucity of giving is the affliction of one who cuts himself off. But why have I done that? Why *have* I become a recluse?

He stood in the dense sunlight gazing at his porch, at the tattered chair and the old table with its worn dusty goods. All at once this shabby evidence of his days seemed a profoundly naked display, a pitiful collection of junk to be left behind one day as proof he had lived here. He crossed the porch and wandered through his rooms, aware there was almost nothing in them. They were so bare it was as if no one at all lived here, or at best some transient putting up for a night or two.

Bell felt exhausted, drained. He went out the back door and fled to his grape arbor to escape the waste of his life. This shabby emptiness . . . what was the use of it? Tajar had been so pleased to see him, but Tajar remembered another man who had gone by a different name in Egypt, a clever and determined man of great power, the secret leader of the Monastery whom Tajar recalled with respect . . . looking back.

But of course Bell wasn't that man anymore. Tajar was. It was Tajar who helped people to do more and be more, who gave back light from the darkness of the times, who smiled merrily and kicked up little puffs of dust on the difficult road to somewhere, while Bell lapsed ever deeper in his dream of a crumbling nowhere, a recluse in timeless Jericho, absorbed in the rhythms of the sun and the swelling hum and shade of his orange grove.

This house, this life, thought Bell. This unspeakable shabbiness . . . *it's appalling.*

In fact it was so appalling it made him smile. For even Bell was sometimes surprised at how far he had gone in creating his own world, where everything was in harmony with his being.

◆◆◆◆◆◆◆◆

When Abu Musa arrived late that afternoon for the daily shesh-besh session with Moses the Ethiopian, Bell was still sitting in the grape arbor, his round single eye a full stop in the question of the universe.

What's this? thought Abu Musa. Off by himself without even a large empty glass of arak in his twisted claw? Only the memory of a lost love in Jerusalem could keep our resident holy man from a drink at this time of day. Obviously he needs a jolt. Even a holy man can doubt himself.

Stealthily, Abu Musa went up on tiptoe. Bell was too absorbed to hear anything but he did sense a movement and all at once he saw Abu Musa's great noble head, dark-skinned and white-maned, gazing solemnly down at him from among the grapes at the end of the arbor. There was no body with the head. The foliage hid that. There was simply Abu Musa's huge serene face among the sun-streaked grapes, a magnificent vision of mankind adrift amidst nature's fruits.

My God, murmured Bell with a start.

I am black but comely, O ye daughters of Jerusalem, boomed the head. *Look not upon me that I am swarthy, that the sun hath tanned me.*

The head wagged roguishly and disappeared. Laughing and sighing and snorting all at once, Abu Musa came waddling into the arbor and settled his bulk on a bench. The quotation was from the *Song of Songs,* he said, good King Solomon's discourse on love and lovemaking. Moses had taught it to him and he particularly liked that phrase, *O ye daughters of Jerusalem,* because it suggested the sensual mysteries and flowering courtyards of a sumptuous harem. Solomon had had innumerable wives and concubines, he added, and surely it was a wise king who replenished his wisdom regularly in the heat of summer afternoons.

Bell smiled. In his roundabout way Abu Musa was reasserting his belief that nothing revived the spirit so well as love and lovemaking. But given Bell's status as a hermit and holy man, Abu Musa quickly moved on to his second-best solution for any problem, which was a tale. Abu Musa loved to tell stories and he now launched into a convoluted account of Crusader ruins in desolate places. According to him, the reason the Crusaders had lost out in the Holy Land was because of their underwear. Most of them had come from France and Germany and had insisted on wearing the same heavy sheepskin underwear they had used for the cold damp winters at home.

In the long summers we have here? asked Abu Musa. Tufts of sheepskin squeezed in under all that tight-fitting armor? Can we even begin to imagine the intolerable itching?

Abu Musa shuddered at his own description. Quickly he reached down to give his genitals a thoughtful scratch and realignment through the loose folds of his faded blue galabieh. In other words, he concluded, it's futile to bring your prejudices with you when you go in search of the Holy Land. That's not what *the land* is about.

Bell laughed. What is *the land* about then? he asked.

Abu Musa looked even more thoughtful. Dust and oranges? he replied. A dream of man's spirit freed at last from the fervor of fanaticism? Cool water and shade and the talk of friends at the end of the day? For a wise king, hot summer afternoons of love. And for a holy man, smiling on all this because it is right and good.

And yet nowhere in the world has there been more fervor

and fanaticism than here, said Bell. And why is that, when all great men of all religions have always preached otherwise?

Why? said Abu Musa. Because great men understand dust and oranges far better than the rest of us. Because they know man *is* dust and oranges. Because they know all the rest of it is simply the clatter and dice of a shesh-besh game, a run of chance and skill which we all play and refer to as life . . . clatter and dice, dice and clatter. So come now. Moses and the very finest chatter await us on your front porch, and you and I know a man is always in the right place when he's in Jericho. . . .

◆◆◆◆◆◆◆

That evening after the shesh-besh players left, Bell recalled the glorious vision of Abu Musa's smiling face among the sun-streaked grapes. Long ago, after the First World War, his war, Abu Musa had been briefly, joyously married. His happiness, and hers, had known no measure. His young wife had wanted to give him a son and she did, but she had died in childbirth and then a few years later the child had also died, so there was nothing. Over half a century ago. And all that time Abu Musa had honored the love in his heart with his gently lustful daydreaming, an inspiration for poetry and good humor and erotic tales, a memory to be embraced and treasured, the indomitable dream of an epic lover. Could one ever be sure, wondered Bell, who the real king was?

And again that night as so often, Bell thought of Yousef lost somewhere above Jericho in the vastness of the Judean wilderness. Oddly, it seemed to him, he also found himself thinking of a man he hadn't seen in some years, the mysterious adventurer from Damascus, Halim.

Why had Halim come to mind? Bell thought about it and decided it had to do with Tajar's unexpected visit. The connection seemed simple enough. The last time he had seen Tajar, three decades ago beside the Nile, Tajar had been leaving on a mission to Damascus. And as it happened Bell knew only one man in Damascus, Halim, the Arab patriot Yousef revered and had always wanted so much to meet.

Bell smiled to himself in the darkness of the grape arbor where he had gone once more to sit. Tajar, Halim, Yousef . . . why was he suddenly trying to make something of these associations? The connections were only in his own mind. Moreover, it had been years since he had thought this way. It was Monastery thinking, he knew, the mirrors and reflections of the secret world of intelligence which he had left behind long ago in Egypt, only briefly resurrected today because of the appearance of Tajar. For Tajar was still a traveler in that other world of secret knowledge and probably Halim was too, although Halim lived across the river on the other side of the Great Afro-Syrian Rift that ran through Jericho. Halim and Tajar were enemies, of course, in the implacable temporal struggle of Arab against Jew.

And Yousef? Also a traveler in another world, but one that was even more obscure and inaccessible than espionage—the stark, sun-blasted landscape of lunar chasms called the Judean wilderness, where his human soul could know no bounds or comfort at all. Ineffable was Yousef. A spirit lost to the regular ways of men.

Tajar, Halim, Yousef . . . Three totally different reflections of the fabled land where all great men had always preached freedom from fanaticism. It was Monastery thinking, but the more he thought about them the more he connected them in his imagination: a Jewish masterspy in Jerusalem, a Moslem patriot in Damascus, a Christian schoolteacher hiding in the caves of the Judean wilderness. Yet the connection had no reasonable basis. It was bizarre and arbitrary. With their conflicting dreams and journeys, what could three such men possibly share? How could they have anything in common, other than fate perhaps?

Other than fate. As if that were not enough.

Abruptly, Bell laughed at himself. Poor Tajar had merely

wanted to look up a piece of his past. That was the purpose of his visit to Jericho, and why was Bell now conjuring up mysteries around the poor fellow, imagining connections that didn't exist? Was it simply because he had failed to mention that he knew Halim, Tajar's enemy in Damascus?

I'm being as convoluted as Abu Musa, thought Bell. I'm thinking in some kind of Jericho time.

Bell stirred in the warm darkness and his gaze drifted up toward the stars. But *are* we finally all secret worlds? he wondered.

SIX

Colonel Jundi's offer was the most extraordinary among many that Halim had received over the years. Long ago Tajar had told Yossi that a measure of the operation's success would be the length of time the Runner could function in Damascus without being recruited by Syrian intelligence. That the Runner would eventually have to become a double agent was never in doubt. It was inevitable because the more successful he was as Halim, the more attractive he would be to Syrian intelligence. Their hope was to delay it as long as possible, so that Halim would be recruited by the Syrians at a higher level.

Tajar's task was to allow this strategy to continue to exist within the Mossad. Again and again he had to convince successive directors of the Mossad that it was right for the Runner to refuse opportunities which often appeared extremely inviting.

To do this, Tajar relied on his intimate knowledge of the way the Syrians disorganized intelligence—the perennial nature of their twelve secret services. Since the Syrians didn't have a paramount intelligence agency that was going to survive as an entity, argued Tajar, it wasn't worthwhile for the Runner to devote himself to one of them. If the Runner accepted a position with a Syrian agency the Mossad would benefit for a few years, but then the Runner's reputation would suffer with the next realignment of power in Damascus, where no one was more suspect than the intelligence agents of the last regime. The Runner's independence, his ability to maneuver and make friends among the new men, whoever they might be, was far more valuable to the Mossad than any short-term gain.

The argument made sense and Tajar was allowed to have his way. The closest he ever came to losing out was when the KGB established the headquarters for its European terrorist campaign in Damascus. The Mossad's need for immediate operational information, then, was so urgent that the long-term benefits of the Runner operation might well have been sacrificed to it, if the right offer had been made to the Runner at the time. But as it happened, the KGB found it impossible to run a secure campaign from Damascus and soon moved that headquarters to Cyprus.

From a personal point of view, Tajar couldn't help but be relieved. Once more it put off the time when the Runner would have to become a double agent, with all the complications that meant. For Tajar had never envisioned the Runner operation as merely a penetration of an Arab capital. To succeed in Tajar's terms the Runner had to be pure in his support of the Arab cause. He had to be a genuine idealist—what Tajar himself might have been if the history of the Middle East had taken a different course after the First World War, when Tajar had learned to run through the multiple cultures of Jerusalem as a boy. Of course Tajar never expressed his idea in this way to the directors of the Mossad. With them he used arguments based on the terms of espionage, which were also true. But the Runner himself had always understood it, and it was the special nature of this vision that had inspired Yossi from the very beginning.

It was never easy for Halim to turn down these offers from the competing secret services in Damascus. Nor was it just the Syrians who approached him. As his reputation grew among the Palestinians, his potential value was recognized by the intelligence agencies of other countries. In Beirut especially, where he went on routine business in connection with his export-import company, he often found himself having chance meetings and chance introductions which weren't what they appeared to be. The ruling Baathists of Iraq, ostensibly Syria's closest friends and in fact its most relentless enemies, were particularly eager to recruit him. The Iraqis were the most persistent but he was also approached by the Egyptian and French services, a Lebanese Christian faction, and the Iranians of the shah. And there was a tentative inquiry that Halim suspected came from the Mossad itself.

Tajar was greatly amused to hear of this last contact. He looked into it before his next meeting with Yossi near Beirut.

True enough, Tajar told Yossi. Suspicion confirmed. I ran my own little operation inside headquarters and it turns out this man who had his eye on you was actually on the Runner back-up team in the sixties. He didn't think there was a chance in the world that Halim would bite, but his boss was so impressed by Halim's reputation he thought an effort had to be made through that Lebanese who talked to you. A bizarre turnabout, but at least it shows the Runner's security is everything it should be. . . .

With his years of experience, the Runner saw these approaches coming long before an offer was made. What he couldn't always discern was whether the offer would be professional or personal. Syrian intelligence officers often engaged in smuggling and other illegal ways of making money, and Halim as a businessman who traveled was a natural target for their schemes. But Tajar had foreseen this and Halim kept strictly to his reputation as the incorruptible one, an eccentricity in Damascus and one of those odd characteristics that made Halim unusual. To his friends, it was part of the idealism that had brought him back from Argentina in the first place.

When the approach was professional, however, and a Syrian intelligence officer began by appealing to Halim's patriotism, his reaction had to be much more intricate and subtle. With great charm Halim set out to project that quality of vision, almost of naïveté, that Ziad had felt so strongly in the early days of their friendship. Halim spoke warmly of all the important causes and his enthusiasm was real, but he also seemed hopelessly impractical when it came to politics, a dreamer who couldn't grasp the everyday facts of life in the Middle East. Perhaps it was because he had grown up in Argentina and saw Syria differently, not really the way it was. In any case he drifted off into a nonexistent realm of airy concepts and futile abstractions, talking on about Arab unity and the Palestinian cause and the Syrian role in Arab brotherhood. The Syrian officer who had thought of recruiting him would soon be accepting Halim's unspoken claim that it was only bookkeeping and basic engineering that he understood in a practical way. Certainly Halim was a patriot, but he just wasn't suited for a clandestine role. He lacked a devious eye. He lacked cunning and the essential traits of espionage. In political matters he had faith instead of understanding, an innocence that was nearly childlike in its simplicity.

Finally, the Syrian officer had no choice but to arrive at the conclusion so skillfully prepared for him. Halim only looked as if he could be useful in espionage. In fact recruitment was out of the question. Halim was a mystic and such men were always unreliable as agents, although they could be fascinating in other ways. In the end the Syrian intelligence officer went away without an agent, but with an intriguing new friend.

◆◆◆◆◆◆◆◆

Colonel Jundi's offer was different because the times were different. The intelligence situation in Damascus had changed with the advent of the dictator, the man Ziad referred to as *el presidente.* There were still a dozen Syrian intelligence agencies continually shifting in size and influence, but now they all reported to the president, who used this system to absorb the energies of conflict beneath him. Ambitions were played out in intelligence rather than in open politics, and the agencies served to counterbalance each other's power.

Like the president, Colonel Jundi was from the minority Alawite sect. He was a former tank commander who had distinguished himself in the 1973 war. He ran one of the very small secret services that operated directly out of the president's office. His job was to keep watch over the internal affairs of all the Syrian secret services. To do this he used a small number of agents who reported directly to him, most of them professional employees of the various Syrian intelligence agencies, their connection to Colonel Jundi unknown within their own agencies. Colonel Jundi spied on the spies and it was the secret identity of his agents that gave him his power. He moved freely in government circles but was seldom seen at public functions. Naturally he was feared, but within the upper echelons of the intelligence agencies themselves, not in the army or the ministries at large where his true role was unsuspected. Even someone as experienced in gossip as Ziad thought Colonel Jundi was merely a minor military adviser attached to the president's office, an ex-hero with a sinecure. Another Alawite crony, Ziad called him.

Halim knew better. The dictator was far too clever to have less than a superior man in such a position. Halim had great respect for Colonel Jundi. He had met him several times but didn't know him well. His knowledge of Jundi's agency came from secondary sources and was inexact, more suggestive than anything else. Tajar had gotten into the habit of referring to Colonel Jundi as the inspector general of Syrian intelligence. It was an organizational term that a man inside might use, but Halim thought it was probably accurate. The fact that Halim knew so little about Jundi's work was itself an indication of the high caliber of the colonel's operation.

The setting Colonel Jundi chose for Halim's recruitment was as spectacular as the offer itself. Halim didn't keep a car in Damascus. Instead he walked and took taxis, part of the method of operation worked out long ago by Tajar. When Halim had business in Beirut he hired a car and driver for the fifty-mile trip. One autumn morning at the border crossing into Lebanon, a Syrian official asked Halim to step inside the customs shed. This was unusual but of course Halim went in. The official excused himself and Halim was left alone. A moment later a man in civilian dress appeared and presented identification showing he was a major in a Syrian security service. Politely, he asked Halim to accompany him. They went out a back door and Halim was ushered into an automobile with curtains over the rear windows. The major drove over bumpy roads for twenty minutes and deposited him at a small farmhouse high up on a hillside, with a magnificent view of the Bekaa Valley.

It was a simple stone house surrounded by olive trees. Standing in the doorway was Colonel Jundi, also in civilian clothes. He welcomed Halim and thanked him for coming, then led him through the house to a flagstone terrace overlooking the valley. The three of them seemed to have the little house to themselves. Halim and the colonel sat in rough wooden chairs on the terrace, facing west, while the major went off to make coffee. A mild autumn sun warmed their backs. The major brought coffee and retired inside the house. Halim was struck by the serenity of this perch above the peaceful valley, by the stillness and the sweeping beauty of the view. Goats' bells tinkled from some distant crevice in the hills. A thin line of smoke rose far away in the clear sky. The terrace was blissfully remote, rich with the smell of earth and sunshine. Colonel Jundi smiled, gesturing toward the valley.

Syria, he said. Our true boundary in that direction has always been the Mediterranean, since ancient times. Today we have these artificial creations of the West, Lebanon and Jordan and Palestine, these legacies born of British and French scheming at the end of the First World War when they carved up the Ottoman Empire to suit themselves. But though empires come and go, real countries remain. You know all this and you know it's time we set things right, and I think it's time you came to work for me. Now what do you say to that?

Colonel Jundi smiled affably and Halim was astounded. He

didn't know what to say. He stared at the colonel and then stared again at the view. There was a large bowl of purple-black grapes on the table, freshly washed and glistening with drops of water. The colonel plucked a grape and popped it into his mouth. He plucked another and went on munching, smiling at Halim as the sun cast its autumnal glow over the peaceful valley.

They ended up talking for several hours, finishing the grapes together. The colonel called for another bowl which they also ate, one at a time, each man popping a grape when he had a point to make. The colonel excused himself after his third cup of coffee and wandered away to relieve himself under an olive tree, still enjoying the view. Later Halim followed his example. Halim had begun with his usual reservations but Colonel Jundi waved them aside. He knew all about that. Halim's manner and reputation were exactly what the colonel needed. In effect, he wanted Halim to spend more time in Beirut and report on the activities of the various Syrian intelligence agencies in Lebanon. Some of this he said directly, much of it was only implied. Obviously the colonel had regular agents in Lebanon who provided him with specific information on specific subjects. What he wanted from Halim was far more personal: the judgment of an outsider. Halim had the right sort of work and character, the colonel felt, for the kind of assessment he wanted in Lebanon. Halim was known to have refused a number of offers in intelligence and his reputation among the Palestinians was unique. He would not be seen as someone from Syrian intelligence, least of all as Colonel Jundi's man. And that was the most important factor from Colonel Jundi's point of view. Halim was perfect for the role because he was so unlikely.

The colonel said he would give Halim only a minimum amount of training. Halim was to be himself. Above all it was Halim's status as a nonprofessional that made him valuable to the colonel, and the colonel didn't want to jeopardize that.

They would meet at the little farmhouse as they had met that morning, never in Damascus. The colonel would tell Halim what he wanted to know and Halim would report directly to the colonel. He wouldn't deal with anyone else. It wasn't all explained in exactly this way to the Runner, but as a professional he quickly grasped what the colonel had in mind. The Runner was to be the private informant in Lebanon of the inspector general of Syrian intelligence, with all the access that implied.

It was an offer that Halim the patriot couldn't refuse, an offer that the Runner could hardly have imagined. In a way it would do for the Runner operation in the seventies what exhaust systems for bunkers had done for it in the sixties.

Once more Tajar had a great deal of planning to do to adapt the Runner's new situation to the needs of the Mossad, to assure the operation's security, and to safeguard the Runner himself. It was difficult and Tajar was careful never to underestimate Colonel Jundi's abilities, but he was also confident that he and the Runner could make it work as it should.

Sometimes, it seemed to Tajar, idealism could indeed produce strange and wondrous results.

◆◆◆◆◆◆◆

Ziad also found himself with a new job in a different secret service. One weekend the captain he served moved over to another Syrian intelligence agency to work full time in the hashish trade. Since Ziad had proved himself competent as a courier, the captain took him along. Halim's careful warnings to his friend, in effect his training of Ziad for an undercover role, had favorably impressed Ziad's superiors.

Ziad was happy with his new job because it meant he no longer had to travel south of Beirut. He had learned to fear southern Lebanon, now the province of PLO militias and commonly known as Fatahland. Even as a Syrian and a courier for one of the Syrian military intelligence agencies, Ziad had felt the danger there.

Various Syrian intelligence agencies financed different PLO

factions. Other Syrian secret services were conduits for Arab oil money. Many Moslem and Christian factions of Lebanon ran their own operations in the south, either business or intelligence or both, sometimes separately but more often in conjunction with a PLO group. The Iraqi secret services were always busy. There were invisible border crossings between one group's territory and another, often in every village. Armed men jumped up at checkpoints and Ziad was stopped, interrogated, stopped again. He never knew whether he would get through with his briefcase with the false bottom. There were stories of hijackings and robberies, and all day long everyone was waving automatic weapons in the air or pointing them with bored, blank expressions.

At what? For whom? Many of the gunmen were no more than boys. They had thin black hairs on their upper lips. They hadn't begun to shave yet. Did they know what game they were playing? Did they care? Did they know who was giving them their orders that day, or why?

Ziad was used to guns, to army coups and tanks in the central squares of Damascus. But armed men to him meant uniformed soldiers marching in ranks. Discipline was brutal in the Syrian army. For that matter, discipline was brutal in all of Syria, a strict Moslem society with rigid rules of conduct, oppressive but orderly and regulated. To Ziad the anarchy of southern Lebanon was frightening. He couldn't stop shaking when he entered those villages where all the boys and young men were running around with guns. Obviously someone was paying them to do something, but he didn't know what it was. Everything about it terrified him.

So Ziad was overjoyed with his new job, his promotion as he called it. His talents had been recognized and he no longer had to stand in front of the boyish gunmen of Fatahland, humiliated and frightened as he looked down the barrels of automatic weapons. Now he lived like a civilized man, traveling to Beirut and sometimes on to the Christian areas of central Lebanon.

Hashish and a promotion—perhaps Europe and Paris would be next? As usual he confided the details of his work to Halim, who already knew the full scope of the venture he served. Hashish was Lebanon's leading export, a source of enormous illegal wealth. Lebanon supplied the huge Egyptian market and also shipped hashish to black Africa, to other Mediterranean countries and to Europe. Within Lebanon it was a vital political factor to many people. Even without Colonel Jundi's interest in the politics of hashish, Halim would have known all about the notorious new alliance that had just been set up between Syria and Lebanon.

The dictator in Damascus wasn't himself corrupt in a personal way, but he had a younger brother who was. At the core of loyalty was family, even more important than clan or religious sect. The dictator thus allowed his younger brother to maneuver and accrue power in his own right, if he were clever enough to do so. The younger brother had begun close to home. First he organized special army battalions in Damascus to protect the dictator, a palace guard. The special units were under his personal control and all the officers were Alawites, former peasants like him and the dictator, men who owed their good fortune in life entirely to him. After that the younger brother naturally wanted to have his own secret service. To finance it and to have independent funds for other enterprises in the future, he struck up a hashish alliance with one of the leading Maronite Christian families of Lebanon. With the protection and influence of the Syrian dictator's younger brother, the Maronite clan's position would be greatly strengthened to control more of the hashish trade out of Lebanon. The younger brother's specific partner in this alliance was an ambitious and sophisticated Maronite who was about his age, also in his middle thirties: the oldest son of the Lebanese president.

Ziad's boss, the captain, was now employed in the hashish department of the younger brother's intelligence agency. And Ziad, far down the line, was still a courier who traveled to Beirut with sealed envelopes in the false bottom of his briefcase. But now he met well-groomed young Maronite men in expensive hotels, rather than gun-waving Palestinian boys in poor villages. Using Halim among others, Colonel Jundi kept track of the alliance at the top, watching it as carefully as he watched everything else in Lebanon.

As for Halim, he couldn't help but feel sad when Ziad spoke of his new life. His friend was always so eager, so excited as he paced up and down describing it all to Halim, and what made it so terrible was Ziad's absolute conviction that this was actually a promotion, that he was finally being rewarded by life.

Ziad described himself sitting in an expensive café on Beirut's seafront, waiting for a contact who would give him his instructions. It was a sunny winter day and the Mediterranean glistened beside him. Everyone was smiling and laughing, the men in their Italian silks and French tailoring. Exquisite women walked by, breathtaking in their beauty. Gleaming automobiles drew up, their doors opened by driver-bodyguards. On the table before him was a real cappuccino, a real croissant, lovely delicate china. He was holding a copy of *Le Monde*, bought crisp and new in a hotel lobby, and it was all an idyll of true grandeur. Here at last was the great world. Here were taste and comfort and beauty, the very magic of his dreams.

And one scene above all. One small heartbreaking moment that touched Halim so deeply he could never recall it without feeling that tears were coming to his eyes.

It was a glimpse of Ziad in the evening, sitting alone in the lounge of one of those splendid hotels by the sea, one whole side of the room an immense window showing the lights on the Mediterranean at night, the little ships in the distance, the moon. There was laughter and music. A stringed orchestra was playing and people were dancing, smiling at each other. Near Ziad a party was going on, a birthday celebration for an elegant white-haired woman who wore jewels. A handsome young man rose and asked her to dance. It was her son. Everyone in the party cheered and applauded as the son escorted his mother out to the dance floor. They danced slowly, gracefully, and soon all eyes were upon them, for they must have been known to the people of Beirut. In the corner Ziad sat gripping his Scotch and staring in wonder and awe, sweating in his ancient winter suit, hardly able to breathe.

It was so *beautiful,* he said to Halim. That room with the lights on the water behind them, the soft music and the proud way he held her and the proud way she danced, the love and joy in their eyes, this elegant woman and her handsome son. . . .

It was snowing in Damascus the night Ziad described that scene to Halim. They had gone downtown to a favorite neighborhood restaurant, a small place which was all but deserted because of the weather, and after dinner they walked along the river as they always did when they went there. It was cold and no one was out by the river. The paths were new and white, without a footprint, the city unusually quiet under the snowfall. Suddenly Ziad turned and clutched Halim's hand.

Don't you see? he said. I know you've worked hard for what you have in life, but you've also succeeded. People respect you. People admire you. You've built a place for yourself in the world and I don't have that. Other than you, no one will ever care that I've lived. For years and years it doesn't seem to matter too much. You just go on and that seems all right. But then later it does matter and you begin to realize how alone you are, how you have almost no one, and it's frightening. Most of us don't want to be just alone in the end. I know you manage that way but you're different. Most of us aren't like you. Solitude terrifies me. So that's why this is a chance for me. What does it matter if it's an illusion? I know what I look like sitting in one of those cafés in Beirut. I look the way I always look anywhere—ridiculous and awkward and out of place. But even an illusion is better than nothing. *Anything* is better than nothing. . . .

SEVEN

Beirut is the flashy whore of the Middle East, said Tajar, with a hundred major pimps and a thousand major customers. The pimps are armed like Barbary pirates and every one of the customers lusts after a different menu of earthly and spiritual delights. In such a situation you have to expect some kind of trouble. . . .

The gangsters and militias of Beirut began their civil war in a desultory way, about three decades after the French put together a famous ancient coastline and a string of mountains and called it the country of Lebanon. According to the National Covenant, the Lebanese Christians still controlled the government in the middle 1970s, although they were no longer the majority community. Their main partners in power were still the Sunni Moslems, although the poorer Shiites were now the majority Moslem sect. The Druse were in the mountains and the Shiites were in the south, which was controlled by Palestinian militias. Even before the Palestinians arrived there had been eleven major communities. Beyond religion were clan politics and commerce and clan warfare, honor and profit and hatred and fear, and refugees from every lost cause in the Middle East. There were also the agents of dozens of foreign intelligence agencies, all of them spending money and some of them making as much as oil princes.

Beirut was a flashy playground but without much respect beyond the seas. When the Lebanese president came to New

York in 1974, to present the Palestinian cause at the United Nations, his luggage was sniffed for hashish at Kennedy Airport. The Lebanese president was outraged, but it was his son back home who maintained the grand hashish alliance with the Syrian dictator's younger brother.

The Lebanese Christian militias had names like the Tigers and the Giants and the Phalange. In those days they bought their arms in the Soviet bloc, from Bulgaria. Their swaggering gunmen wore large wooden crosses around their necks and had decals of the Virgin Mary on their rifle stocks. They were mostly Maronites, an ancient Eastern church that derives its name from a Syrian hermit and holy man of the fifth century. They also bought arms from Palestinians who wanted to make money. The Palestinian militias were receiving their arms from Iraq and Saudi Arabia and Libya and Syria. The Lebanese Christians felt threatened by the Palestinians, who felt threatened by the Christians and aligned themselves with the Lebanese Moslems.

The fighting began in the poorer neighborhoods of Beirut in the spring of 1975. There was looting in the souks, which spilled over into residential areas. The battle of the hotels began that autumn. Each side occupied the upper floors of luxury hotels on the shorefront and fired artillery and rockets crosstown. Streams of brilliant red tracers lit the night sky over the city. During the day the firing stopped and the coastal highways were crowded with cars as people rushed back and forth to do business. There were truces at the end of the month so people could get to banks and cash their paychecks.

Pauses in the fighting were also a useful time for taking hostages. Armed gangs set up makeshift roadblocks and checked identity cards, which listed religion. Hostages were merely a new kind of money in Beirut. They were barter goods like animal skins in a frontier region. If valuable they could be sold outright, if commonplace they could be swapped by lot. Sorting out the money by identity card was easy. Moslem gangs took Christian prisoners, Christian gangs took Moslems.

It was the end of the appearance of central authority and the beginning of rule by militia. Hatred and fear were now as important as money. The Christians tied prisoners to automobiles and dragged them through their mountain villages while children cheered, until the bodies fell apart. In their areas the Palestinians extracted information by cutting up prisoners with blowtorches and welding irons, a part at a time.

Still, there was business to be done in the new disorder and both sides quickly got down to it. The Palestinians went to work robbing the main banks, which were in their sector of Beirut, and the Christians pillaged the port, which was in theirs.

Eleven major banks were emptied. What every gang was after was the vault where the safe-deposit boxes were kept. Palestinian groups controlled by different Syrian secret services fought gun battles with each other in the streets for the right to break into the different banks. At first they tried to dynamite their way into the vaults, but they didn't know enough about it, so underworld professionals were flown in from Europe to do the job. The Christian militias, meanwhile, pillaged the port of its goods, most of which were subsequently shipped off to be sold in Iraq—with more profits for innumerable middlemen.

These stupendous robberies cost very little life. Killing and profit weren't always connected in Beirut. But outside the city it was a time of massacres, of women and children machine-gunned in villages—Christians by Palestinians and Moslems, Palestinians and Moslems by Christians. In Beirut everyone hurried through the streets and alleys carrying cheap cardboard suitcases, trying to escape somewhere with something. In the Levantine manner, both sides claimed every defeat was a victory and every atrocity an act of heroism.

The Syrian dictator was a fierce enemy of the PLO leadership. He had been helping the Christians but still the Christians were losing. Lebanon was disintegrating and no one in the Middle East wanted Palestinians and Moslem leftists to take over the country, at least no one with money or military power that counted, not the Saudis who heavily subsidized the Palestinians, and not the Syrians or the Israelis.

It was time for a peacekeeping force. The Syrian dictator offered his good offices. An arrangement was made through the Arab League and two Syrian army divisions were sent into Lebanon in 1976, to save the Christians and put down the Palestinians.

Halim's respect for the dictator's maneuvering had greatly increased since he had gone to work for Colonel Jundi in Lebanon. As Halim said to Tajar: Only a very clever mongoose actually gets invited into the pit to keep order among the snakes.

◆◆◆◆◆◆◆◆

In fact Halim was horrified by the savagery of Lebanon. He talked about it with Tajar when they met near Beirut. He talked about it far too often with Ziad in Damascus. He even talked about it with Colonel Jundi at their frequent meetings in the little stone farmhouse overlooking the Bekaa valley. Halim had always thought he knew about war and death and brutality. He had learned about killing as a young man, and since then there had been years and more years to live with the reasons offered up to explain it by wise men, by cynical men, by commonplace frightened men.

He knew it was mostly meaningless. Grand causes were generally the cover: patriotism, family and tribe, honor. Or very personal causes: patriotism, family and tribe, honor. But even war at its purest, war in the desert—two groups of men who agreed to be soldiers and went off to hunt each other like animals through the wastes—even then most men were suddenly dead to no purpose, forever struggling up the wrong hill when the bullet came, or crouching terrified in a hole somewhere and gazing sadly at their left boot, their right boot, lost in a vast unspeakable loneliness at the moment the shell struck.

All that he knew. But the vicious chaos of Lebanon? These cruelties a thousand times a day? This boundless hatred and fear and self-destruction?

◆◆◆◆◆◆◆◆

In Damascus, in the great central room of Halim's crumbling old house, Ziad stood in front of the fire with his hands out, trying to warm himself and quell his shivering. It was another winter, a year after they had taken their long somber walk in the snow beside the river. Gone now were Ziad's illusions of Beirut, the city of soft music and dancing and gentle laughter, of beautiful lights playing in the night on a Mediterranean harbor of sunsets. The heavy armor of Syrian tanks had brought a ceasefire of sorts to the Lebanese civil war, but what was gone was gone and there was no hope of peace.

Only the little area in front of the fire was warm and bright. The heat glowed on their faces but the rest of the room was a dim cavern of cold and darkness. Huge shadows loomed on the distant walls, distortions of the fire and the drafty room and the agitated gestures of Ziad, whose every movement before the fire set off giant configurations in the gloom. Halim was sitting beside the fire watching his friend and watching these unfathomable designs play across the ceiling and leap up the walls. Outside the wind howled through the garden, crackling the stiff fronds of the palm trees. Every so often a crash sounded through the gale as the wind tore away a branch and hurled it at the night. The whole house rattled and creaked, its very stones uneasy. Halim thought of the solitary broken statues in the darkness beyond the verandahs, each one alone in its grove and blind to the wild fury of the storm, solemnly guarding its secret memories of Greece or Rome or Byzantium.

I'm scared, Ziad was saying again. I've never been so scared. I used to think it was bad before but that was nothing compared to now. They kill people for no reason. They do things to them first, over and over and over. I want to stop going there but I know I can't just say that. My captain wouldn't even laugh at me. He'd just pick up something and hit me over the head, hit me two or three times and stare at me. What do I have to complain about? I have a job, don't I? I get paid, don't I? I'm Syrian and not Lebanese, aren't I? Why am I whining? What do I have to whine about? . . .

As so often, it went on until a late hour in front of Halim's fire. Ziad was deeply disturbed and drinking more heavily. His shoulders twitched and his hands moved in rapid little jerks as he smoked cigarette after cigarette. And then there was the relentless wind, the huge room dark beyond the little circle of light, the blasts of cold night air and the hulking restless shadows which never stopped roaming the walls with their fantastic shapes.

Halim tried to comfort his friend. There wasn't much to say in words but he said what he could, and he knew the act of sharing Ziad's fear was itself important. That alone was a kind of escape from despair for his friend. Halim understood this well enough, having long had the benefit of this sort of comfort from Tajar.

So in a way these long winter evenings beside Halim's fire could have been part of any friendship. Ziad was terrified by his place in life and Halim as his friend gave him what he could: attention and love, the strength of sharing, the embrace of his heart. In a small fire's glow, he helped keep back the dark immensity of the night.

But beyond that, it surprised Halim how much time he spent worrying about his friend. His own trips to Lebanon were frequent and complicated. His tasks were grave and there was always danger. Colonel Jundi was an extremely competent professional, a man of nuance who placed heavy demands upon him. It was true Halim had always been a solitary person who liked to be alone inside himself, but he still had to work very hard to satisfy Colonel Jundi and also be the Runner. It was never easy and whenever he left his house on another journey, there were always many details to consider each step of the way. To do less, to neglect any of the details, would be fatal.

Yet at home, crossing the great central room or roaming the verandahs, he found himself thinking again and again of Ziad: picturing some everyday event in his life, recalling an expression on his face or a nervous movement of his hands. These images returned obsessively to Halim, as if he were somehow compelled to see his friend's life more clearly than his own. Why was this so, he wondered? Was his friend's life a reflection of his own, or did his mind at least see it that way? Some kind of different and opposite image, as in a mirror? Because it was easier to see things in Ziad, rather than admit to them in himself?

The irony of this to Halim was enormous and unexpected. Knowing himself was the essence of the Runner, his strength and protection, and in appearance the Runner had never been more successful. Through his work for Colonel Jundi, he was providing the Mossad with highly detailed information on Syrian activities in Lebanon. Syria was the occupying force and the Runner knew everything its intelligence agencies did in Lebanon, often before they did it. He kept watch on their manipulations for Colonel Jundi and passed on the information to Tajar. His secret material had never been more valuable to Israel. Surely it was inconceivable for the Runner to succeed so well in Damascus and Beirut, against all the professionals, and yet falter due to his friendship with an insignificant little man like Ziad?

The very idea astonished Halim. And it was profoundly troubling to him that the Runner operation should suddenly seem fragile—not through any objective concerns, but because of the tricks of his own imagination.

He loved Ziad far too much to think of his friend's life as pathetic. But he did find it infinitely sad, and in the end the brutal ways of Lebanon could only lead to disaster for his friend, a terrified messenger scampering back and forth between ruthless warlords, a little man lost among powerful and monstrous forces. With all his heart he wished there were some way he could really help Ziad, some way to lift him out of his life.

But it wasn't that way for either of them. Halim knew that, and he also knew his friend's destiny seemed all too clear. Yet still the deeper doubts haunted the far corners of his mind. Why was he confusing the fate of another with his own?

EIGHT

There were also startling disorientations from *over there* which served to remind Halim that espionage wasn't the ultimate subterfuge in life, that the deceptions perpetrated by love could be far more devious and profound.

The specific news brought by Tajar was that Yossi was a secret grandfather. Even Anna didn't know of the birth of the child. Assaf hadn't told her and probably never would. The revelation astounded Halim. More than ever he felt remote in his role as the Runner, as if he were off on some interminable desert journey and a messenger from the distant past had suddenly come riding into camp with this improbable announcement from beyond the horizons.

In fact it was a summer evening and he was sitting with Tajar in a shuttered room south of Beirut, less than a hundred and fifty miles from Jerusalem. The squat concrete farm building, near the coast, was serving as a safehouse that night. He and Tajar met more often, but for shorter periods of time, now that Halim was skulking around Beirut for Colonel Jundi. It was hot in the small room and a fan played over them, the noisy hum of the cicadas outside occasionally rising above the steady whir of the fan.

Tajar himself had only recently learned all this from Assaf. Of course he did know Abigail, unlike Halim, who was hearing of her for the first time, so quickly had that come about. And yes, Tajar was also amazed by the intricacy of it.

Tajar's account went back a few years.

Assaf was now a history instructor at the university in Jerusalem. As a graduate student he had become very close to the professor who was his academic adviser, and to the man's wife and two young children. He spent time at their house and became part of the family. He played with the children and helped the wife when his professor was away at conferences. Imperceptibly over time, the wife and Assaf drew closer in a different way. With the opportunity so often there, they eventually became clandestine lovers.

The husband learned of the affair only after his wife became pregnant. The two of them considered their lives and the lives of their young children, and agreed to hold onto their marriage for the time being. The baby was born, a girl, and there was no question Assaf was the father. In the end the husband and wife decided against divorce. Instead they were reconciled. Only the two of them and Assaf knew the truth about the daughter, and they resolved to keep it secret for the sake of the family. Assaf agreed to have nothing to do with any of them ever again, not with the daughter and not with the family. The secret was to be inviolable and so it was for some years. Unknown to Anna or Tajar, Assaf went on alone carrying his painful burdens of unspoken loyalty and love, his terrible guilt and regret.

Then that summer Assaf had fallen deeply in love with a young American woman, Abigail, who had arrived in Jerusalem as a journalist and immediately come under the spell of the city's light and sun and history. Abigail adored Jerusalem and Assaf was an inseparable part of it for her. The intensity of their feelings was obvious and even Anna was convinced it was the great love of Assaf's life.

He's devoted to her and I can understand why, Tajar said that night near Beirut. She has intelligence and charm and believes in the rightness of causes. She also has that marvelous American gift for optimism. Of course she's young, and since she grew up in America she's been protected from many things. I'm told this state of grace she's in is known as the sixties generation in America, but you can't fault her beliefs or her courage, or her youth. She'll get where she's going, I have no doubt about that. And even as it is her feelings aren't all that foreign to me. It seems a hundred years ago now, but when I was her age I remember feeling pretty much the way she does. . . .

Assaf's love for Abigail caused a crisis of conscience. He felt he had to tell Abigail of the child who was his and not his, yet to do so seemed an unpardonable betrayal. In despair he sought out Tajar and told Tajar everything.

He wanted absolution, said Tajar. After all he's still young himself, older than Abigail and a strong boy, but young. Children and a family of his own have come to mean a great deal to him. It's what got him into trouble and I suppose it's easy enough to understand. So this matter of the daughter who's his and not his was assuming enormous proportions to him. To someone else it might not have seemed so grave, but it did to him because of the way he is and because of Abigail. Well naturally I told him to tell Abigail the whole story, which was an immense relief to him. The two of them are good for each other and they're getting on wonderfully. The problem now is that Abigail has some notion she never wants to get married, even though she loves him. She'll live with him but she doesn't want to be married. It has nothing to do with Assaf's past, but with her own. Some set of ideas she has, something to do with her own upbringing. Alas, we all have our own ghosts to exorcise. But they're young and with time, who can say. In any case, that's how I learned of all this. . . .

Tajar paused in the shuttered concrete room and looked down at his hands, grown hard and broad from pushing his crutches all these years. The fan turned slowly. Halim was also gazing at those hands and he realized Tajar must know exactly what he was thinking. Tajar always knew. He never hid his feelings from Tajar. They had talked about Beirut and he had spoken of Ziad, as he always did, and now in turn he had heard about Assaf.

Tajar sighed. He looked up, a questioning expression.

Yes, said Halim, our decisions from long ago do live on in the lives of others, don't they? And they assume directions we could never have foreseen or imagined, a will of their own. Assaf and his secret child? Assaf and the family he wanted so much to be part of and became part of in a wholly impossible way? This confusion of the heart and these dreadful complications between him and his Abigail now that he has found the woman he loves, who loves him? When we're young we ask ourselves where it will end, but of course it never does. It has no end. Deep in the past and lost in the future, it just goes on and on . . . this forever mysterious espionage of the human heart. But why do you feel he'll never tell Anna? They've always been so close, sharing everything. And they're so much alike.

That's all true, said Tajar, and I think the reason is simply because he wants to spare her the pain of an illusion. Her family all gone long ago in Egypt, having never remarried, Assaf her only child—for Anna, nothing in the world could mean so much now as having a grandchild. And Assaf knows that, so he spares her this lost hope.

Halim nodded. All at once Assaf had become a much more complicated person to him. He realized he couldn't understand what Assaf had done because it wasn't something he would have done.

The affair with the professor's wife was a terrible mistake, he said. Didn't Assaf sense the betrayal in that when it was happening?

I would say he was very confused in his emotions back then and got them wrong, replied Tajar. I would also imagine a psychiatrist could work out a weighty structure of technical terms to explain it, but what of that? The fact is Assaf was being himself at the time. In the course of it he made a serious mistake, and the outcome was wretched. Certainly Assaf feels wretched about it.

Halim felt chastened. For years he himself had been a secret father, given to guilt and remorse. What was so strange about

Assaf, in completely different circumstances, stumbling into the same dark corner?

You forgive the failures of others with such ease, he said.

Tajar seemed surprised by the remark. He thought about it a moment, then smiled sadly.

If that's so, it's only because my own failures have been so catastrophic, he replied. When I was Assaf's age I had to bear the memory of whole groups of people who had been lost because of my blunders. Now *that* was failure and those mistakes were truly *terrible.* To my mind, forgiving oneself is the hardest thing any of us has to face, since no life can measure up.

To what? asked Halim.

What we would have it be, replied Tajar. What we promised ourselves, when young, it would be. We all know that promise is genuine and eternal and foolproof, but nonetheless it turns out we are not.

◆◆◆◆◆◆◆◆

At another of their meetings near Beirut, Tajar spoke of his renewed friendship with Bell. In particular he described his first dinner at Bell's house. For Halim this evoked nostalgic memories, since he recalled with great fondness the times he had spent at the house in the orange grove in Jericho, more than a decade ago now.

◆◆◆◆◆◆◆◆

Darkness had already fallen when Tajar turned up in Jericho that summer evening, only his second visit to Bell's cottage. He intended to stop for just a few minutes and perhaps have some coffee. He was on his way down the Jordan Valley from the north, driving back to Jerusalem. But Bell urged him to stay for dinner and, since it would be late by then, to sleep over on a cot in the living room.

I leave the house at first light for my walk, said Bell, my circle tour of the valley out toward the river and back. So you can be up and on your way early, and in Jerusalem before most people are having breakfast.

It was more convenient for Tajar to drive down to Jericho in the evening and thus that became the pattern of his visits. He left Jerusalem before the sun set and dropped down through the Judean wilderness in the cool of twilight, arriving in Jericho soon after dark. Bell served dinner and afterward they sat out behind the cottage under the grape arbor, talking until a late hour. Bell welcomed the company. And as Assaf and Yousef and Halim before him had fallen under the spell of the hermit's quiet ways, so Tajar came to anticipate the pleasure of these hours spent with Bell in his oasis near the Dead Sea.

Anna wasn't surprised that Tajar had become so friendly with Bell. She only wondered why he hadn't looked up Bell sooner. Were you being shy? she asked him merrily.

Tajar smiled. I'm always shy with holy men, he said. It's just not seemly to go banging into the life of someone who's considered a holy man. Besides, this hermit-in-residence happens to reside in Jericho and Jericho runs on a different time. Jerusalem is old but Jericho is three times older, and who can imagine such a thing? In Jericho you might greet a neighbor in the morning, then a dozen years later you might greet him in the afternoon and ask him how he is that day. Down there time isn't going anywhere, in other words, and neither are you. Bell says Abu Musa thinks he's three hundred years old and maybe he is. The corn gets harvested in May. Bell also says Moses the Ethiopian thinks he's living in the age of King David and maybe that's true too. What makes sense in such a place? Jerusalem is timeless, but what then of a place that's three times older than timeless? Surely it must be another realm altogether. Yes?

Anna laughed. It amused her the way Tajar talked about Jericho and she enjoyed hearing his descriptions of Bell and the house in the orange grove. But no matter how softly Tajar approached the subject she wasn't ready to think of meeting Bell again herself. Perhaps someday, she replied vaguely, reluctant as always to revive the past.

But that first evening at Bell's cottage when he was invited to stay for dinner: Tajar could never have imagined anything like it. After Tajar accepted, Bell wandered off to the tiny room at the back of the bungalow which served as his kitchen. Tajar had seen the emptiness of that room with its two rusty gas rings, and he preferred not to think what might come out of it that evening. Instead he perched himself regally in Bell's tattered chair on the front porch and gazed out at the shadowy orange grove, imagining it to be his portion of paradise in the hereafter, a sleekly dark old god smiling in the night.

From time to time he heard Bell clattering around in the far-off kitchen. What on earth was the hermit conjuring up back there for his unexpected guest? Last month's impregnable bread and the month-before-last's rock-solid goat's cheese? A bowl of last year's hardtack crumbs topped by a moldy dried date with a side dish of ramrod-hot green peppers, the thin slippery kind shaped like a horn of the devil, to obliterate all taste and detonate nature's needs? Perhaps an ancient green onion the hermit had found hiding in a corner of the kitchen and was now busily stripping of its long gray roots? God alone knew but no matter. Tajar had survived on desert rations before and whatever the hermit put before him, he was sure he could manage it. The first rule in such a situation was to have a mug of scalding tea at hand. Once cleansed and softened, even a fistful of last year's locusts would go down. Alone in the desert, the prophet Elijah was said to have smiled a blissful smile when Providence and crows had provided him with such fare. Smile and swallow: then as now the rule of the desert. Hermits were notoriously austere creatures, known for their single-eyed vision of other worlds.

And in any case dessert would be delicious. God also made

mangoes, an undeniable fact. In Jericho, oasis of fruit trees, dessert was a gift from heaven.

The distant banging eased off in the kitchen. Bell drifted out to the porch and apologized for the delay. Would Tajar care to step inside? Tajar nodded resolutely and gathered up his crutches, determined to face hardship with grace.

Candlelight greeted him at the door. He found himself staring at a magnificent spread of curries and steaming rice, fortified here and there by glistening bowls of homemade chutneys, mango for sweetness and three shades of fiery lemon to burn through the jasmine-scented evening. The array of rich dishes covered the unpainted wooden table in the barren living room, which was also the dining room and later to be Tajar's bedroom. Two sun-bleached wooden benches sat facing each other across the candlelit table, the bare floors swept clean by gentle breezes scurrying through the house. Packing crates hung in the corners with stacks of worn books. High up on the walls immobile geckos, friendly little lizards, awaited any stray insect that might wander in through the doors and windows, which were all thrown wide to the restless fragrants of the night.

My God, what's this? Tajar asked in amazement.

The finest curries in Jericho, said Bell, quietly pleased with his handiwork. Also the only curries in Jericho. In the past they flourished here but the secret was apparently lost. Dig in.

Tajar did so and ate with gusto, helping himself to everything again and especially to the chutneys. How could he have known he was so hungry? Bell ate right along with him, scooping up mounds of food.

Delicious, said Tajar between mouthfuls. But is it possible Jericho was known for curries in other eras?

It must have been, replied Bell, heaping more rice on his plate. Two thousand years ago, say. Picture an adventurous Indian trader following the ancient spice route along the coasts of Arabia and up the Red Sea. He lands at Aqaba and joins one of the camel caravans making its way north to Damascus, through deserts and more deserts and finally through the desolation along the shores of the Dead Sea. Then one evening the caravan comes swaying into Jericho and all at once the trader raises his eyes and looks around and thinks: Isn't this it? This has to be it. Why go any farther in life?

Tajar laughed. Oh I see, he said. Of course that does make sense. I'm sure a trader or two did turn up here from India and found it to his liking and decided to stay on. Do you like to recall such a thing?

I do and I do so all the time, replied Bell. But just imagine how distant, how remote Jericho was then for a man from India. Much farther away than the moon is for men today. It was more like another galaxy, another corner of the unknown and unimaginable universe. Yet here he sat, this traveler in time, perhaps right here where we're sitting now. The oasis has always been small because there's only a limited amount of water. And the shade is the same and the desert roundabout is unchanged, as are the sun and the moon and the stars at night. So then, what thoughts filled the long evenings for him?

I suppose you know this imaginary traveler quite well, said Tajar.

Bell smiled. It's one of the advantages of living in a small place, he said, which is also the oldest village on earth. When you think of it, an extraordinary variety of people have sat right here where we're sitting in the course of Jericho's ten thousand years. Quite astonishing, really. . . .

◆◆◆◆◆◆◆◆

Halim laughed at Tajar's wonderful description of his first curry dinner in the house in the orange grove. Halim had once enjoyed those grand curry banquets at Bell's, and he also remembered Bell's make-believe Indian trader. Born himself in India and long a man without a country, Bell was very fond of his imaginary story of an Indian traveler who had decided two thousand years ago that Jericho was his place in the world.

So Halim was cheered and his mood lightened by Tajar's account of Bell. But there had also been another part to the encounter which Tajar chose not to mention in the safehouse near Beirut: Bell's ominous prophecy concerning Halim. That had come after the curry feast when Bell and Tajar were sitting out back, sipping coffee in Bell's grape arbor.

Bell brought up Halim. Bell didn't have to mention that he had known Halim once, but he had thought about it and decided he wanted to mention it. Why withhold the truth? That would have been Monastery thinking.

Tajar, for his part, was intensely curious. Several times in the long history of the Runner operation he had spoken to men who knew Halim strictly as Halim, Europeans as well as Arabs. But never to someone like Bell, whose opinion he so greatly admired. Bell went on to describe his friendship with Halim over a decade ago, when the two of them had taken long walks out of Jericho at dawn and at sunset.

A man with an intense inner life, said Bell. I realize that as a Syrian, he's your enemy. Doubly so perhaps, since you both move in secret worlds. And I also realize you may know much more about him than I do, if he is a professional as I suspect. But as I recall we can never know enough in the secret worlds, can we? There's always more to be gleaned, a new view or a different insight, some odd fact that may reveal a new dimension. . . . Well then, I have to say first of all that you'd like him. He'd appeal to you immensely. He's thoughtful with a wide heart. He has vision and never fools himself. He's not naïve or cynical, and yet . . . he may lose himself in the end.

The suddenness of the words startled Tajar. Why? How? he asked.

I don't believe he knows defeat as well as you do, said Bell. Whatever it is he does, I fear one day he'll feel it hasn't been enough—in his own eyes. He'll feel he has failed himself, taken a wrong turn perhaps. The thought will haunt him and eventually it may push him over the edge. I say *fear* because he's a good man and I'd be sorry to see it come to that. But you realize I'm not talking now about intelligence agencies or Arabs and Israelis. I'm referring to another kind of secret world.

I understand, said Tajar. The world of Jericho time, as your friend Abu Musa likes to call it. But obviously you care for this man Halim and your feelings about him seem very specific. Why do you feel about him the way you do?

Bell pondered the question. I can't really point to any one thing, he said at last. A man like Halim is always a mystery to anyone who hasn't known him day to day for years. Some people are like that, as you discover especially in the intelligence business when you try to put together a coherent dossier on a man. Sometimes the deeper you dig, the more you realize all your informants are recalling a different man. It's strange but Halim makes me think of Stern, that agent in Egypt whom we've talked about.

Abruptly Bell laughed in the shadows of the grape arbor, startling Tajar anew. What is it? asked Tajar.

A Jericho breeze in the brain, said Bell. I was about to follow Abu Musa's example and say . . . Let me tell you a tale. Well why not? I will. One of the places where Halim and I used to go on our walks toward sundown was the Omayyad palace on the outskirts of town. Earlier than sundown really, for the light. Those splendid ruins, you know them of course. It was the mosaic that was our destination. Surely you know that too. . . .

Tajar nodded. He knew it well. The small palace had been built in the eighth century as a winter residence for the Omayyad caliphs of Damascus. But an earthquake had destroyed it only a few years after it was completed, and then the caliphate had moved with the wealth of Islam to Baghdad, so the site had remained quietly in ruins ever since, a dusty jewel lost in the sands of Jericho. Of the magnificent artistic creations which must have adorned the palace in sumptuous detail, only one survived, but this excavated remnant was complete and of pristine beauty, its subtle colors perfectly preserved by the sands of centuries. This treasure was a raised mosaic floor at the end of an oblong room, the polychrome mosaic rounded at the top as if to represent a portal into the earth, a gate to the world as seen from the sky. Perhaps it had served on special occasions as an alcove at the end of the room, a dais where a dignitary could sit when receiving guests.

The mosaic depicted a pomegranate tree as the Tree of Life. The thickly seeded fruit, an ancient symbol of fertility, hung heavy on the branches. On one side beneath the tree two slender gazelles grazed with raised heads, feeding on leaves, while on the other side of the tree trunk a third slender gazelle was caught in the same pose by a huge lunging lion, which had just landed on the gazelle's back and drawn first blood. A motif of pomegranate blossoms circled the entire mosaic. The greens and browns of the tree, shading in and out, and the flowing lines of the softly brown animals were of awesome delicacy, realistic and stylized at once.

It was the most beautiful mosaic Tajar had ever seen. The serenity of the spreading tree, all-encompassing in its majestic reach, contrasted sharply with the scenes in conflict beneath it, the two gently feeding gazelles on one side, the powerful outstretched lion claiming its kill on the other. The one was idyllic and pastoral, oblivious to any danger in the timeless rhythms of nature, while the other cut through life with opposite extremes of brute force and infinite longing: the ferocious fixed gaze of the lion ripping with its jaws, its bloody talon marks slashing across the tender flanks of the victim so suddenly struck from behind, the sad startled eyes of the little gazelle as it looked up at the leaves in what had become, at that very instant, its last moment of life. The emotions in the mosaic seemed to crowd together and yet remain separate—a commanding Tree of Life sheltering unbounded cruelty and beauty.

The mosaic fascinated Halim, said Bell. We would sit there and look at it and before long his imagination would be roaming in every direction at once, back and forth through history to all those ancient and not so ancient peoples who have unrolled their banners and come marching this way in search of Jericho, our not quite forgotten Garden of Eden, the Egyptians and Assyrians and Babylonians and Persians, the Greeks and Romans and Byzantines and Arabs, the Crusaders and Mamelukes and Turks, the Israelites before and the Jews more recently, and the many other less remembered tribes whose movements remain obscure, whose empires were never born. Yes, the mosaic fascinated Halim and evoked many moods in him, many emotions and memories. I've always found peace when I sit beside it, but not so Halim. To him it was deeply disturbing, finally. Yet he always wanted to return to it and so we did, many times.

Bell fell silent but Tajar said nothing, waiting. Perhaps there was more?

I asked him once what troubled him about the mosaic, Bell said at last. He told me but his answer was a little too succinct. Quite possibly he didn't fully understand it himself, then.

What did he say? asked Tajar.

He mentioned the lion's gaze. Not the ferocity of it but its *fixed* quality. That was what seemed to bother him.

NINE

With the Syrian army on hand in Beirut to suppress the Palestinian and Moslem militias, the Maronite Christians were free to take on each other and act out a play within the play of self-destruction, a civil war within the civil war. At stake as always was money and power, called territory by the Maronites in gangland style, what Tajar referred to as Lebanon's Mafia imperative.

The elderly leaders of the Maronite factions were all in their seventies and eighties. For decades these aging clan chieftains had tirelessly plotted against each other as one or another of their number had managed to ease himself into the presidency, by way of unscrupulous deals with his deadly enemies. The play had always gone on because the presidency was good for only six years of plunder. Wisely, the French had made reelection to the presidency unconstitutional, in order that the keys to the treasury might keep moving from gang to gang. The difference in the late 1970s was that the Syrian army had put down the Maronites' enemies, and the Maronite factions were very heavily armed. Both the Syrians and the Israelis had been providing them with weapons since the civil war.

Among the most powerful Maronite chieftains was one who had always been squeezed out of the presidency at the last moment, a stiff and impeccable man known to everyone as Sheik Jean-Claude, very dapper in his dark blue French suits.

Although the mask of the old man's face was now as dry and set as an Egyptian mummy's, the sheik had begun life as a pharmacist and had been known in the 1930s as Jean-Claude the condom, because his pharmacy in the brothel district was conveniently open at odd hours, the better to do business. That was long ago but a certain raffish aura still clung to the ancient visage of Sheik Jean-Claude, who had seen it all so many times that his expression never changed, and whose hard-earned transformation from a condom to a sheik in the course of a busy half-century was very much in the admired Lebanese manner of achievement.

Sheik Jean-Claude embodied the Francophil element in Maronite thinking, which liked to believe that Lebanon wasn't really in the Middle East at all, but rather just off the south coast of France, a spicier Riviera. The opposing view was held most strongly by the Maronites of the north, who did think they were situated in the Middle East, in fact right next door to Syria. The northern Maronites were accustomed to getting along with the Syrians and even doing business with them. Thus the former Lebanese president whose son ran the Lebanese side of the Middle Eastern hashish alliance, along with the Syrian dictator's younger brother, was a chieftain of the north.

Sheik Jean-Claude had never quite managed to maneuver himself into the presidency, but he still had hopes for his sons. The eldest son and heir apparent, Zozo, was killed in a boating accident at the beginning of the civil war. While waterskiing off Beirut, he was swamped and ridden over by an unidentified speedboat. Sheik Jean-Claude's aspirations then passed to his second son, Fuad, and his third son, Nazo, who dropped his childhood nickname and reverted to his real name, Naji, which Sheik Jean-Claude considered more respectable for a possible presidential candidate.

Both Fuad and Naji had become local leaders during the civil war. Fuad was more interested in political organization, like his father, but Naji loved the casual flair of paramilitary uniforms and devoted his time to Sheik Jean-Claude's militia.

Both brothers were also active in various commercial ventures, in order to pay for their political and military enterprises. Fuad dealt in smuggled whiskey and automobiles and ran some profitable joint businesses with the chief of PLO intelligence. He was friendly with many Lebanese Moslems and had close connections with Syrian intelligence, who supplied him with arms. Naji dealt mostly in hashish and smuggled gold. He despised Moslems, got his arms from the Israelis, and had close connections with the Mossad.

Naji, always smartly dressed in well-tailored camouflage fatigues, became the official commander of his father's militia. He was only twenty-eight at the time and his preferred food was Mars bars. Naturally Fuad still had his own troops which he controlled, separate from Naji's. There were also many other private armies financed by the Arab powers, who all found Lebanon a convenient place to do their killing, without disturbing the precarious political situations they invariably faced at home.

One June morning Naji launched a fateful attack against the summer palace of the clan chief of the northern Maronites. The ex-president himself was in Beirut and Naji's target was the man's son and heir, the most prominent Lebanese of Naji's generation and Naji's most serious Maronite rival, both in politics and in the hashish trade.

For Naji, whose experience was mostly in street killings, the attack on the summer palace was a well-planned military assault. His rival, the ex-president's son, went down shooting in the kitchen, killed along with his wife and their three-year-old daughter and the family dog.

◆◆◆◆◆◆◆◆

And so it went as the gangsters in Lebanon shot and bombed their way into the eighties. Halim met with the lieutenants of these clan chieftains, as well as with Palestinians and Lebanese Moslems. He also dealt with many Syrian intelligence officers who ran operations in Lebanon, and with the countless agents they employed—all for Colonel Jundi. He knew Lebanon could have managed a vicious civil war on its own, but how much more vicious it was with the country stuffed with arms and serving as a killing ground for everyone else's causes, with Syria on one side and Israel on the other and the PLO in between them.

In time Naji became more and more closely aligned with the Israelis. First the Mossad dealt with him, then Israeli generals, then the new Israeli prime minister himself. The Syrians had entered Lebanon on the side of the Christians, but in only a few years the Christians had turned around and were fighting the Syrians, more or less led by Naji.

It was easy enough for Halim to see what was happening. The Israelis had a grand new scheme which would make Lebanon right for them: the Maronites in control, the PLO crushed and Syria out of the country, a peace treaty, an open border. And Naji was the tool who would bring these wonders to pass, with the help of the Israeli army. To Halim it made no sense at all. It ignored everything he knew about Lebanon.

It was also obvious to Halim that his reports to the Mossad had become irrelevant. The extraordinary access he had in Lebanon, the information he acquired for Colonel Jundi and passed on to Tajar, had seemed spectacular only a few years ago. But it was entirely meaningless now that the Israeli government had already decided on its course in Lebanon. And not only the Runner but Tajar himself had become irrelevant to the Mossad. Tajar was a man of subtlety in Middle Eastern ways, and to him the grand new scheme for Lebanon was preposterous. As Naji organized new shoot-outs around Lebanon and was praised by those in power in Israel, Tajar more than ever seemed a man of the past. As usual he spoke his mind, and like the messenger who brought unwanted news he was ignored and isolated in the Mossad as a result.

Halim knew all this. They talked about it one night at a meeting in another safehouse on the coast.

It is what is, said Tajar. I've served a long time and eras change. We used to wonder about it but it does seem, finally, that Israel is to become part of the Middle East after all. People in this part of the world have always had a thin grasp of reality. It's a place of wish and fantasy. You either believe absolutely, which generally means religion, or you make-believe with equal fervor. Either way there's not much room left in the middle for men like me. It's dangerous to always call defeats victories, as we do in this part of the world, but what is it that leads us to embrace these fatal illusions? Is it the desert with its harsh extremes that promotes fanaticism? Everything is so much itself in the desert. Is that why man gets viewed with such disastrous simplicity? In all my life I've never seen anything so horrifying as Lebanon. Even religion is merely a metaphor for what goes on here. The Maronites fear the Moslems, but they're just as quick to kill Maronites from the next village, and the Moslems are the same way. And where are the Palestinians to go? Or are they simply *to go,* as the Turks said to the Armenians when I was a child. How much easier it is when evil has a name, when there *is* an enemy. But Lebanon isn't like that, unfortunately for all of us, and worst of all for the people who live here. Being Israeli or Syrian may be difficult, but it's nothing compared to being Lebanese. . . .

Halim was aware that in fact he was now working primarily for Colonel Jundi. His reporting was no longer of any particular use to the Mossad and to Israel, but it was extremely valuable to Colonel Jundi and therefore to Syria. He said as much to Tajar.

Yes, I suppose that's true, replied Tajar. And it does seem like some kind of unbelievable reversal of cause, of loyalty. But it isn't really, not to my thinking. Look at it another way. I can't use the word *succeed* in Lebanon, because no matter what anyone does here now it can't be called succeeding. But if Colonel Jundi and the Syrians were somehow able to keep things together in Lebanon, that and only that might keep the Israeli army out, which would be a blessing for us and an enormous triumph for the Runner operation. The Syrians can't win here. No one can. There are no winners in such a place. To come in means to lose. It will be a disaster for the Syrians here, but it will be a far greater disaster for us, to us, to come in. If we do we'll be just another Middle Eastern country playing the Middle Eastern game: illusion, power, suppress where you can, dominate those you can dominate. And coming in on the side of a man like Naji, this heroic defender of his minority faith, is fantasy pushed to madness. So I see your work for Colonel Jundi as immensely important in an unexpected way. Strangely, it's as important as anything the Runner has ever done. You're serving Israel, Yossi. But you're doing it in a murky and difficult world where truth can be its opposite. . . .

When Halim left Tajar that night he found himself thinking of the persistence of the Arab-Israeli wars, with their steady recurrence every seven to ten years, or about the time it took for a new generation of men to exert their influence on affairs. Yes, but it isn't just that men forget, thought Halim. It isn't as easy as that. The tragedy is that our greatest human treasure —memory—so often glitters locked away out of reach, the one gift we can never quite give to another, even to those we love most.

He was staying that night with a Syrian officer, an acquaintance who had taken over a villa in the mountains above Beirut. He had to go to another meeting in the city before he went up to the house, so it was very late when he got there. He was exhausted, as he always was in Beirut. The watching and the listening, memorizing every nuance of what he saw and heard —there was never any rest when he left his garden in Damascus and took the road of descent down into the hellish chaos of Lebanon.

It was almost three o'clock and he had to be up again in three hours. Still, he didn't feel like trying to sleep. The somber conversation with Tajar had disturbed him in many ways. The house was quiet and he poured himself a brandy to take out to the terrace. Some specific memory was rumbling around in the back of his mind, trying to push itself up into consciousness. He was too tired to think of it but he settled into a chair on the terrace, hoping the memory would surface and release him to go off to bed.

In the distance below was the harbor, peaceful and beautiful with the lights on the sea. All harbors were beautiful at this silent hour in the darkness. And beyond it the great black expanse of the Mediterranean reached out to an infinity of stars.

Suddenly he saw it. The image was there in front of him with perfect clarity. It was thirty years ago at the little settlement in the Negev and he and Anna were sitting side by side in the central hut, counting out bullets. It was night and a single kerosene lamp burned overhead. Other men and women were there. They were all there except for those on guard duty, about two dozen of them. Only Yossi and one other Palmach soldier had had any military training. The rest were just men and women, like Anna. The Egyptian army was expected in two or three days and they were all sitting together and counting out the rounds for the few old rifles they had. They were also deciding who would take over each rifle—in the second case, in the third case—if the man or woman assigned to the rifle could no longer fire it. After that Yossi would fill some bottles with the last of their precious petrol, so that he and the other Palmach soldier would at least have something to throw at the armored cars or tanks, if the Egyptians came with them.

How solemn they were as they went about these tasks to defend the little settlement which they all knew would fall. How pure the dream had seemed to them then, how simple and right and good. And they had succeeded, that was the wonder of it. They had held out and defended their settlement for one whole day, a miracle. And to Halim . . . Yossi, looking back, that single day in the desert seemed the greatest triumph of his life. Never again had he known such exhilaration, such a sense of pure victory as when darkness came to protect them that night.

Only thirty years ago and now there was this. There was this tormented city at his feet, half-destroyed and torn by war and more war. There were Naji and his gangsters and all the other gangsters. And there was the Runner, as clever an agent as the Mossad ever had, working as hard as he could for Colonel Jundi, the utterly ruthless inspector general of Syrian intelligence.

He drank off his brandy. He had always believed in himself and his cause, but lately he had begun to wonder how long the Runner could go on running. That only really mattered to him and to Tajar. If it did happen that he saw the end coming, should he speak of it? He was inclined to think not. After all Tajar had done for him, a smile and a wave seemed the better way. The rest, all the rest, Tajar would certainly understand.

TEN

Ziad was painfully morose that last winter, the winter of 1982, the fortieth year since Anna had fled from Egypt. He still worked in Syrian intelligence as a courier for his old hashish department, its senior employee both in age and in years of service, a true survivor who had managed to hold on to his battered briefcase with the false bottom as his department had moved from agency to agency and been regularly raided and absorbed and realigned and reintegrated, in keeping with the law of changing fortune for Syrian secret services. Ziad had also served under many different men. His original captain had been purged years ago. Other captains had disappeared into prison and a few had been transferred to the Golan Heights. The last captain before the present one had simply not turned up for work one day, the victim of some unrevealed intrigue.

Ziad's hashish department always served the dictator's younger brother, no matter which intelligence agency it happened to be in at the moment. The turnover in captains was continual because they were at a level where the temptation to do a private deal was great. If they took a chance and succeeded, they made a small fortune overnight. Ziad always referred to the officer he was serving as *my captain.* They lasted for longer or shorter periods and were cruel and ambitious men. Colonel Jundi had their secret services penetrated at a higher level and the danger of their work was extreme. But the potential profits were so enormous there were always new men eager to take their places.

Ziad himself might easily have advanced beyond his lowly status if he had been willing to take chances. But Halim was forever warning him against it, and Ziad was too timid for that in any case. Ziad loathed his trips into the Lebanese mountains. He feared the Maronites he visited and hated the way they treated him. Before he left Damascus he was so depressed he could hardly speak, and by the time he returned he was so hysterical he had to drink himself into a stupor in order to quiet down, as if each trip were an unexpected reprieve from death.

With Halim that last winter he was morbid and manic at once. His humor knew no bounds. He laughed wildly with tears in his eyes and joked as the tears ran down his face. He grinned and gestured extravagantly, making fun of himself. But still the tears kept coming and eventually, as the night wore on, his pathetic face crumpled into undisguised despair.

In the afternoon when he and Halim were strolling along the river in Damascus, he would suddenly look over his shoulder to see that no one was near them in the thin winter sunlight. Then he would clutch Halim's arm and lean close and giggle.

Have you noticed that *el presidente* has promoted himself? he whispered. He's now having the newspapers compare him to the illustrious Salah al-din, the greatest Moslem warrior who ever lived. And with careful reminders that it was this military genius who defeated the Crusaders and finally threw the foreign devils out of the Middle East. At first I thought: oh dear, is he really going to become as powerful as all that? But then I thought: oh no, there's nothing to worry about, it's just another mild case of terminal megalomania. National leaders in this part of the world always get that. It's when they begin comparing themselves to God that you have to worry. *That's* when the trouble starts and you get upheaval on a colossal scale. . . .

Or on a sunny winter weekend as the two of them sat side

by side in overcoats on Halim's verandah, a bottle of brandy between their thronelike chairs, Ziad would suddenly interrupt their silent drinking with another terrified giggle.

In Lebanon they say that Syrian torture is considered the cruelest in the Middle East, he whispered. But how do people arrive at such conclusions? Is there a way to measure these things? What of our brothers the Iraqis who also have a progressive Baath party in power? *Their* president is known as the butcher of Baghdad, and doesn't that mean progress is everywhere? . . . Why do I fear Naji and the Maronites so much? Are they worse than anyone else? It's irrational, I know, but fear's like that. It starts with something specific and becomes general, which is called anxiety. Which is my state of mind, precisely. When are the Israelis going to come in and take Lebanon off our hands? Isn't it time for the Americans to fly by and bomb it into the Stone Age? Aren't the Russians even a little interested? Could the French be talked into taking it back? Doesn't *anyone* want it? . . .

Halim didn't see Ziad often that last winter. They were away from Damascus at different times, or Halim was too busy when he was in Damascus. But Halim did see Ziad in Lebanon once during those last months of his friend's life, the only time that ever happened.

It was in the mountains north of Beirut. Halim had gone to a village stronghold to meet a Maronite sub-chieftain who was an enemy of Naji. The man had dealings with the Syrians and Halim was there for Colonel Jundi, under the cover of some suitable business, to find out more about a certain Syrian intelligence officer. As he was led into the villa he saw a row of men sitting on a bench in an anteroom, waiting their turn, each man with a briefcase between his feet. One of them was Ziad. Ziad looked up and quickly looked down again, staring hard at the floor. His face was wet with sweat. In his heavy old winter suit he looked like a poor petitioner from the village, some tenant farmer who had put on his best clothes and come to beg the landlord for an extra tenth of his crop.

Halim kept on walking. He was ushered into the sub-chieftain's library and had his meeting. He was asked to stay for lunch, but lunch in Lebanon could take three or four hours and he gave an excuse. The house was richly furnished with expensive carpets and furniture. There were gardens and a swimming pool. It was the kind of mountain retreat that became known as a summer palace in Lebanon, if the owner managed to shoot his way to the top in Beirut.

Later, Ziad gave an account of that day to Halim.

He had been sweating heavily in the anteroom because he was wearing long underwear. It was cold in the mountains in the winter and he had to wear long underwear to keep warm on the trip up to the potentate's village. But when he finally reached the potentate's waiting room, naturally it was hot. Potentates were rich and their houses were well-heated. Sometimes he had to wait for hours and his long underwear began to smell. At least it began to smell to him. As for his old suit, that already smelled of a thousand lonely nights in Damascus and Beirut and the back streets of poor Lebanese mountain villages, all those places where he had spent the last ten years of his life as a messenger . . . watching life. Because that was what he did, wasn't it? He was always looking at life from the outside and was never a part of it. He was always peeking in at it and yearning to be *in there* somewhere, clumsy in the way he came across to people, awkward and out of place and inept. There was no denying that, was there? A whole decade of his life spent carrying messages to Lebanon in fear and loathing, always hiding inside himself and wishing for something better, damning them all because he was trapped, terrified when anyone looked at him or spoke to him and asked him who he was . . . *Who am I? I'm Ziad, the anonymous failed spy from Damascus. Before that I was an anonymous failed whore of a journalist, and before that I was a boy sitting in a tiny cavelike room above the souk in Damascus, dreaming of the world, dreaming of being someone when I grew up. But it didn't work out that way and I never did become someone, and you might as well shoot me now.*

That's who I am. . . . So finally, after waiting and sweating and waiting some more in the sub-chieftain's anteroom, a man came in and looked at Ziad. He was a young man about half Ziad's age, a junior thug. He laughed arrogantly and came striding up to Ziad and slapped a Lebanese pound-note on Ziad's wet forehead. The pound-note stuck there, glued to Ziad's skin, and Ziad knew he was being called into the presence. He was next. The chief thug would see him now. Ziad got to his feet, feeling weak and sick and ruined. He shuffled forward, thinking: this is me, this is my life. He kept swallowing, trying not to throw up out of fear. His feet made squishing sounds in his shoes. Cold sweat was running down his arms, his legs. The pound-note was still stuck to his forehead and what was he supposed to do with it? Was it safe to peel it off and hand it back to the junior thug, or would that be an insult? Perhaps he was supposed to go inside this way and appear in front of the chief thug with the money glued to his forehead. A kind of sign: I'm a whore and I sell myself to get by in the world. He knew that once he was inside he had to cringe and look frightened in front of the chief thug, but that was easy. That was the way he felt. But what about the rest of it? Different thugs liked different kinds of obeisance. How should he behave with this one? Should he do a little dance of excitement, like a boy who had to make water? Should he grin and joke that he smelled like a soggy ram left out alone in the rain too long? Or should he compliment the chief thug on his French cologne and his excellent taste in carpets looted from Beirut homes? No, that was all haphazard. Better to fall back on basic local behavior when meeting a Middle Eastern dignitary. Look humble and fearful and gaze at the chief thug as at a great light, while muttering over and over, *God be praised, God be praised.* . . .

Thus Ziad's day at that well-guarded villa in the mountains where Halim had been casually asked to stay for lunch, which would have meant fine French wines in the glassed-in terrace overlooking the gardens and the swimming pool. Ziad ended his description by warning Halim about that particular Maronite sub-chieftain. Ziad had heard rumors that the man was not to be trusted. That he might be making some kind of deal with Naji to sell out his Syrian friends and go over to the side of Naji and the Israelis.

Halim listened sadly, in silence, to this warning. Of course he knew all about the man. That was his job. And in fact the man *was* making a deal with Naji, and it would have been better for Ziad to stay away from that sub-chieftain's village and never go there again. It might be dangerous for any Syrian to be within the man's reach when the deal was set and he betrayed his Syrian contacts and made some gesture to prove his new allegiance to Naji and the Israelis.

Halim knew all about that. Colonel Jundi knew all that. This kind of intrigue was a morning's work for them. They were professionals. But Halim couldn't say anything to Ziad, and even if he could, what difference would it make? Ziad didn't decide where he would go in Lebanon, or when. He didn't have any control over it. *My captain* decided that. And who could say? Perhaps it was even better that poor Ziad knew nothing about the trouble ahead other than some vague rumor. What he didn't know he couldn't fear. And yet even now here he was still loyally trying to help Halim, trying to warn his friend.

The thought of that cut deeply inside Halim, and once more he felt useless. He was failing Ziad, perhaps fatally so. But there was nothing he could do about it.

◆◆◆◆◆◆◆◆

There was nothing special about their last evening together. Of course they didn't know it was their last evening, so there was no reason for it to be different from any other. They were to meet downtown and have dinner. It was to be an early evening because Halim was just back from a visit to Beirut and still exhausted from his trip. Halim had work to do at the office, and it was decided that Ziad would wait for him at the hotel bar on the top floor of the office building.

As it happened Ziad hadn't been up to the hotel for a long time. The barroom was still the same with its wood paneling and potted plants and ceiling fan, not turning now, and the bowls of peanuts that came with the drinks. To Ziad, though, it seemed much shabbier than he remembered it from the times when he had sat here and waited for his friend—*the gaucho* then, the enthusiastic young idealist from Argentina—to finish his paperwork on the balcony and come in and plan an evening on the town. But yes, that had been a long time ago, over twenty years. As he had done then, Ziad sat near the window watching the light of the sinking sun slant into the room. When Halim finally did show up Ziad had a crisp new copy of *Le Monde* open on his lap, a glass in his hand, an untouched bowl of peanuts at his elbow. Ziad was smiling and relaxed, happy for once, his fond memories of the room having evoked a magical nostalgia in him. He raised the bowl of peanuts in greeting.

You see here a man on top of the world, said Ziad. Twenty years ago I sat in this place and didn't know my good fortune. I wonder if you'll ever be able to appreciate how I felt then, drinking real Scotch and plundering bowl after bowl of free peanuts? It was sheer joy, and more. You showed me the world. Just watching you and seeing your confidence in things was a marvel for me to behold. Oh yes, *good days,* my friend. The very finest life has to offer. . . .

They went on to one of Ziad's little restaurants, which was Halim's too now. Then they walked along the river, stopped for one more coffee, parted. Halim took a taxi home and it was as simple as that. A quiet evening between two friends. A commonplace evening toward the end of winter, 1982.

◆◆◆◆◆◆◆◆

Colonel Jundi told him of the killing.

Halim was returning from Beirut one winter morning when

he found the colonel's man waiting for him at the border crossing. It was unexpected. He and the colonel didn't have a meeting scheduled. He got into the curtained automobile and they set out across the hills.

A dismal rain had been falling since first light, a hard steady downpour that threatened to go on all day. Deep pools had formed in the ruts of the mountain road and there were washouts on the curves. The major was a new man who had only recently joined the colonel. He drove slowly, picking his way with care. In the distance an occasional goatherd huddled beside some outcropping of rock, which gave little shelter. Halim caught sight of them through the curtains. The land was bleak and the lonely men looked cold and miserable. At last the car came bumping into the yard of the little stone farmhouse. Halim pulled his coat around him and made a dash for the door.

Colonel Jundi was waiting for him in the main room, standing with his back to a crackling open fire. He must have just come in from a walk across the hills, because his trousers were steaming and his boots were caked with mud which hadn't yet dried. The room smelled of wet wool and wood smoke and that special sweet fragrance that came from wild mountain bushes, which were used to supplement fires in the hills where wood was scarce. Halim greeted the colonel and went up to warm himself at the fire. He noticed that a bottle of brandy stood on the table, which was unusual. The colonel poured two glasses and handed one to Halim. Colonel Jundi seldom drank and never during the day. Halim knew the brandy was meant just for him and the colonel was joining him out of courtesy, because it wasn't proper to make a man drink alone. Gravely, the colonel faced him.

I have bad news, said the colonel. Your friend Ziad is dead.

Naturally, the colonel knew all about Ziad. To him the friendship had always seemed strange because the two men had been so unequal. Halim was an unusual man in every respect and Ziad hadn't been at all. Halim was gifted and would have been a success anywhere, while Ziad had been mediocre and would have failed anywhere. Still, friends could be oddly balanced and the colonel knew these two men went back to the time when Halim had first arrived in Damascus from Argentina.

The colonel's account was terse.

The Maronite sub-chieftain had finally made his about-face switch to Naji. In doing so, as a gesture of his new loyalties, he had rounded up the Syrians in his area. Ziad had the misfortune to be spending the night in the village. He was pulled out of bed and taken away without being allowed to dress. There were five Syrians in all, minor figures like Ziad. The next morning they were found hanging naked from a makeshift gallows in the central square of the village. There had been torture and mutilations. Huge, deep crosses were cut in their chests. It wasn't known whether the carving had been done before or after death.

But now it doesn't matter, said Colonel Jundi. Your friend's suffering is over and he rests, his pain gone. Ours is still with us, but our concern must be for the living. . . .

There were other words from the colonel but Halim didn't really hear them. He left the little farmhouse and was driven back to the border crossing, where he went on to Damascus. It was raining as hard as ever when he arrived home. It was cold and he kept his overcoat on although he had no intention of going anywhere or doing anything. He was too restless to sit in front of a fire and warm himself, so he poured brandy and wandered around the house with the glass in his hand, listening to his footsteps echo.

At the end of the central room, the almond tree outside the window-door was in full bloom, its white and pink flowers bravely set against the gray skeletons of the garden. It was by far the first tree to bloom, recklessly throwing out its flowers in the very deepest gloom of winter, long before the other trees had sprouted even a tentative bud. In the rain and cold its beauty was always astonishing, an unexpected cry of abandon and hope, its delicate colors calling forth the memory of a season that seemed far away. And impossibly out of place in the bare gray desolation of winter. Even now the beautiful little flowers of the almond tree were past their peak and falling, broken by the hard rain.

All afternoon the rain pounded down on the house. Darkness came early but Halim didn't turn on a lamp. Toward evening a wild electrical storm broke over the city. First hail pelted the verandahs and then fierce thunder and brilliant flashes of lightning crashed across the sky, lighting the great central room and the garden in a pure white intensity which abruptly went black. Only the flowers of the almond tree survived in the darkness. Another flash of unworldly light lit the garden and Halim caught a glimpse of a solitary broken statue beyond the gray trunks of the trees, the stone streaked and weathered with half its head gone, one eye staring.

He was glad the storm had come. The explosions of lightning and thunder soothed him by screaming his own emotions at the night. It was wild and chaotic, a war of the gods in heaven, and its awesome crashes exactly reflected his own black, shattered mood.

ELEVEN

Halim traveled to Lebanon much less that spring, then stopped altogether. Part of the reason was operational: Colonel Jundi's priorities were changing and Halim's reporting was less vital to him at the moment. The colonel expected an Israeli invasion of Lebanon by the summer, which meant the Syrian secret services would have to deal with a regular army in the field, not just the murky intrigues of Lebanese tribal warfare. The term of the Lebanese president ended in September. Colonel Jundi expected the Israeli army to be in place well before then to assure Naji's election.

Not that that particular piece of chicanery matters, the colonel said to Halim. If Naji's elected, he'll be killed. It's too much to expect us to put up with someone like him next door.

Halim also traveled less to Lebanon because of Colonel Jundi's concern for his well-being. The Runner's double life for Colonel Jundi over the years in Lebanon—and beyond that his triple life for Tajar—had cost heavily. Halim had been working without letup since the beginning of the Lebanese civil war in 1975. Increasingly he had come to rely on alcohol to sustain him, which worried the colonel. To him, Halim had always seemed a man of impregnable balance and moderation. But he had himself seen the impact of Ziad's death on Halim, and Halim's profound emotional response had made a deep impression on him. It was only then, during that dismal rainy morning at the stone farmhouse on the border, that he had fully come to realize how exhausted Halim was. Nor was that all. Something else had suddenly struck him. For a moment he had wondered if he knew Halim as well as he thought he did.

It was the depth of Halim's emotion that caused the colonel to wonder. Halim was successful and had innumerable friends. The Palestinians in particular revered him for his integrity. Was it also possible, then, that he had felt so isolated in Damascus all these years that the death of his oldest friend could have such a powerful effect on him?

Of course it *was* possible, thought the colonel. There were reasons why even a man like Halim might feel isolated. Living a secret life—the fact that no one really knew him—was only one of them. Halim's sense of isolation didn't have to mean an espionage connection. Halim had grown up in Argentina and that could be the cause of his estrangement. Or it could be some peculiarity of character. A man who was revered and felt he didn't deserve it might feel estranged, especially an idealist like Halim who believed so strongly, who *wanted* things so much. Colonel Jundi hadn't achieved his high position in intelligence through any lack of understanding of human nature. He knew the Halim-Ziad friendship could have been exactly what it always appeared to be: an odd congruence of two unlike people, brought about long ago by chance.

So it wasn't that Colonel Jundi suddenly had doubts about Halim's loyalty or patriotism. There was nothing as specific as suspicion, and at the moment he had a hundred serious matters in front of him. Israel would soon be invading Lebanon. The PLO would be smashed in the south. The Syrian army might be attacked. Naji would be gunning for the top in Beirut, backed by Israeli tanks. What of the Shiites and the Druse and the anti-Naji Maronites, all the dozens of factions and armed militias? The civil war in Lebanon had already gone on for seven years and it might go on indefinitely, if everyone kept feeding in arms and agents.

Colonel Jundi was hectically busy. Furthermore, he was very fond of Halim in a personal way. He liked Halim's frankness and modesty and determination. Halim had worked hard for the colonel in Lebanon and worn himself out. He looked haggard. He was living too much on alcohol. He detested Lebanon and the death of his friend had overwhelmed him temporarily, a final event which made the weight intolerable.

Thus Colonel Jundi felt more than sympathy. His concern for Halim was deep and genuine. He praised Halim and urged him to spend more time in Damascus. He also urged him to take a rest from his businesses, which would be interrupted by the invasion in any case. The Israelis would have their futile adventure with Naji. They would lose in Lebanon and pull out. After that there would be time for Halim and the colonel to sit down and see what was next for the two of them, together.

Halim agreed and thanked the colonel. The invasion was imminent but he also felt the Runner had gone as far as he could in Lebanon. He had been working for Colonel Jundi for almost a decade, and to his mind, he had failed finally. Israel's coming war in Lebanon was the failure. The Runner had traveled far but as with Ziad, it hadn't worked out in the end.

With his great experience, Halim was also aware of the doubt he had placed in Colonel Jundi's mind. He knew he could easily have overcome that doubt in the years ahead, if there had been years ahead. But that didn't concern him now because he was no longer thinking of a future for the Runner in Damascus. Instead, at last, Halim now saw the Runner's long journey coming to an end. Soon, very soon, it would be time for a final smile and a final wave to Tajar.

Years ago in front of the fire in the great central room of his house, during the second winter of the Lebanese civil war, he had listened sadly, helplessly, to the outpourings of Ziad's heart and watched the shadows of Ziad's terror loom on the far walls of the room like some primitive dance of death in a cave on the edge of the underworld. He had felt very close to Ziad then, so close he had wondered whether he might be in danger of confusing Ziad's destiny with his own.

Yes, well, his friend had given him many things over the years, far more than he ever knew. And wasn't it strange how all of this had ineluctably come to pass for the Runner? Even with the most careful planning and all the will in the world, there never seemed a way to know which little moment from the past would mysteriously blossom into a man's inevitable, entire future.

When did it begin, I wonder?

But when did *what* begin? Which part of the intricate scheme of things? The sordid nightmare of life which was Lebanon? His complex feelings for Ziad? A man's estrangement from his country and culture?

And that was just it. For years he hadn't had time to ask himself that kind of question, which a recluse like Bell pondered day in and day out. Yet once there had been long leisurely hours when he and Bell had explored it together in the ruins of the Omayyad palace in Jericho, sitting beside the magnificent mosaic of the pomegranate tree with its three gazelles and its lion.

Before the Six-Day War. Yes, Halim remembered those times very well.

◆◆◆◆◆◆◆◆

Yossi saw Tajar only once that spring. There had been little reason for them to meet after they had both come to accept the fact that the Runner, now, was working primarily for Colonel Jundi. Tajar had far more cause than Colonel Jundi to be concerned about the effect of Ziad's death on Yossi. He knew how close they had been and how Yossi had identified himself with Ziad in strange and unpredictable ways.

But Yossi had no intention of making the meeting dramatic. On the contrary, he wanted it to be as ordinary as possible. Of course his self-discipline in the face of hardship had always been phenomenal.

They met in a safehouse on the coast near Beirut. Yossi was in a reflective mood, relaxed and calm. Tajar was reassured. He felt Yossi was managing very well under the circumstances.

After talking about Ziad they went onto other subjects, which pleased Tajar. With the death of his friend, it seemed natural that Yossi should be looking back over his life and recalling other times. Tajar thought it a good sign. It also encouraged him that Yossi asked about Anna, as if he were reaching into the past to find a place for his strongest memories. Tajar was relieved and chatted away.

There had been great changes in Anna's life, Tajar said. All at once she had become very prominent as a painter. Now she exhibited abroad, and every dealer in Jerusalem had to have her works on hand in order to be taken seriously. Success had come in a short time, brought on by the changes in the Jerusalem landscape.

For years Anna had been painting the hills around the city as she had first seen them: a scattering of almond and olive trees, the stray ruins of a stone house clinging to a slope, a crumbling gate without walls opening onto empty fields, the sparse geometry of an Arab village, a donkey path winding away through the centuries. Now these scenes of a simpler Jerusalem were treasured as tiers of concrete apartment buildings crept out from the city and covered the hills, penetrating even the once lonely wastes of the Judean wilderness, for so long a primeval moonscape of wind and sun and nomads.

It all happened so quickly in the heady optimism after the Six-Day War, said Tajar. First the hills were transformed to look like modern Western suburbs, then highways were strewn around to connect them. But gradually people realized what was being lost and longed to recall the real Jerusalem, the old Jerusalem, and there were Anna's paintings as she had been doing them for years, so simple and powerful in their economy, a beautiful dream of a city unchanged for millennia, worn old with hope. Well in no time at all the house on Ethiopia Street has become something of a shrine, especially for rich Americans dropping over in the summer. They arrive at Anna's door dressed for a Florida outing but ready to assume a reverent manner—the Holy Land, after all—and parade along Anna's walls to buy views of the *real* Jerusalem of their imagination, to take back to their modern suburbs at home. Anna finds it embarrassing to be making money out of nostalgia. She's always shy around her paintings and not accustomed to the attention being shown her. Once or twice I've been sitting in a corner when a group of tourists arrives and the stares I get are most curious. Some crippled old smiling Arab? A faithful retainer kept on the dole even though he's not much use anymore? But artists are known to be eccentric so the visitors are respectful, just in case I'm some questionable friend of the great lady. A fine sunny day, the men say heartily, and I nod with pleasure. Of course. Even mute old Arabs enjoy a fine sunny day. I've thought of stopping a couple of them on their way out, blocking them into a corner with my crutches like some mad ancient mariner of the desert, then fixing them with wild eyes and whispering: *Listen, I was the first chief of the Mossad, let me tell you my tale. . . .*

Tajar laughed merrily, impish to the end.

But poor Anna, he added with feeling. Success is truly a burden to her. She welcomes the recognition but she'll always be uncomfortable with strangers. They think she's withdrawn and aloof when she's just being shy. . . .

Tajar also had good things to say about Assaf and his Abigail. After a difficult time they seemed closer than ever, even though Assaf still longed to have a child with her and Abigail was still opposed to marriage.

She and Anna have become great friends and surely that's good, said Tajar. She also likes to talk to me for some reason. We have long intimate discussions on Anna's balcony when Anna's working. I guess I'm something of a key to Assaf's past for her. She asks about you and Anna's brother David, and I'm supposed to unlock all the secrets about how Assaf became what he is. I tell her there are no secrets about that and Assaf is still her best source, but she thinks I'm just being inscrutable and finds some other way to question me. I like her more and more. Of course she has fears to overcome, unlike the rest of us at that age, or this age. . . .

Bell also came into the conversation along with the shesh-besh partners who haunted his front porch, Abu Musa and Moses the Ethiopian, and Assaf's unfortunate schoolteacher friend from after the Six-Day War, Yousef, who was still a fugitive somewhere in the caves of the Judean wilderness. They spoke of many things from the past but not of the future. Yossi gently hinted it wasn't a time for that. He would have the rest granted him by Colonel Jundi, then they would see.

Tajar felt this was just as well. Certainly he had no desire to discuss what the next months would bring in Lebanon. The Runner's reports had all gone to the director of the Mossad, but what did it matter? The course was set and Israel's grand plan for Lebanon was under way. There was to be an end to the Palestinian nationalist cause and Naji was to be Lebanon's new national savior.

So Tajar and the Runner talked of where they had been, not where they were going. Yossi preferred it that way and Tajar, for his part, was encouraged by the Runner's quiet strength. Characteristically, Yossi left him that night near the coast with a smile and a wave which warmed Tajar's heart.

At least he has survived the dreadful years in Lebanon with his spirit whole, thought Tajar. At least there's that.

TWELVE

Halim spent most of his time that spring sitting under the fig tree at the end of his garden, watching the tangled vines and bushes and trees come to life. Of all the trees, the fig grew its leaves in the most peculiar way. One tiny leaf appeared at the very tip of each of the larger branches, perhaps a few dozen in all. After several days a small green bud thrust out at the base of each single leaf, a messenger for the future fruit. Then rapidly in the next days the vivid greenery burst out from the ends of the branches and marched in triumph back toward its source, the grayish-black tree trunk of winter.

He had an extremely erotic affair with a young Italian woman which lasted a few weekends. She was younger than Assaf, still in her twenties. She worked for an airline and would arrive at his door in her uniform, demanding no more than a bath and some hashish to smoke, then they would make love all weekend. They also made love under the fig tree when its leaves became full. Once she had lounged there laughing and naked in the golden light of late afternoon, redolent with love's smells, and raised a languid hand to the tree's hard little fruits.

Do you know what fig is slang for in Italian? she asked. No? A wise man's breakfast. . . .

Even while it lasted he thought of her as *the Italian woman*, which was how Ziad would have referred to this magnificent creature. It was a Ziad kind of fantasy, a daydream of a ravishing young woman from Europe who flew into his life as if by magic, who was convulsed by sex and wanted nothing but sexual excess for the short time she was with him. An affair without prologue or consequence, without explanation, an abandoned celebration of lust that would have reaffirmed all of Ziad's glorious fantasies on the erotic possibilities of life, on the irresistible nature of lovemaking, on the final triumph of joyous bold sex over loneliness, an erotic feast that was always *just here* while it lasted and always just for now.

After a few weekends she left to fly a different route elsewhere. A slip of paper arrived in an envelope with a drawing of a fig tree and a sun and a moon above it. In the upper corner an airplane sped away, trailing tears. She hadn't written any words and there was no signature.

As brief as it was, he knew he could have loved this wonderful young woman. A woman who was capable of giving so much, whatever the circumstances, was a rarity to be treasured. If he had met her a year ago or six months ago, who knew what might have come of it? But he had met her exactly when he did. Why? Because she sensed her abandon was safe with him? Without a future to study it, to understand it and reduce it? Was perfection only there when you disregarded it and considered nothing, calculated nothing, weighed nothing? Clever people and grocers, she had said, weigh everything.

An idyll in the grand manner, then, a perfect sexual encounter. *The Italian woman* come and gone, and a last banquet of sensuality . . . Ziad's exquisite daydream briefly made real under Halim's fig tree.

What a superb taste of life. He smiled at the splendor of it.

◆◆◆◆◆◆◆◆

Out of habit he continued to rise early, even though he seldom left his house and garden. One morning at first light he wandered out into the garden and found a dead man.

The man was sitting under the fig tree where the garden furniture was. He wore a greasy cloth cap pulled down tight on his head and a ragged winter overcoat buttoned up to his neck. His trousers were rolled up to his knees, leaving his thin legs bare. He wore no socks and his tattered shoes were huge, without laces. The tongues of the shoes curled up and the soles curled down, making the shoes look like a clown's prop from a circus. The man's eyes were closed and his face was frowning as if he were deep in thought, but the unnatural pose of his body left no doubt he was dead. Halim telephoned the police.

The odd thing was he knew the man, or knew him by sight just as thousands of people did. For years he had seen this tall thin derelict haunting the sidewalks of downtown Damascus, often near the central post office. He was a stooped man with nervous eyes who was always peering intently down the street. He dressed the same in summer and winter and seemed oblivious to anything around him except a smile, which caught his attention at once if he thought it was directed at him. Then he grew agitated and muttered angrily. But when he was ignored he became calm again.

The derelict's heavy overcoat looked grotesque in the stifling heat of summer, the exposed gray flesh of his legs painfully cold in the hard wind and rain of winter. People learned to walk past him without disturbing him. He hovered close to buildings and gave the impression that he was about to make a decision to break away and head off down the sidewalk. Sometimes he even took a few forceful steps forward, gazing intently into the distance. But ten minutes or two hours later he was still in the same place, doing exactly the same thing. Like other people Halim assumed someone looked after him because he was more or less clean, except in winter when his bare legs were caked with mud.

The police were apologetic when they arrived to remove the body. They said the derelict normally kept to the busier downtown streets during the day because he liked to be among people who were hurrying in every direction. Then when it grew dark he went straight home to his slum, bothering no one. He was a harmless man who had been deranged for years, cared for by his sister.

Later that morning Halim received a telephone call from the district police superintendent, a friend, who said it was very unusual for the derelict to have strayed into a good residential area. As for him climbing over Halim's wall to sit down and die in the garden, well, there was no explaining that. Some manner of breeze in the mind of God, as the old saying put it. The superintendent also apologized for the awkward incident.

◆◆◆◆◆◆◆

Halim often thought of Bell that spring. More and more he had come to admire Bell's achievements as a man, his humility and wisdom and acceptance of himself despite his horrible disfigurement. The fact that Bell hadn't intended to become what he did in no way lessened the accomplishment.

If Halim had been given a choice now to be positioned anywhere he wanted in life, he would have chosen himself as he was, making a new start in Bell's house with the young Italian woman. Yes, why not perfection? Why not everything? He would have feasted on the fruits of life and sat on Bell's front porch, in Bell's orange grove with its dust and sunlight and hum of insects in the morning, with that magnificent woman singing somewhere nearby.

Certainly he would have chosen Jericho, not Jerusalem and not Damascus.

When he was a child growing up in a village near the Euphrates, both Jerusalem and Damascus had been mythical cities to him. Now at the other end of life, knowing one of them was enough. A man heard many myths but lived only one in the end.

Jericho, still and always, was a different sort of place. Jericho had never had great temples or been the throne of empires. Armies ignored it and aspiring tribes passed it by. Conquerors searched elsewhere. Of all the dreams of man it was the oldest. It was the kind of place, valuable for its balsams, that Mark Antony would present as a love-token to Cleopatra, who would then turn around and rent it for a good price to Herod, who enjoyed it for its sun. Herod had wanted to escape the winter rain and cold of Jerusalem. Mark Antony was thinking of empires and Cleopatra of rent and meanwhile Jericho slumbered on, an oasis in the Great Rift of the world's affairs where one millennium was not so very different from another.

After all, a town that was ten thousand years old didn't have to concern itself with passing fancies. Jerusalem and Damascus with their mighty deeds and ruins, their mighty passions and vigorous causes, went back not half so far in time.

◆◆◆◆◆◆◆◆

Thinking of Bell and Jericho also led him to think of Bell's surrogate son, Yousef, the young Arab schoolteacher who had befriended Assaf for one autumn and winter and spring after the Six-Day War. Since then Yousef had been a fugitive hiding in the Judean wilderness, an exile in his own land, an idealist who had sought this wholly personal and futile way to live the cause of his people in freedom. For all that time, nearly fifteen years, Yousef had done nothing but survive in the wilderness, hiding in caves and wadis and never lifting a hand toward anyone, almost never seen. By now he would surely have to be a little mad, touched by the awesome extremes of solitude in those desolate wastes.

In the security reports submitted to Tajar by the Shin Bet, Yousef was referred to as *the green man,* the code name given him long ago by Tajar. *The green man* was a traditional Arab name for the prophet Elijah. At the time Tajar assigned the code name it had been a quiet tribute to an unusual friendship, and a suggestion of the spiritual nature of Yousef's gift to Assaf after Assaf suffered his near-fatal wounds of the soul in the Six-Day War. To the Shin Bet *the green man* was a crazed Palestinian hermit of no operational interest whatsoever, whom they occasionally heard about third- or fourth-hand, via their informers. When they did hear news they passed along the report to the Mossad, as requested, wondering how even a low-level desk man in the Mossad could be concerned with such a totally useless figure. If they had suspected the recipient of their infrequent reports on *the green man* was a man as important as Tajar, they would have been astounded. But within the Mossad Tajar kept his interest in Yousef hidden, and only Tajar and Yossi had ever been aware of the private significance of the code name.

During their last meeting near Beirut, Tajar had mentioned how this code name from another era had strangely acquired a reality of its own. For it seemed that in the Arab villages near the Judean wilderness, the fugitive Yousef had in fact come to represent a kind of Elijah to some of the more superstitious villagers, an elusive spirit in the wastes for whom children left tiny caches of food in secret places when they were out tending their flocks of goats.

◆◆◆◆◆◆◆◆

Halim smiled. He poured himself more brandy under the fig tree. Tajar's long-ago code name for Yousef had reminded him of Tajar's habit of suddenly dipping into history without warning, without preface. Tajar had always been famous for that. Sometimes when he first mentioned something you couldn't quite be sure whether he was referring to yesterday or to a thousand years ago.

The green man, Elijah, wandering the Judean wilderness in this day and age?

It sounded odd to Halim but it had always been Tajar's own particular way of recognizing things, of giving them a shape and a size that made sense to him. Of course memory was also like that, as Tajar liked to point out.

It's as free and erratic as a butterfly . . . Tajar's phrase.

Once in Geneva two decades ago, in the middle of a discussion on dead drops in Damascus, Tajar had abruptly begun talking about the pyramids of Egypt. Yossi had listened to him in astonishment. What was the connection? What had sent Tajar careening off to Egypt? Had he suddenly thought of the pyramids as history's ultimate dead drop? Solid stone proof of man's insatiable desire to have a secure secret place, at last, to hide in? Tajar, meanwhile, had gone on to marvel over a statue of Cheops he had seen in the museum in Cairo, the only known representation of the pharaoh who had built the Great Pyramid as his mausoleum. According to Tajar the statue of Cheops was tiny, no bigger than a man's finger.

Just imagine it, Tajar had said. In the desert the Great Pyramid, six million tons of fitted stone perfectly piled into place, immense and incomprehensible. And in a museum five thousand years later, this minuscule presentation of its creator. Alas for poor Cheops. He wanted to be remembered as the weightiest king in the history of the world, but as it turned out some minor craftsman undid him with an hour's work. *We see him.* And there he is, as big as a finger but no bigger. . . .

Halim smiled under his fig tree. He remembered laughing in Geneva and asking Tajar what on earth had caused him to think of Cheops in the middle of a discussion on dead drops. Tajar had said something, but he couldn't recall his fanciful explanation now.

◆◆◆◆◆◆◆◆

Memory . . . Tajar's butterflies.

There in his garden that spring Halim was trying very hard to see the Runner's life as right in the end. He knew the Runner's days in Damascus were over. He had accomplished much but the Runner's role was for running, and Halim knew he had already pushed his endurance more than enough. It was a younger man's vocation which demanded a young man's eye and skill. Spies didn't grow old in their work. They went inside like Tajar or found an oasis on the edge of the desert like Bell, or died with their mask on like Ziad. But where could he go?

He felt like Bell at the end of the Second World War—a man without a country. Bell was English but he had never really lived in England. He had grown up in India but then his past had been denied to him and he couldn't go back there because of race and war and circumstance.

Israel wasn't Halim's home. Even when he had lived in Israel he had felt out of place, and how much truer that would be now after nearly twenty-five years as an Arab in Damascus. He had served Israel with honesty but Israel as an idea, a concept, perhaps as Bell had served England while living in India and Egypt. For Bell, that hadn't meant there was an England to go back to.

Where then? Some Arab community in South America? In North America? Sitting with the other old men in an Arab coffeehouse on Atlantic Avenue in Brooklyn, playing shesh-besh and reminiscing about the old country? Recalling Tajar's humor and sneaking off one afternoon a week to ride a subway to a Jewish neighborhood of Brooklyn where he could back some frightened schoolboys into a corner and whisper to them with wild eyes, like some mad ancient mariner off the docks: *Listen, I was the greatest secret agent the Mossad ever had, let me tell you my tale? . . .*

He laughed at himself. It was marvelously ridiculous, and also sad and hopeless. But what then? A new identity and a new life in Hong Kong? A new identity and a new life in New Mexico? On the edge of the Gobi desert? On a hillside in the Hindu Kush?

He was trying hard to make light of the end of his role as the Runner. He was trying to believe he might be going somewhere—not just leaving Damascus and this house and this garden. He had known profound friendships over the years and he wanted very much to honor Tajar and Ziad as they deserved to be honored, and not to feel regret or sorrow. All the choices had always been his, so regret and sorrow were wrong. A smile and a wave was the way to honor his friends, but he also knew these gestures had to be real.

To honor them he had to honor himself, which was the hardest thing for any man to do alone in the end. Tajar did it but he wasn't alone. He had Anna and Assaf and Abigail. Bell managed it but he wasn't quite alone. He had Abu Musa and Moses the Ethiopian. Ziad hadn't managed it, and he had been alone.

◆◆◆◆◆◆◆◆

The green man.

The idea came to him between Cheops and Herod. Merely a glimpse of an idea at first, a suggestion which slowly took shape. In his garden beneath the fig tree that spring, between Cheops and Herod: *the green man.*

There was a majestic simplicity to it. In fact Yousef had always wanted to meet him. The obscure fugitive who lived like an animal in the wilderness had always yearned to meet the revered visionary from Damascus: Halim the incorruptible one, the conscience of the Palestinian cause.

Over the years men from the West Bank had turned up in Halim's garden with Yousef's humble request. They weren't sophisticated men. They were men from villages near the Judean wilderness who respected Yousef's reputation, such as it was. They were simple farmers and goatherds to whom the fugitive Yousef meant something. To them Yousef was a symbol of freedom, a spirit of resistance. All these years Yousef had never left the land, never forsaken it, but he was willing to do so and cross the Jordan to the east if it meant he could meet Halim.

It was strange, thought Halim. Subterfuge was strange, and illusion and reality and myth, and love. Tajar had always said the Runner had to be a genuine idealist in order to succeed in Damascus, and so he had been and so he had succeeded. Yet

Yousef was also a genuine idealist, although of a completely different sort. Much had come from the Runner's idealism. Had anything come from Yousef's?

A little perhaps. In a few poor villages of Palestine, some Arab children dreamed as a result of Yousef. He gave them a kind of hope, and a hope and a dream were always a hope and a dream. *The green man?* Elijah? Something might come of it someday, who could say. . . .

The idea shaped itself slowly, over brandy, in his garden beneath the fig tree. First he decided he would meet Yousef. Then he decided the place to do that was not on the Jordanian side of the river, but in Israel. He would cross the river to the plains of Jericho: the spy who came home to the promised land.

That part of it amused him. Not even Moses had managed to make that crossing. God had said no to Moses. Moses had already come far enough. He had journeyed long and well through the wilderness, but here was an end to his wanderings: a view of the promised land. . . .

So the Runner would stand on one of the mountains of Moab and look down on the valley and the river to the west, and when darkness came he would slip across the river to the plains of Jericho. Yousef had pledged himself never to forsake his homeland, and Halim would honor that pledge by going over to meet him on the other side, Yousef's side. It would also be a way to honor Yousef for what he had once done for Assaf. The finer meanings of all this would be unknown to Yousef, but that didn't matter. Halim was doing it for himself. Tajar would also understand this final gesture.

Halim even knew where he and Yousef could meet. There was a small, abandoned Ethiopian monastery on the banks of the river. As a child Yousef had gone there for picnics with his brother Ali, now dead, and with Bell and Abu Musa and Moses the Ethiopian. There the Runner and *the green man* would sit in the darkness and rejoice at the end of their long journeys through the wilderness. And since they would both be at home on the plains of Jericho, together on the promised side of the river, neither of them would ever have to set out again.

Halim made a telephone call. A Palestinian friend was to come by that evening. Once the message got through to Yousef, the reply would come back to him quickly in Damascus. He only hoped it could be arranged before summer, so he wouldn't have to hear about Lebanon.

THIRTEEN

Bell had seldom seen Yousef during the last decade. Once a year on a moonless night Yousef might turn up in the ruins of Herod's winter palace on the outskirts of Jericho, a silent ghost in the darkness. The rest of the time Yousef kept to his caves up in the wilderness, hiding far back in the deeper ravines and the more inaccessible wadis.

Yousef went barefoot and was pitifully thin under his rags. He had lost most of his teeth which gave him the gaunt sunken look of a man without flesh. His legs and arms were covered with running sores, infected bites from the minute creatures that gnawed on him in the caves where he lived. He was not so nimble now but always alert, like an animal, his gaze suggesting a simpleminded attention. To Bell, he looked a generation or two older than Assaf. Sadly, Abu Musa had been right. The Yousef they knew had been lost to them long ago.

When Bell saw him that spring—the spring before Israel went to war in Lebanon—Yousef talked much more than he usually did. He also asked questions about Jericho, about the fields under cultivation toward the river, about military patrols along the border. He even reminisced about the wonderful excursions they had all once made together down to the little Ethiopian hermitage on the river, floating in eerie silence across the plains in the grand old steam-powered touring car driven by Moses in his flowing yellow robes and racing goggles, those trips likened by Bell to a journey on a flying carpet. There by the hermitage, Ali and Yousef had played in the water for hours under the watchful eye of Abu Musa, while Bell daydreamed over a book, until Moses finally finished his duties around the place and they all sat down to an epic picnic on the banks of the Jordan. For a moment Bell's heart leapt at these fond memories. Was Yousef at last thinking of leaving the wilderness?

But no, he had promised to tell Bell before doing that and there was no hint of such a decision. It was just a sudden stirring of nostalgia, thought Bell, as he watched Yousef begin the long climb up to the desolate hills. And so Bell left the ruins of Herod's winter palace and wearily made his way back to his orange grove, the bleaker vistas of his life hard upon him as they always were when he saw Yousef.

◆◆◆◆◆◆◆◆

That spring was a gloomy time for Tajar. Israel was preparing to go to war and all the Mossad's resources were directed toward Lebanon. An apocalyptic sense of purpose had seized the government, which seemed mesmerized by the ease with which it was going to achieve so much at a single blow.

Tajar opposed the invasion and was so outspoken he was excluded from almost everything in the Mossad. Even the Runner's reports were not highly regarded, perhaps because they reinforced Tajar's arguments. The Runner said flatly that the Syrians would never allow the Maronite Christians to dominate Lebanon. But the answer to that was that the Syrians could do nothing about it because Israel was far stronger than Syria, army to army. In any case, like Tajar, the Runner was sometimes known to see things from an Arab perspective and there was no place for that now.

The Mossad sent teams of agents in and out of Beirut and Tajar was kept away from planning. Ignored and isolated, he retreated more than ever to Jericho and the unworldly serenity of Bell's orange grove.

◆◆◆◆◆◆◆◆

Early in June, late in the afternoon, a bedouin boy was scrambling up a ravine in the Moabite mountains of Jordan, overlooking the Jordan Valley. Every few moments the boy stopped to peer and to listen. During the long day when the sun stood still above the barren plains of Jericho, there was never any danger of a goat straying. But as soon as the sun stirred from its throne above the valley and edged westward, then an animal might wander and lose itself, lured by the instinct of return—to a place, even an imagined place, what men called home, all animals felt it—an instinct which had been obscurely triggered by this tiny promise that darkness was coming.

His grandfather had taught him that. The boy moved nimbly up the ravine. He had been out on these slopes with his family's black goats for over eleven hours. The walk from the tent to the east, begun at first light, had taken another two hours. The animals had been fresh and hungry then and it would take longer to lead them back, but he wasn't worried yet. There was still time to find the lost one and be home by nightfall. She had strayed before and he knew her ways.

The boy encouraged himself by dreaming of adventure. Miracles could happen in this valley. When his grandfather was a young man, a bedouin boy in the hills across the valley had sought a lost goat and discovered a cave with ancient earthenware jars protruding from the dust. The jars had contained not gold but something which turned out to be even more valuable—brittle parchment with strange writing on it. That goatherd boy had broken off a piece of the writing and taken it with him. The fragment found its way to more and more important people and eventually the boy's family was made rich through his discovery of the Dead Sea Scrolls. That was in his grandfather's time. Who could say what might happen in his?

The boy stopped dead. He was peering down into a smaller ravine and saw there a man who was just sitting, gazing west out over the valley. The man looked like a bedouin, a very poor bedouin, ragged and dusty as if he had been living alone in the wilderness for a long time. The boy's first impression was that the stranger was a fugitive. He knew who was to be seen in these parts and this man didn't belong. It even flashed through the boy's mind that this might be the fabled *green man,* a wild creature of the wastes of whom he had heard, an unworldly presence who was both spirit and holy man. *The green man* was said to dwell on the other side of the valley in the mountains to the west, but who could be sure where a spirit wandered? Perhaps he had flown over here during the night.

The boy stared only a moment. Whether this was *the green man* or not, the boy knew better than to approach strangers in these gullies. The border with Israel was just down below. A fugitive who sat in the mountains of Jordan so close to the border, looking west toward Palestine as if waiting for darkness, was enough reason not to search here for the missing goat. The second miracle of the Dead Sea Scrolls would have to wait for another day. This wasn't the time to discover ancient fragments of history more precious than gold.

Silently the boy withdrew, backing down the way he had come. . . .

In fact the stranger had seen the boy's flock earlier and knew there was nothing to fear. A bedouin child tending goats would keep well away and speak of what he had seen only to his family, that night. Such was the rule for the children of nomads near dangerous enemy borders.

The stranger would have been taken for a bedouin by anyone, but his age betrayed him as a man out of place. The white stubble of a beard stood out on his lean dark face. To the boy this had given the stranger the desperate look of a fugitive, although actually it served to soften the man's gaunt, weary features. But in any case he was out of place in these ravines, whichever desert he was from, since only goats wandered here without a secret purpose and only children minded them.

As for the stranger himself, he wasn't feeling at all out of place but that was because he was gazing across the great empty valley at the green patch on its far side, imagining he was there. The green patch was the oasis of Jericho with its luxuriant fruit trees and cascading flowers, a little up the valley at the foot of the opposing range of mountains, which marked the easterly reaches of the Judean wilderness. He had chosen this sheltered lookout because he could view the oasis from here without having the glare of the Dead Sea in his eyes. Now the sun was sinking toward the far horizon and casting shadows of the wilderness back over the lifeless deep-blue waters, but earlier the sea had been a mirror too brilliant to behold. And this perch in the hills of Moab was also directly above a certain spot—two small huts invisible from here—which lay hidden within the thin line of green foliage winding down the middle of the pale barren valley to the Dead Sea, the banks of the little stream which was itself the border. Now the vast empty plains were also coming alive with subtle shades of color as the sun sank lower and gave the magical oasis in the distance an even more intensely green hue in the day's afterglow.

He thought of it that way—*a magical oasis.* Green was the color of Jericho, of the Prophet's banner and paradise. And it was none other than Jericho that Satan had spread before Jesus to tempt him in the wilderness, as Abu Musa was so fond of recalling.

Give pause, Abu Musa would say, looking up from the shesh-besh game on Bell's front porch. How could it be that Satan hoped to win the soul of Jesus by offering him Jericho? Why didn't Satan offer Rome and Persia and the other great empires? But the answer must be obvious. In those days serious people must have been much more like me, intent on the real fruits of life. So there was the choice of choices two thousand years ago. Did one choose Jericho or eternal life? Which was it to be?

A familiar portent, a sparkle of devilish joy, would creep into Abu Musa's eyes . . . But might they not be the same thing? he would whisper. Isn't that also a possibility? And are you now thinking we may be in deep sand here? Well it's true we are, just as Jesus was when he was standing up on the Mount of Temptation behind us. And Jesus had to choose then and we have to choose now but I insist on choosing both, on having *all of it,* because to me eternity and a life lived in Jericho are one and the same, deliciously so. . . . Whereupon a massive grin would erupt on Abu Musa's old face and his huge body would heave with silent laughter, while Bell raised his glass in salute to homegrown theology, and Moses the Ethiopian smiled benignly and went on sniffing a fragrance of jasmine that was passing his way. . . .

The sun had slipped below the horizon on the far side of the valley. These rich memories of Bell's front porch, of Bell and Abu Musa and Moses, had never been more vivid to him. He could feel these memories in a thousand different ways. Jericho's greenery had turned dark and somber in the twilight beyond the desolate plains. And so what did Jericho mean to him, finally?

Bell's life, of course. He knew that was what he had always wanted in the end, but it was too late for that now. He had gone too far, too long. He had missed somehow and would never know Bell's life. Once long ago there had been exhilaration and success, a very grand success in the Six Days of creation. And then there had been despair which he had overcome, and sadness and loss and all of it come to this—a dream of Jericho glimpsed from afar. From empty verandahs through long days and nights that spring, since the death of Ziad at the end of winter, he had looked down into the tangled gardens of memory and seen the broken statues of his life, solitary and silent and discolored by time, a mystic's solemn companions.

So perhaps it was as Ziad had often claimed and there was

far more than just a touch of the mystic to him. Perhaps that had even been necessary in order for him to have been the Runner. Mysteries and mysticism and espionage, esoteric codes and rituals and undeciphered identities, unsuspected rites—weren't such things always likely to travel together in the mythical caravans of these ancient lands? He thought of Bell and his long-ago Monastery in Egypt, where Bell had been the enigmatic grand master of the secretive Monks and Tajar had been one of the novitiates. I see your role in Damascus as that of a *working mystic*, Tajar had once said to the Runner.

He thought of Ziad's wistful smile and his sad dreams of a longed for, an eternal *over there*. . . . If it works it can go on forever, Tajar had said to the Runner in another lifetime, when he was young, and certainly it had looked like forever then.

Night fell. Darkness graced the ravine, the hillside, the mountains of Moab. Night was a welcome friend come to hide the expanse of barren desert stretching between him and the distant lights of tiny Jericho, that beautiful dream in the moonless deep of the immense chasm at his feet. It was time now and he left his perch, his lookout, to make his way down to the valley floor. He went with great care. There was an exact route to follow and he had to move swiftly without delay, without a wrong turn. He reached the dry cracked plains and hurried on.

Once he thought he heard a muffled beat whispering to him in the dark stillness. Could it be the famous drum of Moses the Ethiopian thumping in the night, carried on some errant breeze from Jericho? But no, that was impossible. Jericho still lay miles away and Moses's little chapel was in the very heart of the oasis. Even if Moses were beating his drum in Jericho the dense fruit trees would absorb its rhythms. It was his own heart he heard as he trotted over the wastes.

The low line of foliage, with the stream and the border, lay ahead. He had but to cross it and make his way a few hundred yards upstream to reach the spot where the small huts stood, the place where Yousef had been brought for picnics as a child.

He admired and pitied Yousef and had much to thank him for. His own son was whole because of Yousef, who had lived with a purity he himself had only pretended to. But of course accomplishing things was partly pretense, and purity was also a kind of madness. What he wanted tonight was to bind his existence to Yousef and unite their secret purposes. That this had to happen in death would be their own private breach of time, not suicide but a final and necessary transverse of identity. That he was making the decision for both of them was as it must be. He couldn't avoid it. So here was the last border, the final crossing, and it wasn't for innocents. It seemed unlikely they would have more than a minute or two together, if they were able to meet at all. But if he actually did reach that poor confused soul he would take his hand and tell him that his own real name was also Yosef, which was only the beginning of an astonishing secret history they shared, a tumultuous tale if they but had time to recount it. . . .

He waded into the water, walked the few yards across, climbed up the other bank.

The Jordan. He had crossed the river and here was the promised land. On these same desolate plains of Jericho, long ago, the prophet Elijah had left behind the secret despair of his fate and risen to eternity in a chariot of fire, a whirlwind into heaven.

He hadn't gone very far upstream when he heard the engine of a desert vehicle. It didn't sound far away but perhaps he had heard it before and willed himself to ignore it. At that moment a searchlight must have been switched on as the vehicle churned forward, the beam pointed down to sweep the gullies and reflecting off the sand, for all at once an eerie glow leapt up over the landscape in front of him. The glow was diffuse and illusionary, not penetrating the darkness overhead but clinging close to the earth as if the desert were surrendering a host of pale memories to the night, a last remnant of sunwracked noons. He even stopped moving for an instant, so hypnotizing was this haunting illumination with its looming shapes and dancing shadows. But now the dance suddenly quickened as the eerie glow gathered strength, and he began to run and run harder and harder, flying over the earth.

There were shouts off to his left and he saw the first of the little huts which stood by the shore upstream. A figure, an unworldly ghostlike figure, emerged in the uncanny glow beside the hut. It was Yousef, that strange apparition from the Judean wilderness, and he was looking around the clearing with a childlike curiosity, bewildered and frightened, not knowing what to do. The warning shouts were closer and louder, the glow to the land swelled brighter. There were also sharp thuds off in the darkness, what might have been warning shots at the stars. As he ran he smiled and waved at the ghostly figure and Yousef must have understood something, for he too seemed to smile as he came around in front of the hut. Yossi ran even harder and called out the single word of recognition, his final cry—their name, the man they both were—here at the end of time on the edge of the promised land, waved and smiled and raced on, but he was still only running toward the hut when the first burst of bullets chattered out of the night.

He stumbled, saw Yousef smile, then nothing. Yousef, confused, a ghost with welcoming arms stretched wide in the pale night light, almost reached him. But then another burst of small flames chattered from the darkness and the ghost shuddered, knelt, settled lightly in a fluttering of rags a few yards away as a last bullet ticked at the dust between the two crumpled bodies, beside the little stream trickling down to the Dead Sea.

◆◆◆◆◆◆◆◆

One evening at the beginning of June Tajar was visiting Bell when a jeep drew up outside Bell's gate. It was a moonless night and they had just finished another of Bell's superb curry dinners. The two of them were still sitting at the table, facing each other in the candlelight. Bell was talking about India. He knew Tajar's gloomy mood those days and suspected it had something to do with Lebanon, so as best he could he distracted his friend. The arrival of a jeep at the gate didn't surprise Bell, although it had never happened before. Bell had no telephone and obviously Tajar would have to leave his whereabouts known to someone.

The gate clanged and they heard a man advancing through the orange grove. Tajar only had time to reach for his crutches, not to rise, before there were steps on the porch and the man appeared in the doorway. He was a young army captain in fatigues, armed. He glanced at Bell and addressed Tajar.

A call from one of your men, sir. *The green man* has been killed near here at the border. Near the river, by one of our patrols.

What? Trying to cross over to Jordan?

It seems not but there was a mix-up. Another man was killed with him and that one had come across—*from* Jordan—which is what caused the mix-up. A Syrian, apparently.

Bell saw his friend's eyes open in horror.

A Syrian? How do they know?

He was carrying papers, replied the young officer. I can—

Tajar was heaving himself up on his crutches. His bench went over with a crash and he was hobbling toward the door. The officer disappeared ahead of him and Bell heard the gate clang, the jeep drive away. It had all happened in a minute or two.

Bell sat for a time and then began clearing away the dishes. He washed them and cleaned up in the kitchen, put the food away, started to boil coffee and then thought better of it. Usually he went to his grape arbor after dinner but tonight he returned to the front porch and sat in his chair with a glass of arak, the decanter on the table beside him. Not that he expected to see Tajar again that night but he felt his place was here, facing the orange grove and the front gate and the road. It was a silent night of stars and the gentlest of summer breezes.

The green man . . . Elijah?

That had to be Tajar's code name for Yousef, of course. The ghost of Yousef gone at last, released from his suffering in the wilderness by a mix-up near the border, near the river, shot by an Israeli army patrol. That was why Yousef had asked Bell questions about the land near the river and border patrols, because he had intended to go there.

And a Syrian killed with him by the river?

For some reason Bell was sure that could only be Halim, the man Yousef had always hoped to meet someday, the mysterious adventurer from Damascus who had once spent long twilights with Bell beside the beautiful mosaic in the ruins of the winter palace of the Omayyad caliphs.

The look of horror in Tajar's eyes?

Yes, there was no doubt in Bell's mind that Halim had secretly been Tajar's man. And chance and fate and desire—who knew in what combination?—had brought Halim across the river to meet Yousef on the plains of Jericho, where they had both been killed.

Bell raised his glass and gazed through the clear liquid at his orange grove. And to think he had once linked these three men in an illusionary chain of being . . . poor Yousef, poor Halim, poor Tajar.

Gazing through his arak, Bell thought of the ancient Egyptian belief that to repeat the name of one who is dead is to cause him to live again.

FOURTEEN

Nearly three decades had passed since Tajar had conceived the beginnings of his audacious master plan for the Runner operation and taken the first quiet steps to set it on its course. Years had gone by before the vast scope of the plan had become apparent and even then only four men, the directors of the Mossad past and present, had shared the intricacies of the operation with Tajar: Little Aharon, Tajar's competitor in the Mossad at the beginning, Generals Dror and Ben-Zvi, and now General Reuvah.

The Runner operation had been the most ambitious penetration in the history of Israeli intelligence. For nearly twenty-five years the Runner had been an influential citizen of Damascus, respected as a Syrian patriot, admired as an Arab visionary. The operation was also the most closely guarded secret in the history of Israeli espionage. Only the four directors of the Mossad had ever known, with Tajar, the true identity of the Runner—that he was an Israeli, an immigrant from Iraq who had learned to pass as an Arab, a soldier who had distinguished himself in the 1948 war when the state was founded.

Tajar had spent the days after the Runner's death gathering facts from the Shin Bet, the border police, the soldiers involved in the shooting. Still shaken and somber, still crushed by the enormity of his loss, he sat in the office of the director of the Mossad one night, alone with the director.

General Reuvah was a blunt squat man of great tenacity, a

former paratrooper and hero from the Yom Kippur War, when he had fought on the Golan Heights against the Syrians. Like Colonel Jundi, he had distinguished himself as a tank commander in that war. Tajar had never worked out a common ground for friendship with General Reuvah, perhaps because they differed too widely in their views, perhaps simply because Tajar was beginning to find unbridgeable the gap between himself and these younger and younger generals.

General Reuvah had never disguised his lack of sympathy for Tajar's ways, nor Tajar his disagreements with the general. But the general did understand death all too well, particularly the deaths of comrades who were also friends. And the Runner had been the Runner, Tajar's magnificent and unique creation from long ago, so there was much to unite them that evening. Indeed, all at once they both felt extremely close to each other —and lonely. They also knew that as unlike as they were, a powerful bond would always exist between them.

Of the facts, there was little to say. Certainly there had been a mix-up and it was always better to sit down and ask questions, if that could be done. But a border at night? The sensors picking up a figure moving through the Israeli no-man's-land toward the river? Another figure moving through no-man's-land on the other side of the river and then crossing the Jordan into Israel? A patrol dispatched and warning shouts in the darkness, warning shots in the darkness, men running in the darkness? . . . No, there was nothing to say about that other than to ask one simple question: what was the Runner doing on the plains of Jericho? So they put aside the facts from that fatal night and instead talked about the Runner, or rather the general quietly asked questions and Tajar talked about the Runner.

And when you saw him in Lebanon the last time? . . .

Yes, it's easy enough now to imagine I saw things and ignored them because I preferred to, for both our sakes. The signs were there—aren't they always in retrospect? Of course we had talked about him leaving Damascus someday and where he might go and what he might do. It's true he never thought of coming back to Israel to live. He thought in terms of a visit perhaps, then going on somewhere else to live, somewhere so far away and foreign to him that he could always be a stranger and never have to fit in. As for *the green man,* Yousef, the Runner had known about him for years, ever since Yousef and his son became friends after the Six-Day War. Yousef had always wanted to meet him. It was Yousef's great dream and there's no question he would have tried to cross the river to fulfill it, if he had been asked to.

But instead? . . .

Yes, instead the Runner came over to our side. The meeting was obviously going to be in that little abandoned monastery, or hermitage, beside the river. Just a few huts, really. The property still belongs to the Ethiopian church. An ancient anchorite lived there for decades. Do you know the story?

No.

The anchorite was an Ethiopian monk who had lived beside the river since Turkish times, said Tajar. After the Six-Day War the army moved him out. Abba Avraham was the anchorite's name, mostly deaf and so shrunken with age he was little bigger than a child. Close to a hundred, by all accounts. He chanted prayers through all his waking hours, rather loudly because he was deaf. I'm told you always knew when he was nearby because he sounded like a gently buzzing bee. The army took him to the Ethiopian monastery in Jericho where a couple of monks were living, but the next day he was gone. During the night he had walked back to his hut beside the river. An officer tried to explain to him that the river was now a border, a military area and out-of-bounds, but ancient Abba Avraham wasn't having any of it. All he knew was that his tiny hut beside the river was his place in the world. John had baptized Jesus there and that was where he belonged. The Ethiopian monk in charge in Jericho, a giant old eunuch called Moses, pleaded with the anchorite and all went well for a time. It seemed ancient Abba Avraham would stay in Jericho. But then one morning he turned up missing again and sure enough a patrol found him collapsed out in the desert, buzzing very weakly, half-dead from exhaustion, on his way back to the river. Moses was in tears. I can't lock him up, he said, and if I don't he'll just keep trying to go back until it kills him. Well as it happened ancient Abba Avraham didn't recover from that last trek. He was mostly unconscious when they brought him back to Jericho and a few days later he died . . . trailing his hand in a pan of water which Moses had placed beside his cot. In *his* mind anyway, Abba Avraham's mind, he had gone to heaven straight from the banks of his holy river. With Moses's help, of course.

It sounds like a tale from some other age, said General Reuvah.

Yes it does, replied Tajar. And so the Runner decided to come over to our side for his meeting with Yousef, a matter of only a few yards, after all. The river isn't much of anything at that point. In fact I've never known anyone who wasn't astonished at seeing the Jordan for the first time. To be so small, just a quiet little stream a few yards across and shallow and warm, and yet to be so famous. It's always imagined quite differently, as a great river, and the crossing of it surely a momentous event. *Chills the body but not the soul, hallelujah*— as the American song says, getting it exactly backward. And so the Runner wanted to cross it and he did, and he even carried papers with him to show he was a Syrian . . . if anything happened.

If anything happened. Tajar had added those words in a whisper. Now he bent his head, looking down at his hands. The general waited a moment before speaking, and when he did it was as if he were speaking to himself.

I assume he knew about our sensors, said the general. He would have to have known about borders.

Tajar still gazed at his own hands. Of course the Runner had known about borders. That was his profession. And he had known sensors sounded alarms that brought soldiers. He had also known Jericho was only fifteen miles from Jerusalem and that the border near Jericho was therefore very tightly guarded. . . . And at night? With troops dispatched immediately? It could only mean sure bursts from automatic weapons if an infiltrator didn't stop at once, as ordered. No one could expect to cross the river there by chance, to trespass without the full, expected response.

Oh yes he knew about borders, replied Tajar. And he knew about that one.

Again the general paused before speaking.

Perhaps what we call in the army the silently wounded, he said. I've seen good men go on for years and then suddenly for no reason, what appears to be no reason. . . . But it's foolish for me to speculate about the Runner. I never even met the man and you knew him . . . well, forever. No one else ever really knew him at all. Not for thirty years anyway.

Tajar nodded. He gripped his hands together and gathered his strength, pushing on. He mentioned Anna and Assaf and talked for a while about both of them.

It's up to you, said General Reuvah. If you want to talk to them you can, but of course they can never share the secret with anyone. Do what you think is best, just let me know what you decide. No one else is going to know and nothing will ever be said from here about the existence of the Runner, or the fact that there ever was a Runner operation. Officially and unofficially: *nothing.* There'll be some talk within the agency about a mysterious operation having ended, and a few of our most knowledgeable people may discreetly try to find out which important Arab diplomat has been dismissed lately, or has retired or dropped out for some other reason. But even within our security services no one knows the identity of the Syrian who was killed with *the green man,* nor will they try to find out, since we took over the case immediately and *the green man* was no one of importance to them. So on our side, nothing. An end. The security services in Damascus will want to find out what happened to Halim and they will. They'll find out he went to meet Yousef across the river, and they'll see it as another of his quixotic gestures on behalf of the Palestinians. He covered himself in Damascus, dropped hints as we know and said things, particularly about his despair with Lebanon. So now, for them, this will only add to the legend that Halim was the true conscience of the Arab cause. In a way he always prepared them for something like this. His refusal to get involved in factions, staying above that and then deciding all at once to cross the river to meet someone as inconsequential as Yousef—it will all fit for the Syrians, Halim being Halim right to the end. What an extraordinary agent he was, just perfect in his disguise. Even when he decided . . . to do this, he prepared it and covered it and made it seem natural and plausible, inevitable even. Yes, that's what would strike me if I were a Syrian intelligence officer reviewing the life and death of Halim. The inevitability of it.

Tajar looked up from his hands. The general was saying all this because he deeply felt the need to talk about the Runner, to praise and honor and remember him. And since he couldn't speak of Yossi as a man and a friend, he did the next best thing and praised and honored him as a professional. Tajar realized this. To him these thoughts could have sounded crude and belittling, but he recognized General Reuvah's good intentions. He was also grateful the general had so carefully avoided dwelling on the one simple question concerning the Runner's entry onto the plains of Jericho. For there was no answer to it except that this had been the view given to Moses three millennia ago, his glimpse of the promised land which God had said he could never enter.

They talked for a long time. Eventually Tajar gathered up his crutches and pulled himself to his feet. He would be leaving the Mossad now, his work done. Yossi's grand rabbi of intelligence was retiring. To others in his work Tajar had always appeared to be the fortunate one, the gifted and the blessed. He was a legend without rival, the patriarch of Israeli intelligence, the incomparable survivor whose mysterious trail spanned nearly half a century of success and adventure, stretching all the way back to Baghdad in 1936. There were tears in the general's eyes as he stepped forward to embrace this small crippled figure, so weighed down with grief.

The Runner was the most valuable agent Israel ever had, said the general.

Oh yes, whispered Tajar. . . . He was that too.

◆◆◆◆◆◆◆◆

It was a quiet June evening when Tajar sat down with Anna and Assaf in the spacious high-ceiling room of the old stone house on Ethiopia Street, and there recounted the story of Yossi's secret journey through the years, beginning in Argentina a quarter of a century ago. Tajar spoke by candlelight, slowly and lovingly going into detail as best he could, careful to dwell on small moments which might help them recognize Yossi from their memories, bringing to life in the shadows these echoes of Yossi's dedication and struggle, his lonely triumphs and far more lonely defeats, from the grand successes before the Six-Day War to the growing darkness of the later years, a steady advance in the footprints of time which had finally ended in a fatal crossing of the Jordan to meet Yousef on the plains of Jericho.

Neither Anna nor Assaf interrupted him during all this long tale. When he was finished Anna rose and went to stand in the doorway to the balcony, her back to the room, looking out at the night. Assaf seemed to have a thousand questions at first, but soon he too sought refuge in silence, the enormity of these revelations far beyond the grasp of a moment.

After a time Tajar went off to the kitchen to make coffee. Assaf followed him down the corridor to bring it in. On the way back from the kitchen, carrying the three little cups on a tray, Assaf stopped in the middle of the great room to stare with a quizzical expression at the candlelit photograph of Yossi on Anna's desk, over by the balcony window, trying to comprehend a small part of what he had heard. Tajar, hobbling along behind him, paused to follow his gaze. It was the photograph of Yossi in his paratrooper uniform at the age of twenty-nine, handsome and smiling somewhere in the desert, taken a month before the 1956 war broke out and Yossi was supposedly killed in the Mitla Pass in the Sinai. At that moment Anna turned in the balcony doorway and smiled at them both, a strangely enigmatic smile in the candlelight. Her hands came up as if to welcome the two men, or to hold them.

Assaf with his offering on a tray and the solemn figure of Tajar leaning on his crutches, Anna smiling and reaching out, the photograph off to the side between them: for a long moment the three of them stood motionless in these attitudes, facing each other and memory, silently fixed for all time in the large airy room they all loved, a grave and ancient tableau as if from some dimly remembered rite.

It was Anna who broke the silence.

You see it doesn't surprise me in a way, she said. Tonight we've heard nothing but fantastical things, a kind of display of magic. And yet in a way none of it surprises me because everyday . . . *so seldom do we know the worlds where we walk.*

Tajar and Assaf weren't aware of it but these were Yossi's words which Anna was resurrecting, spoken long ago when he and Anna had sat on a little desert hill watching the sunrise in the Negev, sifting through their fingers the riverborne, seaborne, wind-driven sand which had come all the way from the upper Nile to lie at their feet, the two of them rejoicing in that quiet place at the dawn of the world.

FIFTEEN

That summer Israel went to war in Lebanon and Bell died with his eye open, sitting on his front porch gazing at the dust and oranges of his life.

Abu Musa found him.

Late one afternoon the old Arab turned up at the regular time, wheezing and sputtering as he gave Bell's gate a kick and sent it clanging open on its hinges—his usual warning to Bell that the drowsy siesta hours were giving way to the demands of serious shesh-besh and society, to inscrutable Ethiopian chants and clouds of hashish smoke and interminable monologues on a princess and God and a holy river, on lust and castles in the sky and all manner of growing things.

Yes, the social hour in Jericho. Scandal and gossip and disreputable intellectual mayhem in the lowest and oldest village on earth. Surely no self-respecting holy man could survive without it?

Cradled in Abu Musa's arm were masses of bright red mangoes, oozing and sticky with juices, fresh from one of his trees. Bell liked to claim that the ambrosia of the ancient Greeks, the food of the gods of Olympus, had in fact been nothing more unworldly than ripe juicy mangoes. Was it true? But if the ancient Greeks had really been so dedicated in their quest for knowledge, thought Abu Musa, why hadn't they settled down right here to eat ambrosia while working out their laws of man and nature, their philosophies and sciences and their epics of tragedy and comedy? If they were so wise, why had they left Jericho and pushed on east dreaming of Persian and Indian and Bactrian empires? Pure folly and so much for the Greeks. Because in matters of knowledge, obviously, a man could go no deeper than the lowest and the oldest, which in fact was right here.

Around his ample stomach, Abu Musa's pale blue galabieh was darkly stained from the juices of the mangoes cradled in his arm. At the end of his arm, in his hand, blossomed an orange-red fistful of fiery flamboyants, also from one of his trees. Abu Musa was never quite sure which one of the three kings of the Orient he was meant to represent in Bell's abstruse scheme of things—who could fathom a holy man's thoughts? But he never doubted he *was* a king and was always careful to arrive for the social hour bearing gifts for the other two kings, who would be grateful and thank him for them. Then Bell would slice mangoes and Moses would delicately arrange flamboyants behind his ears, framing his huge chocolate face in an orange-red halo, and while they were busy with these matters he himself would be free to launch another fascinating account of his day in Jericho.

Today he was feeling especially fine because he had been visited by a mysterious and complex dream during his siesta, a beautiful dream incorporating large parts of his life and filled with symbols and grand events and sensuous delights, a dream of fruit trees and lions and gazelles and many colors, of vast deserts and a distant oasis and all of it never ending . . . even now it puffed him up to think of it. Abu Musa's heart glowed. How many refills of his nargileh would it take just to begin such a tale?

Bell's gate clanged open and Abu Musa's eyes narrowed with cunning. Perhaps he should tantalize his two friends? Merely hint at the splendors of his dream and spread the telling of it out over a week? But might not there be other dreams between now and then? Was it wise to wait and fall behind? Or would either of his friends even tolerate delay once he had fired their imaginations? He could see Moses gently nodding on the other side of the shesh-besh board, pretending to chant prayers under his breath while he was secretly gulping down every word. And he could see Bell smiling beside them in his tattered chair, pretending to daydream with a glass of arak while secretly listening for every exciting new turn of events. They would insist, of course. They would demand to hear, *immediately*, the entire intriguing drama of his dream from beginning to end.

Abu Musa was sweating heavily. Even in the late afternoon the summer heat was ferocious out there in the sun by the gate. Wheezing and plotting and smiling to himself with his armload of mangoes and flamboyants, he wallowed into the hermit's compound and went crashing through the orange grove with his head down, to emerge in the clearing in front of the porch. Here, over the years, he had been known to break into wild dances when his joy and his sorrow were too great for words. How well he knew this clearing.

He raised his head. Bell was looking at him and smiling, lean and austere in white and sitting where he always sat on his porch, the claw of his bad hand gripping a half-empty glass of arak and resting on the table, which was cluttered with the usual bowls of fruit and piles of worn books and the two decanters of what looked like water to prevent dehydration. Abu Musa beamed and was about to shout a greeting when an invisible blow struck him.

Bell's eye. There was no life in Bell's eye.

He tiptoed up to the porch and placed his armload of fruit and flowers on the table. He raised Bell's hand from his lap, his good hand, and held it, feeling for a heartbeat, then gently replaced it. He passed his fingers over Bell's face, closing the single eye. A great sob escaped him. He clutched his chest and staggered back into the clearing in front of the porch, where he fell to his knees. Still Bell sat facing the orange grove, smiling and gripping his glass, his eye now closed. Abu Musa moaned and swayed back and forth on his knees, raising his head and lowering it, his hands groping in the dust and throwing dust over his head, more and more dust to mix in the fading sunlight with his anguish and tears and soft cries.

Before long the gigantic shape of Moses the Ethiopian arrived in bright yellow robes to cast a shadow over the clearing. Moses let out a huge yelp and at once whispered praise to God and thanksgiving to God for the infinite variety of His gifts, His blessings. Then solemnly Moses began to chant the Psalms, *repeating David* as it was known in his language, and with Moses chanting in the darkness and Abu Musa kneeling and moaning and throwing dust over himself, so it went on and on in the gentle embrace of the summer night.

SIXTEEN

His heart just stopped, Abu Musa said to Assaf. At some moment very soon before I turned up he took a sip from his glass and put it down on the table, thought of something and smiled and . . . went. Moses is inconsolable, sentimental old monk that he is. He insisted there be a service. Is that proper, I said, with the body already gone and buried? But Moses insisted and you know how he is when he decides something—*immovable.* He's so *big,* a fact of nature like a mountain or a desert. He just sits there and refuses to budge. Most of the time he's content to let his mind drift along with his chants, mulling over his memories of his little princess and his dreams of a holy river nearby, even if it is inaccessible. But this time he wouldn't be deterred and there was no arguing with him. A service for Bell, he said, and on his front porch, and either you beat the drum or I'll hire a pair of ragamuffins off the street to do it. Well what could I say? I knew it was all decided because when Moses gets it into his head to break out his great African drum, we *will* have drumming.

The drum Abu Musa was referring to—known to everyone in Jericho as *Moses's heartbeat*—had been brought to the Holy Land from Ethiopia by the tiny Ethiopian princess who had also brought Moses himself to the Holy Land. It was long and thick and handsome with the shape of a hollowed-out tree trunk, from which such drums must once have been made.

Stretched hides were lashed over its ends and the smooth wooden sides were intricately decorated with abstract designs painted in red and green and gold, Ethiopia's national colors. A tall man with long arms could just manage to sit with the drum across his lap, one end of the drum resting on the ground, and thump both drumheads with the open palms of his hands—two thumps with the right hand followed by one with the left hand was the usual beat . . . *thump-thump boom.* The great drum was primitive in appearance and Moses claimed its shape and design hadn't changed in thousands of years.

No question about that, Abu Musa had once whispered to Bell with a wicked gleam in his eye. Of course its shape hasn't changed in thousands of years, but I don't think primitive is the word to describe it. *Basic* would be more like it. Moses is much too spiritual to know what he has there, but that drum's not fooling me. Nor, I suspect, did his little princess have any doubts about what it represented. That *thing* gives a shape to little boys' dreams, little girls' too. Call it the staff or rod of life or call it the tree or drum of life, what does it matter? In any case, call it *life.* Without that none of us would be here. Long and thick and handsome and booming? Ah, how well I know it. The thought of it, the fact of it, the meaning and memory of it, plagues my days and haunts my nights. Moses doesn't realize how fortunate he is to be able to devote his energies to higher realms. He chants to it, but the rest of us? But for that *thing,* I could have been a saint. . . .

The great drum was used only on the most sacred Ethiopian Christian feast days, and even then few people ever saw it except for Moses and his two or three elderly fellow monks, only heard its dull throb swelling out into the night from the Ethiopian chapel next door to Bell's house. On those special nights all of Jericho would quietly pulsate in the darkness for hours, from sundown until first light, and everyone would sleep especially well because the primeval rhythms of the drum were exactly what sleep required. Clever rogues, these Ethiopians, Abu Musa used to say. Their muffled *thump-thump booms* in the night take us all back to better times, reminding us of the blissful eternity we once spent dozing away in our mothers' wombs, before all our troubles began.

So Moses's service for Bell was planned and announced and the day came, and a small crowd of Bell's friends and neighbors from Jericho gathered in his orange grove, where they sat scattered around under the trees in the shade. Assaf and Tajar were there, and even Abigail and Anna. Bell's front porch looked the same as it had when Bell was alive. The doors and windows of the little bungalow were all open and deep shadows stirred inside the rooms. Bell's old straw hat lay in his tattered chair on the porch, and it was in front of this chair that Moses had positioned himself in the clearing. There he stood in his bright yellow robes with his congregation spread out behind him, leaning on a tall staff with a mass of flamboyants tucked behind his ears, monotonously chanting above the beat of the drum.

Moses was chanting in Ge'ez, the ancient language of his church's liturgy, and naturally no one could understand him. Before the service Abu Musa had suggested that perhaps, just this once, Moses might chant in Arabic. Otherwise no one will have any idea what you're up to, Abu Musa had said, and Bell didn't know Ge'ez, so wouldn't Arabic make more sense? But Moses, always self-assured in matters of prayer, had replied with a broad smile and a quotation: Religions in general tend to be in foreign and archaic tongues—who said that? Bell said it, Abu Musa reluctantly had to admit, thereby resigning himself to hours of incomprehensible Ge'ez, which was surely as foreign and archaic a language as anyone in the orange grove was ever likely to hear.

Abu Musa had started out on the drum, sitting near Moses's feet in the clearing in front of the porch, but after a while he caught the eye of a tall young man from the village who came over to relieve him. Beating the drum was hypnotic work, Abu Musa had found. Moses might be used to it, but Moses was a monk and this sort of thing was his business. For Abu Musa the regular beat of the drum was profoundly sleep-inducing. Again and again he had found himself nodding off as he thumped away, slipping back into a dreamy paradise aided by Moses's monotonously soothing chant. Clearly it wouldn't do. No one understood Moses's chants but everyone understood a drum beat. He got the young man to relieve him, lumbered to his feet and staggered back into the shade of the orange grove, sweating heavily. He rested on a tree and wiped his face with the sleeve of his galabieh. Many of the people in the orange grove already seemed fast asleep, lying stretched out facing the porch with their backs propped up against the trees. Did Moses know? wondered Abu Musa. Would he care? Would Bell?

Next to Abu Musa stood the small man on crutches who had become so friendly with Bell during the last years. Assaf had introduced them that morning but they hadn't yet really had a chance to talk. The small man was about half Abu Musa's size. Now he gestured toward the people asleep under the orange trees and whispered up at Abu Musa.

It seems thoughtful prayer and sleep have much in common, he said.

It's true, Abu Musa whispered back. Bell used to say the same thing. Serenity, prayer, peace of mind, sleep—they all partake of the same gentle breeze, he used to say. But I hope you don't find this scandalous. Are you Christian?

No, whispered Tajar.

Good. I mean I can't imagine what a Christian would make of this service Moses is putting on. Facing the porch like this as if it were an altar, and specifically facing Bell's old straw hat in that shabby chair as if it were a chalice. Surely it must be sacrilegious. I don't know what's gotten into Moses. Do you think any of this is allowed? Mightn't a flight of Christian saints swoop down and whisk us off to Purgatory? Mightn't the Pope? Oh dear.

It may be an Ethiopian variation, whispered Tajar. A vestige from the African past. Old beliefs live on, don't they? Even in distant lands?

I hope you're right, whispered Abu Musa. I wouldn't like to think that Moses, at his age, could be getting himself into trouble with his superiors. He's too old to be going off on his own and founding a new religion. Once upon a time, perhaps, when he first put on his racing goggles and got behind the wheel of that enormous touring car with the Lion of Judah on its prow. If he had decided then to set out on his own across the desert, who can say? But that was centuries ago when his little princess was still alive and he was young with his life ahead of him. It's best to be young, I always say, when founding a new religion.

He's the biggest man I've ever seen, whispered Tajar.

Also the most determined, replied Abu Musa. It's very dangerous to play shesh-besh with him. Eunuchs have extraordinary powers of concentration which become dispersed in the rest of us through sexual innuendo.

I see. And what will become of your shesh-besh games now?

We intend to go on playing, whispered Abu Musa. Moses is adamant about it. Every afternoon we'll turn up here at the regular time and sit on Bell's front porch and play. Of course our conversations won't be the same because Moses always believes anything I tell him and I always believe anything he tells me. It was Bell who asked questions and straightened us out.

Abu Musa wiped his face with his sleeve. The sweat was still pouring off him.

It must be hot work beating a drum in Jericho today, whispered Tajar.

Today or any day, agreed Abu Musa. But when you live in the lowest and oldest village on earth, you have to expect some heat. You don't look so young yourself. Do you understand dreams?

A bit. What kind are we referring to?

The ones that come during sleep, whispered Abu Musa,

bending down more to get his mouth closer to the ear of the little man on crutches. Once more Abu Musa mopped his face.

This *heat,* whispered Tajar. But dreams, you say?

Yes. You see I had one the day Bell died.

Ah.

During my siesta that afternoon. I was on my way here, hurrying over to tell Bell and Moses about the dream, when I found him. He was sitting right where you now see his hat, sitting and smiling with a glass of arak in his hand and gazing out at the orange grove, at just about the spot where we're standing now. It was uncanny. He looked exactly the way he always looked.

Ah.

A thin man, Bell, and he always sat very erect. I could never understand why he was so thin when he ate so much. Those immense curry dinners, for example. You know about them. He served them to you, he served them to me and Moses, he served them to Assaf and to others in the past.

Others?

There was his Syrian friend some years back, the man from Damascus. Bell also made curry dinners for him. And after that, almost every week it seemed, there was the Indian trader passing through. Before you turned up in Bell's life, of course, and took the trader's place.

He once told me about an Indian trader, whispered Tajar, but I thought the trader was imaginary. I also thought he was speaking about something that might have happened two thousand years ago. Was there really an Indian trader?

Abu Musa nodded thoughtfully and wiped his face with his sleeve, still bending down to keep his head close to Tajar, who craned upward. The buzz of their whispering voices was easily hidden by the incessant beat of the drum and Moses's powerful chant, by the hum of insects in the orange grove and the gentle snores rising from the spectators asleep under the trees.

Assuredly the Indian trader *did* exist, whispered Abu Musa. Not for us to see him but in Bell's mind. Once a week Bell would announce that the Indian trader was due that night and excuse himself early from the social hour, to go into his kitchen to make preparations.

Ah, I see.

Thump-thump boom.

To make curries, in other words, which he would then eat alone, in the company of the Indian trader who existed in his mind. And you know how he ate when one of his curry dinners was in front of him: like a camel that had been lost in the wilderness for forty years. So I always asked myself, why did he remain thin?

And the answer?

A mystery to the end, whispered Abu Musa. One of God's mysterious gifts to a holy man. And there were other mysteries. My dream the day he died, for example. The very afternoon he died. It might even have been no more than a few moments before he died. There is a rumor that we sometimes have a vision before we die and in this vision our entire life passes before us in an instant, which is perhaps the instant it took us to live it. For one moment, in other words, we are given to see everything, all we are and were and have done and have been. Are you familiar with this rumor?

Yes.

Well that's what happened to me, whispered Abu Musa. I had that kind of utterly comprehensive dream and hurried over to tell Bell and Moses about it, to enlist their help in explaining it to me—not realizing at the time that it was a dream to sum up a life—and what did I find? I found Bell smiling as if a pleasant thought had just come to him . . . smiling and dead, so I closed his eye. Only later, after reconsidering it, did I realize the dream was his, not mine. It was *his* life I had seen in its entirety, not my own, which was why so much of the dream had seemed mysterious to me and slightly askew. So that's a more important mystery. Death came to him but the dream came to me. Nor is that all. The day after Bell's death I told Moses about my curious dream, and it turned out that exactly the same thing had happened to him.

Thump-thump boom.

What? You mean Moses also dreamed Bell's life? whispered Tajar.

Abu Musa smiled and mopped his face. So Moses claims, he whispered, but he might just be following my lead. In spiritual matters our monkish Moses has always been notoriously susceptible to suggestion, including his own. Just look at this service he's putting on for Bell. Wouldn't any serious Christian be scandalized by it?

I'm not so sure anyone would find it amiss, whispered Tajar. And in any case *I like it.* I like the drum and Moses's chants, and I like the people dozing under the trees. Everyone seems to be enjoying himself and that's a fine tribute to Bell. In fact, I feel nothing but elation.

Abu Musa's eyes flashed. An immense warm smile burst over his dripping, sweaty face.

But that's *wonderful*, he whispered. I like it too and *elation* is just the right word. And we feel this way, you and I, because we have both had the vast good fortune to have known this compassionate, genuine, hard-drinking holy man whom we are here to honor. Surely God has never fashioned finer handiwork, don't you agree? But come now, *at once.*

Where?

Abu Musa had seized Tajar by the shoulder and was propelling him out of the shade and into the clearing. The dazed youth on the drum had been relieved by another dazed youth who thumped on. Moses also droned on and most of the friends and neighbors in the orange grove were now definitely asleep. Tajar looked over his shoulder and saw Anna sitting with Abigail and Assaf under a tree near the gate, watching him with startled eyes. Abu Musa dragged him right up beside Moses.

Welcome him, he's one of us, whispered Abu Musa, tugging Moses's robes.

Moses broke off his chant and turned and smiled. He reached down and put his hands under Tajar's arms and lifted him up off the ground as if he were a child, raising him up in the air to his own eye level. Tajar's crutches dangled at the ends of his arms. Moses pulled Tajar in and hugged him and noisily placed a kiss on each side of his face.

Welcome, said Moses, beaming. Then he lowered Tajar down to the ground and turned back to face the porch and the tattered chair and Bell's old straw hat, resuming his chant. Abu Musa nodded happily and sat down at Moses's feet, once more taking his place at the drum. Tajar hobbled out of the clearing and through the shade of the orange grove toward Anna and Abigail and Assaf, who were all silently clapping. Anna held his hand when he sat down beside her.

Bravo, she whispered. But what did all that mean? It looked like some special little ceremony. Have you joined something?

Tajar nodded, smiling.

It seems I've become the third partner of a shesh-besh game, he said. I watch and they play. I also comment on what they say. Now and then I turn up here and sit on the porch with them.

Is that all?

All? But the game has no end, Anna. Don't you see? I've been invited to become part of Jericho time.

◆◆◆◆◆◆◆◆

Later Abu Musa came to join them where they sat under the trees near the gate. He was happy they were all there and especially thankful that Anna had come. After chatting for a while he gestured toward the clearing and the front porch.

Look here, he said, you might as well just drift away whenever the spirit moves you. There's no logical time to leave a ceremony like this. Tales may have a beginning and a middle and an end but life in Jericho doesn't, and especially a celebration staged by Moses. When Moses casts a spell over Jericho his chanting has a way of going on and on like his favorite holy river. No doubt there'll be a subtle transformation from one thing to another at some obscure hour today or tomorrow or the day after that—but who can say when it will come? I'm sure Moses himself doesn't know. I'll be sitting at the drum thumping away when I begin to sense that something has changed, that the world is not quite the same as it used to be. And then I'll notice, say, that the insects seem to be humming more loudly in the orange grove than they were. Has my hearing suddenly improved because I'm young again? Am I less dazed than before? But no. I'll look up and notice that Moses's lips are no longer moving, that instead he's just standing there leaning on his staff, pondering the old straw hat in Bell's chair. By God, I'll think, that's why the humming seems louder, because Moses is no longer chanting. So I'll know it's time to give the drum a particularly forceful whack and that will be the end of it, the *final end* of the whole affair. Like Moses, I'll be left limp and tired and elated and satisfied, gazing at the old straw hat in Bell's chair, and so it goes. Life, Bell, a day in Jericho . . . ah yes, and so it goes. Our great friend will have been given a send-off fit for a holy man, Jericho style, and Moses and I will both feel good about it because we dearly loved him. . . . And our friends and neighbors here? These people who are happily asleep under Bell's orange trees? Well in due time they'll rouse themselves as if from a dream, today or tomorrow or the day after that, and stretch their arms and legs and wander home and eat a meal as the sun is setting, and water their fruit trees and stroke the heads of their children or their children's children and say good night and go to bed, where some of them will conceive new life while others give birth and still others breathe a final sigh, and all the while I'll be beating the drum and Moses will be chanting in his incomprehensible Ge'ez and everyone in Jericho will be feeling especially good about everything. But fear not. I'm clever and I've bribed some of the local youths to stay on and share the vigil on the drum with me, so all's well. I'll be able to nap a bit and still do my share of the thumping and our holy man will be properly honored in Jericho. . . .

Abu Musa laughed at the end of his softly spoken speech. But before you leave, he added to Assaf, do take your family for a turn around the village. Surely that's the right way to remember Bell.

Joyously smiling and waving and scratching himself and wiping his face with his sleeve—all of these things at once—Abu Musa said good-bye to them at the gate. Abigail knew Jericho from her visits with Assaf but it was all new to Anna, who had always avoided it when Bell was alive. So Assaf, who was driving, decided to follow Abu Musa's advice and take them on a tour. Just up the road from Bell's house they passed the tel where archeologists had excavated Jericho's huge round stone watchtower, ten thousand years old and the most impressive ancient structure in the world, standing now in a deep pit far below the earth's surface, witness to time's accumulations and the drifting sands of millennia. Across from the tel bubbled Elisha's spring, the source of Jericho's water and the cause of its orchards and flowers. On the outskirts of the village they stopped at the famous ruins of the Omayyad winter palace so Anna could see its exquisite mosaic with the pomegranate tree and the three gazelles and the lion, the ferocious and gentle image of life that had always haunted Yossi. Then Assaf drove slowly through the back roads of the village, down dusty lanes beneath thick greenery, between tumble-down houses half-hidden by fruit trees and banks of flowers and crumbling walls and gates. Tajar smiled and smiled, holding Anna's hand in the back seat.

What a strange and beautiful little place it is, said Anna. So lush and effortless in its splendor but only as far as the water reaches, and then *nothing*. Nothing but empty desert, a different beauty, stark and pure. You can't escape the contrasts of life here, not for a moment. Seeing Jericho like this, it's not difficult to understand how we have arrived at so many of our dreams.

Assaf nodded and Tajar went on smiling, both of them pleased that she was at last sharing Jericho with them. Abigail was also smiling as she gazed out the window, preoccupied by private thoughts.

Once more they lapsed into silence. The mood deepened as

they emerged from the dusty green tunnels and Assaf drove slowly west out of the oasis, climbing above Jericho toward the foothills of the Judean wilderness where the sun was sinking, already casting the first shadows of twilight. Assaf's dirt road gave way to a desert track. He turned off it and they bumped along over hard sand, coming to a stop near the edge of a wadi. The wadi was broad and shallow as it entered the desert plains, but above them it deepened into a steep ravine where it cut upward into the rising wastelands to the west. Jericho lay below them now. Scattered ruins lined the earth near the wadi, the stones worn and bleached white by the sun, what had once been Herod's winter palace. Here great ornamental pools had shimmered in the sun two thousand years ago, when the palace had straddled the wadi and the runoff of the winter rains from the mountains had fed magnificent fountains.

They were above the plains with a view not only of Jericho but of the whole Jordan Valley. To the south in the distance the Dead Sea glistened blue and empty, and to the east across the valley the long ridge of the hills of Moab reared pink and purple and mysterious in the late afternoon sun. The silence was complete as they got out of the car to enjoy the view. Anna roamed by herself over to the edge of the wadi. Down below was a bedouin tent with its sides opened to the breezes, little children playing and dogs and chickens poking around, the few camels of the family grazing nearby on the parched land. Across the wadi a small mosque stood amidst a cluster of mud-brick houses, its thin brown minaret rising straight and true against the awesome blue sweep of the sky. Banana trees grew along the far side of the wadi. Farther up in the sandy hills a string of tiny black dots stretched over the wastes—the family's herd of black goats being led down the mountain by one of the older children.

Surely much of this scene hasn't changed in thousands and thousands of years, thought Anna. It was here long before the palace was built and it's still here, long after the ruins have returned to the desert.

She walked along the edge of the wadi, entranced by the grandeur of the view and the placid routine of the bedouin family down below. They didn't have a view down there, but the wadi provided some meager vegetation for the camels. The family was preparing for night and they would all be asleep soon after darkness came, guarded by their watchful dogs. The camels were already seeking out a place to kneel not far from the tent, their spindly front legs collapsing first and then their hind legs as they awkwardly lowered themselves onto their bellies for the night, the young one close to the mother, the male a little to the rear protecting the calf from the other side. They had arranged themselves so that they faced exactly east, awaiting tomorrow's light. Did they always sleep that way? she wondered. They were unfettered and untied because they wouldn't wander in the darkness and no man would steal a camel. From high up the mountain the string of tiny black dots wound nearer. Now she could make out the small figure of a child running along with the goats, leaping down the hillside after a long summer day in the wilderness. How welcome the open tent must look from up there. How good to be coming home at last. And dogs and chickens and camels and a whole family moving around near the tent . . . surely a joyous moment for the child running down the mountain in the shadows.

Anna too felt great joy then. She was happy with her family and happy with all of it, at peace with herself. She hadn't seen Assaf so lighthearted in years, and Abigail simply glowed in the rich afternoon sun. And Tajar was so proud to be invited to visit the shesh-besh games on Bell's front porch. . . . Yes, there were wonderful times in life, moments of breathtaking beauty.

Assaf was calling to her. She walked back to the blanket where Abigail had laid out their late picnic of olives and tomatoes and cheeses and bread, grapes and peaches and figs. They feasted looking out over the valley, over the intensely green oasis of Jericho and the desolate plains surrounding it, facing east like the camels with the Moabite hills across the way and the Dead Sea off to the south, watching the colors of the world change as the sun sank behind them and offered these final glimpses of a glorious summer twilight over the desert.

As the feast ended Abigail made her announcement. She was going to have Assaf's child. Anna tried to hold back her tears but the tears came anyway. Certainly it was joy she felt, but there was also sadness in her heart. Assaf put his arm around her to comfort her. Tajar made a gesture and Abigail and Assaf left them for a few minutes to wander over near the wadi. Tajar took Anna's hand.

I didn't want to say it in front of them, whispered Anna, but I couldn't help thinking of all the things this unborn child will have to go through someday. It just seemed to overwhelm me for a moment. The things we come to know in time . . . the endless farewells of life. You understand, don't you?

Tajar squeezed her hand. Oh yes, he said. *Memory* we call it, you and I . . . and yes, dear Anna, I do understand.

The hills across the valley dimmed with the last of the day's light. Anna wiped her eyes and looked up. She was smiling now and Tajar smiled with her. He waved for Abigail and Assaf to come back.

And now, dearest Anna, he said, isn't it time for us to make our way up the mountain to our mythical city . . . our beautiful and imaginary and oh-so-real Jerusalem?

ineluctable - Not to be escaped from

der. - [luctare - to struggle
e - from in: not]